ICONS OF THE LUSO-HISPANIC WORLD

1

FEDERICO GARCÍA LORCA

ICONS OF THE LUSO-HISPANIC WORLD

ISSN: 2633-7169 (print)
ISSN: 2633-7177 (online)

The Icons series includes books on a broad range of outstanding individuals – royalty, religious figures, explorers and leaders of indigenous resistance, inventors, scientists, politicians, revolutionaries, activists, authors, artists, musicians, philosophers, film directors, athletes – and occasionally groups of people, who have had a significant impact not only on Spanish- and Portuguese-speaking countries but on a broader, even global, scale. Books in the series offer an expertly researched overview of the impact these icons have made both within and beyond their native regions, considering their achievements, influence on contemporaries, and reception more widely. Focussing on key moments in an icon's life and work, these books trace the acquisition of iconic status. They explore an icon's legacy and image and afterlife(ves), showing how they have been interpreted, appropriated, and at times reimagined. Based on the most up-to-date scholarly research, books in the series explore how and why a Hispanic or Lusophone icon can also be considered an international icon.

FEDERICO GARCÍA LORCA

The Poetry in All Things

Federico Bonaddio

TAMESIS

© Federico Bonaddio 2022

All Rights Reserved. Except as permitted under current legislation
no part of this work may be photocopied, stored in a retrieval system,
published, performed in public, adapted, broadcast,
transmitted, recorded or reproduced in any form or by any means,
without the prior permission of the copyright owner

The right of Federico Bonaddio to be identified as
the author of this work has been asserted in accordance with
sections 77 and 78 of the Copyright, Designs and Patents Act 1988

First published 2022
Tamesis, Woodbridge
Paperback edition 2025

ISBN 978 1 85566 354 1 hardback
ISBN 978 1 85566 420 3 paperback

Tamesis is an imprint of Boydell & Brewer Ltd
PO Box 9, Woodbridge, Suffolk IP12 3DF, UK
and of Boydell & Brewer Inc.
668 Mt. Hope Avenue, Rochester, NY 14620-2731, USA
website: www.boydellandbrewer.com

Our Authorised Representative for product safety in the EU is
Easy Access System Europe - Mustamäe tee 50, 10621 Tallinn, Estonia,
gpsr.requests@easproject.com

The publisher has no responsibility for the continued existence or accuracy
of URLs for external or third-party internet websites referred to in this book,
and does not guarantee that any content on such websites is, or will remain,
accurate or appropriate

A CIP record for this title is available
from the British Library

*For Matteo and Luigi
whom I missed terribly during lockdown,
and for Maria
who accompanied me throughout*

Contents

List of Illustrations ... ix
Acknowledgements ... xi

        Introduction ... 1
Chapter 1   Lorca, the Gitano ... 21
Chapter 2   Lorca, the Modern ... 69
Chapter 3   Lorca, the Feminist ... 131
        Conclusion ... 179

Suggested Further Reading ... 185
Bibliography ... 189
Index ... 195

Illustrations

ILLUSTRATIONS 1 AND 3–12 are reproduced with the kind permission of the Centro Federico García Lorca and the Fundación Federico García Lorca.

1. Young Lorca at his piano at home in Granada in 1919 — xii
2. Antonio Luna, Manuel de Falla, Federico García Lorca and José Segura with a group of children during an excursion in the province of Granada in 1923 (© Archivo Manuel de Falla) — 11
3. Lorca and José Bello taking tea with friends in the Residencia de Estudiantes, Madrid, in 1924 — 12
4. Jorge Larco, Federico García Lorca, Manuel Fontanals and José González Caballero dressed as sailors, in Buenos Aires in 1934 — 16
5. Lorca with Margarita Xirgu and theatre company director Enrique Borrás at the premiere of *Yerma*, Madrid, 1934 — 19
6. Lorca and Buñuel in a paper biplane cut-out, at the festivities of San Antonio de la Florida, Madrid, in 1923 — 70
7. Lorca seated in the back of an automobile in Guadix, Granada, in 1926 — 70
8. Lorca and Dalí standing on the shore at Cadaqués in 1927 — 73
9. Lorca seated with friends at the granite ball at Columbia University in 1929 — 78
10. Self-portrait in New York, 1929 — 122

11. Lorca in Havana with a newspaper boy in 1930   129
12. Lorca with the Barraca troupe in front of a tour bus in 1933   162

The author and publisher are grateful to all the institutions and individuals listed for permission to reproduce the materials in which they hold copyright. Every effort has been made to trace the copyright holders; apologies are offered for any omission, and the publisher will be pleased to add any necessary acknowledgement in subsequent editions.

Acknowledgements

I WOULD LIKE TO thank the Centro Federico García Lorca and the Fundación García Lorca for their kind permission to reproduce twelve images from their archives, including Lorca's self-portrait in New York and the image of Lorca at Columbia University on the front cover. I would also like to thank the Archivo Manuel de Falla for its kind permission to reproduce the image of Lorca standing with Manuel de Falla, Antonio Luna, and José Segura.

Figure 1 Young Lorca at his piano at home in Granada in 1919

Introduction

THE ICONIC STATUS that Federico García Lorca has attained in and outside Spain is bound up with his biography and with events and circumstances succeeding his death in 1936. His murder by Nationalists at the outbreak of the Spanish Civil War, the censorship of much of his work during the years of dictatorship that followed, and the fact that the mass grave in which he was buried has yet to be uncovered, have contributed significantly to the idea of Lorca as martyr for the causes of freedom, truth and justice. So too, since the 1980s, his homosexuality, after years of silence, has been celebrated and presented 'as one of the keys to his artistic output, helping to establish [his] relevance in a new world of pluralism and identity politics'.[1] And yet, while any self-respecting critic would want to avoid engaging in an 'uncritical, hagiographical treatment' of the man and his oeuvre, and retain a healthy scepticism 'of approaches that rely too heavily on the romantic ideas of the "genius"',[2] we ought nonetheless to acknowledge that Lorca would most certainly not have endured as an icon had it not been for the inherent strengths and qualities of his work. For notwithstanding the role his life and death have undoubtedly played in his reception, Lorca's reputation

---

1 Stephen Roberts, *Deep Song. The Life and Work of Federico García Lorca* (London: Reaktion, 2020), p. 8.
2 Jonathan Mayhew, *Apocryphal Lorca. Translation, Parody, Kitsch* (Chicago and London: The University of Chicago Press, 2009), p. 1.

still has at its core the very poems and plays that continue to delight and move readers and audiences alike.[3]

Over the years, critics have sought to increase the visibility of Lorca's lesser-known works – what Maria M. Delgado refers to, in her book on his theatre, as the 'unknown' Lorcas.[4] Some, if not all of these, are products of Lorca's engagement with the aesthetics of the avant-garde and count among the more experimental of his works. Thus, his series of poems collected under the titles *Canciones* [Songs] and *Suites* [Suites] respectively, which he wrote in the early 1920s, as well as his *Poema del cante jondo* [Poem of the Deep Song] – better known because of its connection with a flamenco competition Lorca helped organize in 1922 – are all characterized by syntactical simplification and the eradication of emotionalism in accordance with the early twentieth-century avant-garde's emphasis on impersonal art: a style and approach captured by T. S. Eliot's famous conclusion that 'Poetry is not a turning loose of emotion, but an escape from emotion', and in line with what the Spanish thinker, José Ortega y Gasset, described as 'dehumanized' art.[5] In other words, 'an aesthetic that implied economy, understatement and detachment' (Walters, p. 137).

3 Despite himself 'reject[ing] biography as an explanatory mode', Mayhew (2009, p. 6) concedes that 'Lorca's life and death do play an undeniable role in his reception both in Spain and internationally.' But, as he also rightly observes in respect of Lorca's poetry (although the same applies to his theatre too), 'a poem by Lorca is a work of *fiction*, not a biographical document' (Mayhew 2009, p. 8).
4 See Maria M. Delgado, *Federico García Lorca*, Routledge Modern and Contemporary Dramatists (London and New York: Routledge, 2008).
5 See T. S. Eliot, 'Tradition and the Individual Talent', *The Sacred Wood: Essays on Poetry and Criticism* (London and New York: Methuen, 1986), pp. 47–59 (p. 58); and José Ortega y Gasset, 'La deshumanización del arte', *Obras completas*, III (1917–1928), 5th edn (Madrid: Revista de Occidente, 1962), pp. 353–86. André Belamich, in 'Presentación de las *Suites*', in Federico García Lorca, *Suites*, Edición crítica de André Belamich (Barcelona: Ariel, 1983), pp. 9–26 (p. 9) explains that Lorca began writing his suites at the end of 1920 and completed them in July 1923. Neglected for some length of time, a number of suites were published in 1935 under the title *Primeras canciones* (see Belamich, p. 16). As D. Gareth Walters tells us in *'Canciones' and the Early Poetry of Lorca* (Cardiff: University of Wales Press, 2002), p. 136, Lorca wrote his *canciones* [songs] between 1921 and 1925. They were collected together and published under the title *Canciones* in 1927. Lorca wrote many of the poems of *Poema del cante jondo* in 1921, though the collection was not published until 1931.

As regards his plays, 'Lorca also made great inroads into the theatre of the avant-garde, culminating in his strikingly modernist works, *Así que pasen cinco años* [*Once Five Years Pass*] and the theatrical *tour de force*, *El público* [*The Public*, or *The Audience*]', both products of the time he spent in New York between 1929 and 1930.[6] Yet despite the efforts of scholars and translators to make these and other theatrical works more accessible, when we think of Lorca, it is most likely not the Lorca of *Así que pasen cinco años* or the hermetic *El público* who immediately springs to mind; nor, for that matter, the Lorca of the bio-drama *Mariana Pineda* [*Mariana Pineda*] or the tragi-comic farce *Amor de Don Perlimplín con Belisa en su jardín* [*The Love of Don Perlimplín for Belisa in Their Garden*], to name but a few. Just as it is not the Lorca of *Canciones* or *Suites*, or the Lorca of his first poetry collection, *Libro de poemas* [*Book of Poems*], or the very personal *Diván del Tamarit* [*Diwan of Tamarit*] and *Sonetos del amor oscuro* [*Sonnets of Dark Love*], both of which he wrote in the 1930s. And although we could make a case for Lorca's long poem *Llanto por Ignacio Sánchez Mejías* [*Lament for Ignacio Sánchez Mejías*], the renown of this elegy for his bullfighter friend rests principally, in the popular imagination, on a single line: its famous, emblematic refrain, 'A las cinco [de la] tarde' ['At five in the afternoon'].[7] No. The Lorca who is still best known and, I would suggest, best loved, is not the Lorca of any of these. Rather it is the Lorca of *Romancero gitano* [*Gitano Ballad Book*], his first popular success;[8] the Lorca of *Poeta en Nueva York* [*Poet in New York*], in many ways *Romancero gitano*'s antithesis and often read in juxtaposition with it; and the Lorca of the trilogy of tragic plays, *Bodas de sangre* [*Blood Wedding*], *Yerma* [*Yerma*] and *La casa de Bernarda Alba* [*The House of Bernarda Alba*], with its focus on the limitations experienced by women in the rural areas of southern Spain.

---

6   Sarah Wright, 'Theatre', in Federico Bonaddio (ed.), *A Companion to Federico García Lorca* (Woodbridge: Tamesis, 2007), pp. 39–62 (p. 41). *Así que pasen cinco años*, with its 'surrealist atmosphere', has been read as 'a retreat into the inner world of the psyche' (Wright, p. 53). *El público*, for its part, breaks down the fourth wall, leaving the audience 'metaphorically trapped within the theatrical space' (Wright, p. 49).
7   García Lorca, Federico, *Obras completas*, 3 vols, ed. by Arturo del Hoyo, 22nd edn (Madrid: Aguilar, 1986), I, pp. 551–52.
8   Commonly known in English as the *Gypsy Ballad Book* or quite simply the *Gypsy Ballads*. Because of the pejorative connotations of the exonym 'gypsy' in English, we prefer to use the Spanish 'gitano' instead, a term used not only by outsiders but also by the Spanish Romani themselves. We have capitalized it throughout as we would any proper noun in English.

Now, it would be a mistake to presume that the popularity of these works relative to Lorca's more experimental output is merely a consequence of the latter's complexity or opacity and the former's comparative clarity and simplicity. For example, as Jonathan Mayhew (2009, p. 11) rightly points out, even though *Romancero gitano* 'brought Lorca his initial fame' and 'is sometimes regarded as a concession to popular taste', 'it also contains some of Lorca's most metaphorically dense and difficult poems.' Instead, a better explanation can be found, at least in part, in Lorca's reluctance to make wholesale concessions to the aesthetic demands of the avant-garde. On the one hand, his engagement with impersonal art, right across his oeuvre, is at best ambivalent, so that it is possible to detect, even in his early writing, a reluctance to abandon himself completely to the processes of dehumanization.[9] On the other, despite demonstrating an early interest, Lorca abhorred the formal disorder and abstraction engendered by the unconscious processes of Surrealism, a dominant mode from the mid-1920s onwards. Lorca was clearly not prepared to detach himself completely from the real world, from the people that lived there or from their stories; nor was he prepared to relinquish the principles of order and control and abandon the real world for the world of the unconscious and dream. While he cannot, by any stretch of the imagination, be considered a realist, his conception of poetry and of the theatre emphasized their connection with human reality. In an interview he gave to the Madrid newspaper, *La Voz*, in 1936, he explained that he had never conceived of poetry as abstraction but rather as 'cosa real existente, que ha pasado junto a mí' ['something existing and real that has passed close to me'].[10] And he added: 'Todas las personas de mis poemas han sido' ['All the people in my poems have existed'] (OC, III, p. 671). In the same interview, he also explained that 'El teatro 'es la poesía que se levanta del libro y se hace humana. Y al hacerse, habla y grita, llora y se desespera. El teatro necesita que los personajes que aparezcan en la escena lleven un traje de

---

9 See my treatment of Lorca's poetry in Federico Bonaddio, *Federico García Lorca: The Poetics of Self-Consciousness* (Woodbridge: Tamesis, 2010).
10 Federico García Lorca, *Obras completas*, III, ed. by Arturo del Hoyo, 22nd edn (Madrid: Aguilar, 1986), p. 671. All translations from Spanish into English, of this and other sources, are my own. Christopher Maurer's revised edition of *Collected Poems* (New York: Farrar, Straus and Giroux, 2002), his translations of Lorca's prose, in *Deep Song and other prose* (London: Marion Boyars, 1980), and J. S. Kline's *Four Final Plays* (Poetry in Translation, 2018), available at <https://www.poetryintranslation.com/PITBR/Spanish/LorcaPlayshome.php> have all been helpful points of reference for my own versions.

poesía y al mismo tiempo que se les vean los huesos, la sangre' ['Theatre is poetry that has stepped out of its book and become human. And in doing so, it talks and shouts, it cries and despairs. Theatre needs the characters appearing on stage to be wearing a suit of poetry and at the same time for us to be able to see their bones, their blood'] (OC, III, p. 673).

Lorca was receptive to avant-garde ideas but the foot he kept firmly in reality revealed his tendency towards compromise and a more balanced approach. Thus, he engaged his artistic interests without losing sight of real-life drama. Nowhere is this more evident than in his ballads, New York poems and trilogy of rural tragedies, each, to some degree, the fruit of his ambivalent engagement with impersonal art and its implicit resistance to dehumanization, as well as his defence of order and artistic control. This, in part, explains their popularity over some of Lorca's more experimental production – this together with the possibility that, of all his works, they most effectively combine an interest in the human subject with an interest in poetic craft, the former eliciting deeply emotional responses to a range of dramatic scenarios, including tragedy.

Romancero gitano, for example, contains a huge dose of lyricism that occasionally confounds the narrative, and yet it refuses to abandon altogether the story-telling function of the ballad form that emerged from Spain's popular, oral tradition. Instead, its ballads are replete with memorable characters that, no matter how poetic their treatment, appear before us, each with their own story, as if in flesh and blood: a young boy dying in a blacksmith's forge at night; a young girl running scared from a howling wind; a nun daydreaming as she embroiders in her convent; Romani suffering the onslaught of Civil Guardsmen as they ransack their encampment; feuding gang members wounded in a knife fight; a wounded smuggler seeking refuge in the house of the woman he loves; a couple's tryst on the banks of a river. In this way, humanity reveals itself amidst the collection's elaborate poetic conceits that conjure up emotional depths in terms which, if anything, render the physical presence of these and other characters ever more vivid.

Take, for instance, the figure of Soledad Montoya, in 'Romance de la pena negra' ['Ballad of the Black Sorrow'] (OC, I, pp. 408–09). Soledad (her name means 'loneliness' in Spanish) is configured as the incarnation of sorrow, her very body bearing metaphors that convey a deep-seated anguish: 'Cobre amarillo, su carne | huele a caballo y a sombra. | Yunques ahumados, sus pechos | gimen canciones redondas' ['Yellow copper, her flesh smells of horse and shadow. Smoked anvils, her breasts moan round songs'] (OC, I, p. 408); '¡Qué pena! Me estoy poniendo | de azabache, carne y ropa. | ¡Ay, mis camisas de hilo! | ¡Ay, mis muslos de amapola!' ['What sorrow! I'm turning jet black, my flesh and my clothes. Alas, my linen shirts! Alas, my poppy red thighs!'] (OC, I, p. 409). This combination of physicality and figuration allows Soledad to be emblematic of a sorrow that is not hers alone but belongs to all her race: '¡Oh pena de los gitanos! | Pena limpia y siempre sola. | ¡Oh pena de cauce oculto y madrugada remota!' ['O sorrow of the Gitanos! A sorrow pure and forever alone. O sorrow of hidden riverbeds and distant dawns!'] (OC, I, p. 409). And yet, at the same time, it means she can also be a woman who, in her own right, experiences the anguish of a very personal solitude and despair: '¡Qué pena tan grande! Corro | mi casa como una loca, | mis dos trenzas por el suelo, | de la cocina a la alcoba' ['What great sorrow! I run about my house like a madwoman, my two plaits along the ground, from the kitchen to the bedroom'] (OC, I, p. 409).

By contrast, it is much harder to make out the human forms that inhabit the poems of *Poeta en Nueva York*. This, as we shall see, is an effect of Lorca's depiction of the alienating and dehumanizing consequences of modern city life. It also owes much to the surrealistic devices he employs, the dislocations and seemingly haphazard juxtapositions characteristic of Surrealism ensuring a consonance between the aesthetics of the collection and its social themes. Yet even in the midst of the disorientating images and often unremitting prose of Lorca's New York poems, it is still possible to discern a storyline, both within individual poems and across the collection as a whole. For the first-person voice that dominates the collection provides a singular, unitary presence that ties each and every image to the poet's often harrowing and barely expressible experience of the city. As its title makes clear, the collection is quite literally about a poet in New York, meaning that even the most obscure images can be traced back to the perspective – albeit estranged – of one man in a moment in time and space; a man who is searching for order amidst chaos.

In the poem 'Nocturno del hueco' ['Nocturne of the Void'] (OC, I, pp. 504–06), for example, the poet-speaker, with his insistent repetition of the first-person, singular pronoun, reaffirms his presence even amidst the empty, broken images and the abstruse symbolism that constitute his artistic response to the city around him: 'Yo. | Con el hueco blanquísimo de un caballo, | crines de ceniza. Plaza pura y doblada. | Yo. | Mi hueco traspasado con las axilas rotas. | Piel seca de uva neutral y amianto de madrugada' ['I. With the whitest void of a horse, manes of ash. Pure and bent square. I. My void pierced by broken armpits. Dry skin of neutral grape and asbestos of the dawn'] (OC, I, p. 506); 'Yo. | Con el hueco blanquísimo de un caballo. | Rodeado de espectadores que tienen hormigas en las palabras. | En el circo del frío sin perfil mutilado. | Por los capiteles rotos de las mejillas desangradas. | Yo. | Mi hueco sin ti, ciudad, sin tus muertos que comen. | Ecuestre por mi vida definitivamente anclada. | Yo' ['I. With the whitest void of a horse. Encircled by spectators who have ants in their words. In the circus of cold without mutilated profile. Amongst the broken capitals of blood-drained cheeks. I. My void without you, city, without your dead who eat. Equestrian throughout my definitively anchored life. I'] (OC, I, p. 506).

Poeta en Nueva York, like *Romancero gitano* before it, is a product of the poetry Lorca discerns in human experience, that 'cosa real existente' ['something existing and real']. Thus, the aesthetic differences between the ballads and the New York poems can be explained by their markedly different settings and circumstances of production. The surrealistic imagery and angst-ridden tirades of *Poeta en Nueva York*, written in free verse, are the work of an alien in New York. The orderly ballads of *Romancero gitano* are, for their part, those of a man au fait with the traditions of Andalusia, his homeland. Importantly, the connection Lorca maintains to the human subject in both collections allows him to engage with social realities as well as explore the aesthetic possibilities of his craft. Both *Romancero gitano* and *Poeta en Nueva York* are notable for their representation of minorities against a background of intense racial prejudice, discrimination and marginalization. In the former, it is the Romani of southern Spain; in the latter, the African Americans of New York's Harlem neighbourhood. Additionally, *Poeta en Nueva York* offers a critique of modern life at a time of increasing urbanization and industrialization. Yet the collection is equally important for its aesthetic incursions into the realms of Surrealism and Expressionism, just as *Romancero gitano* is significant for its construction of complex metaphors, partly in homage to the seventeenth-century poet, Luis de Góngora, whose work Lorca and many of his contemporaries famously celebrated in 1927, a year before the publication of *Romancero gitano*, on the tercentenary of Góngora's death.[11]

---

11 As Christopher Maurer explains in his chapter 'Poetry', in Bonaddio 2007, pp. 16–38 (pp. 26–27), 'Lorca's poetic group – the Generation of 1927 – would draw its name from this important event [the celebration of Góngora on the tercentenary of his death], which had wide repercussions throughout the Spanish and Latin American literary world'.

In his trilogy of tragedies, Lorca turns his focus to the condition of women in rural Spain and the inequalities they faced within a traditionally patriarchal society. As always, he is equally attentive to the poetic and lyrical qualities of his work, even in *La casa de Bernarda* which is the most prosaic of the three. Lyricism, as we shall see, permeates the language the characters speak and the songs and lullabies they sing. Lorca's choice of the tragic mode, moreover, brings to his trilogy a vision of the world that is rather more poetic than it is realist, his emphasis on the poetry of life displacing the stark realism a documentary approach might have brought with it. Thus, talk of past feuds and knives at the beginning of *Bodas de sangre* signal the inevitability of its tragic conclusion, as does the very name of the eponymous protagonist of *Yerma* (meaning 'barren'), and the pathetic fallacy of the storm brewing throughout *La casa de Bernarda Alba*. Above all, Lorca's trilogy epitomizes that which, in the popular imagination, is most characteristic of his theatre, as well as of his poetry: 'a search for passionate bursts of life amidst encroaching, stultifying repression' (Wright, p. 40). The paradigm of life versus repression is equally relevant, I would suggest, to Lorca's own resistance, as both a poet and dramatist, to the repression of personality, stories and emotion in art. The fact, moreover, that he is able to combine storytelling with a sustained interest in aesthetics means that often his work also confounds rigid distinctions between high and low art.

Now, to be absolutely clear, the personality, stories and emotion we refer to above cannot automatically be equated with those of Lorca's person. They are, instead, the personality, stories and emotion of his characters. This said, it would be unreasonable not to acknowledge the autobiographical aspect of *Poeta en Nueva York*, albeit keeping in mind the disparity between the tone of Lorca's New York poems and the rather more positive accounts he gave about his experience of the city in letters to his family. Likewise, we should not dismiss out of hand the importance of Lorca's first-hand knowledge of Andalusia and its peoples in our reading of *Romancero gitano*; nor, indeed, when it comes to his rural trilogy. Inevitably, the lyricism permeating the plays will also give rise to interpretations that connect the characters' predicaments and emotions back to Lorca's own personal experience.[12] Yet, despite this, their particularity, I would argue,

---

[12] Yerma's barrenness, for example, was famously related by Lorca's friend, the dancer and singer Encarnación López Júlvez ('La Argentinita'), to his frustrated desire to have children. Leslie Stainton, in her biography, *Lorca: A Dream of Life* (London: Bloomsbury, 1998), p. 397, citing La Argentinita,

lies not so much in biography as it does in the broader historical context of their production; a context that includes both the artistic trends of the day and its socio-political and cultural realities.¹³ We can say the same of his poetry also. Ultimately, notwithstanding his artistic priorities, Lorca's work does tell us something about his view of Spain at the time he wrote or, in the case of *Poeta en Nueva York*, about his experience of New York and modernity.

The very particularity of Lorca's work, especially with regard to the Andalusian setting, risks inviting interpretations that reproduce stereotypical notions about not only southern Spain but the country as a whole (for which Andalusia, erroneously, is often treated as emblematic). For example, there is the notion, dating back at least to nineteenth-century Romanticism, particularly amongst people from outside Spain, of a country populated by bullfighters and flamenco dancers; a country, furthermore, where passion always gets the better of its people at the expense of the principles of reason and logic.¹⁴ Might it be, then, that the allure of exotic Spain is what lies at the root of *Romancero gitano*'s or the rural trilogy's popularity? If it is stereotypical Spain that draws our initial interest, careful reading of Lorca's work ought quickly to dispel misconceptions. Lorca, especially in the case of *Romancero gitano*, wrote painfully aware of the risk that 'la falsa visión andaluza' ['the false Andalusian vision'] (OC, III, p. 340), as he put it, might colour the reception of his work. And yet, as Mayhew (2009, p. 3) argues, what he offers instead is a depiction of Andalusia and its people that is 'complex and multifaceted', 'not a one-dimensional caricature.' Importantly, the particularity of Lorca's settings

---

    tells us how, at the première of *Yerma*, she declared that the play was '"Federico's own tragedy"' and that '"What he'd like most in the world is to get pregnant and give birth".'

13 Paul Julian Smith, in his *The Body Hispanic: Gender and Sexuality in Spanish and Spanish American Literature* (Oxford: Clarendon Press, 1989), ch. 4 ('Lorca and Foucault'), pp. 105–37 (p. 107), advises against approaches to Lorca that treat literature and life as one, as well as the insistence on finding 'in his work characteristics of homogeneity and uniformity by which to link it to the person himself.' For Smith (p. 107), the idea that Lorca's work is 'at once universal and particular' has emerged precisely from approaches to it that invoke Lorca's biography.

14 This Romantic vision of Spain is exemplified by Prosper Mérimée's novella *Carmen*, published in 1845 and later adapted for opera by Georges Bizet. See Prosper Mérimée, *'Carmen' and Other Stories*, trans. by Nicholas Jotcham, Oxford World's Classics (Oxford: Oxford University Press, 1998).

does not preclude readings that also offer a broad, universal significance. Local setting is undoubtedly integral to the appeal of his work, along with the accomplishments of his poetic craft. So too, however, is the universality of his work's themes, such as the oppression of minorities, marginalization, and the tension between society's rules and individual desire. Here, universal meanings are aided by Lorca's essentially poetic, as opposed to realist or documentarist, approach. Additionally, in the case of his plays, his recourse to tragedy ensures his work has resonance for the human condition that extends well beyond the confines of either rural Andalusia or Spain, notwithstanding the details connecting it to a particular locality.

WHILE IT IS not Lorca's person that concerns us here, but rather his work, it is useful, nonetheless, to outline some key moments of his life by which to situate his production.

The eldest of four siblings, Lorca was born on 5 June 1898 in the farming village of Fuente Vaqueros in the river plain known as the Vega of Granada. His father, Federico García Rodríguez, was a wealthy landowner; his mother, Vicenta Lorca Romero, a primary school teacher. In 1907, the family moved to the nearby village of Asquerosa and then, two years later, to Granada, the provincial capital itself. Despite periods of residence in Madrid, Granada would remain Lorca's main family home until his death.

Lorca showed little interest in studying during his formative years in Granada. Instead, as a teenager, he developed an interest in music and writing literature. He took piano lessons and, while registered for an arts degree at the University of Granada, joined a group of local writers and intellectuals, known as 'El Rinconcillo' ['The Little Corner'], that met regularly at the Café Alameda. From around 1917 he began writing poetry and prose, and in 1918 published his first book, *Impresiones y paisajes*. Paid for by his father, this book of prose was inspired by cultural excursions around Spain he had undertaken with other students early in his degree. On two of these excursions, to Baeza in 1916 and 1917, he met the illustrious poet, Antonio Machado, and at the first opportunity

Figure 2 Antonio Luna, Manuel de Falla, Federico García Lorca and José Segura with a group of children during an excursion in the province of Granada in 1923

Figure 3 Lorca and José Bello (second right), taking tea with friends in the Residencia de Estudiantes, Madrid, in 1924

borrowed a copy of his complete works, pencilling one of his early poems in its pages.[15]

As his studies faltered, Lorca left Granada for Madrid in early spring of 1919 in preparation for a lengthier stay in the capital that would begin in November that year and end in 1921. The idea was for him to complete his degree at the University of Madrid, but, true to form, he neglected his studies for other pursuits. Boarding at the prestigious Residencia de Estudiantes [Student Residence], he spent his time writing and networking in the capital's artistic circles. At the Residencia, where he gained a reputation for being a partier and prankster, he befriended the writer José 'Pepín' Bello, future filmmaker Luis Buñuel, and painter Salvador Dalí. He became exposed to the ideas of the avant-garde which would leave their mark on his first book of poems, *Libro de poemas*, published in June 1921. Much of the collection, however, still remained under the spell of Romanticism and Symbolism.

15 See Ian Gibson, *Federico García Lorca: A Life* (London: Faber and Faber, 1989), pp. 47–48, 62; and Stainton, pp. 34–35, 42.

Concerned that he was not focusing on his studies, Lorca's parents demanded he return to Granada, which he did in the autumn of 1921. Back home, he met up with classical composer Manuel de Falla. Keen to 'revitalize the folklore and folk culture of his native region' (Roberts, p. 67), he collaborated with Falla in the organisation of a competition to celebrate *cante jondo* [deep song], a form of flamenco considered the most authentic expression of Gitano and, by association, Andalusian culture. In anticipation of the competition, Lorca wrote a series of poems on the theme of deep song, eventually published in the collection *Poema del cante jondo*. Then, in February the following year, he gave a lecture on the subject of deep song to Granada's Artistic and Literary Centre in order to promote what came to be called the Concurso del cante jondo [Competition of the Deep Song]. The competition was eventually held that June in the Plaza de los Aljibes in the Alhambra Palace. It represented a personal success for Lorca, earning him rave reviews, as did his recital of his poems a week earlier in the Alhambra Palace Hotel (see Gibson 1989, p. 115, and Stainton, p. 102).

In February 1923, after completing his degree (now in Law, not the Arts), Lorca was allowed to return to Madrid and the Residencia. This was the start of a period of intense production that saw him complete the poems of his *Canciones* and *Suites* and start work on a number of plays, including *Mariana Pineda*, which he finished in 1925 and premiered in 1927, along with *Amor de Don Perlimplín con Belisa en su jardín* [The Love of Don Perlimplín and Belisa in the Garden] and *La zapatera prodigiosa* [The Shoemaker's Prodigious Wife], both of which he finished in 1928, though neither was performed until the early 1930s. In 1925 and 1927, Lorca accepted invitations to stay with Dalí at his family home in the seaside town of Cadaqués, in Catalonia. The relationship between the two men was based not only on their common artistic interests but also, it seems, on a strong sexual attraction, although Dalí, for his part, has always denied that the attraction was mutual.[16] Dalí engaged Lorca in his interest in Cubism and then Surrealism, and Lorca's own meditations on artistic practice at this time, such as his unfinished dialogue, 'Corazón bleu y Coeur azul', which he composed in 1927 or early 1928, are the fruit of this interaction with his friend. During the period of his friendship with Dalí, Lorca also turned his hand increasingly to the pictorial arts. Dalí encouraged him to exhibit his drawings, which he did, with the

---

16 See Ian Gibson, *The Shameful Life of Salvador Dalí* (London: Faber and Faber, 1997), pp. 135 and 611.

support of friend and art critic Sebastià Gasch, at the Dalmau Gallery, in Barcelona, between 25 June and 2 July 1927.[17]

Between 1924 and 1927 Lorca wrote the ballads for his *Romancero gitano*. In 1926, in Granada, he delivered his famous lecture 'La imagen poética de Don Luis de Góngora' ['The Poetic Image of Don Luis de Góngora'], which pays homage to the Renaissance poet's creation of complex metaphors. Lorca's lecture displays few if any signs of his ongoing discussions with Dalí on the subject of Surrealism. Instead, the picture he paints of the poetic process is one in which a poet's hunt for new images is dependent on his use of the five bodily senses: sight, touch, hearing, smell, and taste. On 16 and 17 December 1927, Lorca would join fellow poets, including Rafael Alberti, Luis Cernuda, Jorge Guillén, and Pedro Salinas, in an event to commemorate the tercentenary of Góngora's death, organized by the Seville Athenaeum, with the support of bullfighter Ignacio Sánchez Mejías. The group of poets in attendance would consequently come to be known as the Generation of 1927.

In 1928 Lorca published his *Romancero gitano*. The first edition sold out quickly and made Lorca a literary celebrity (see Roberts, p. 116). Dalí and Buñuel, however, were critical of the book, which they saw as being mired in traditional rhetoric and motifs. Their criticism and Lorca's problematic love affair with a young sculptor, Emilio Aladrén, are most likely what gave rise to Lorca's 'gran crisis *sentimental*' ['great sentimental crisis'], as he put it in a letter to Gasch dated August 1928.[18] In two lectures he gave in October 1928 to the Granada Athenaeum, 'Imaginación, inspiración, evasión' ['Imagination, Inspiration, Evasion'] and 'Sketch de la nueva pintura' ['Sketch of the New Painting'], Lorca spoke positively of Surrealism, though in a letter to Gasch from the same period, dated September 1928, he made it clear that he had serious misgivings, insisting that his own work, unlike Surrealism, maintained clarity of consciousness. Lorca explained to Gasch that two prose poems he had recently written responded to his 'nueva manera espiritualista, emoción pura descarnada, desligada del control lógico pero, ¡ojo!, ¡ojo!, con una tremenda lógica poética. No es surrealismo, ¡ojo!, la conciencia más clara los ilumina'

---

17 See Jacqueline Cockburn and Federico Bonaddio, 'Drawing', in Federico Bonaddio (ed.), *A Companion to Federico García Lorca* (Woodbridge: Tamesis, 2007), pp. 84–100 (p. 84).

18 Federico García Lorca, *Epistolario completo*, ed. Andrew A. Anderson and Christopher Maurer (Madrid: Cátedra, 1997), p. 576. On the reasons behind Lorca's crisis, see Gibson 1989, pp. 228–29, 231, and Stainton, pp. 205–06.

['new spiritualist mode, pure, bare emotion, untied from logical control, but – watch out! watch out! – with a tremendous poetic logic. It's not Surrealism – watch out! – the clearest consciousness illuminates them' (*EC*, p. 588). Lorca seemed to want to offer a compromise, accepting that the creative process was not entirely conscious or rational while, at the same time, persevering with the idea that a poet ought to keep control over it. In February 1929, he delivered another version of his lecture 'Imaginación, inspiración, evasión'. Here he argued that there were different ways to escape reason en route to creating poetic realities. He also made clear his own reservations about the path taken by Surrealism:

> Esta evasión puede hacerse de muchas maneras. El surrealismo emplea el sueño y su lógica para escapar. En el mundo de los sueños, el realísimo mundo de los sueños, se encuentran indudablemente normas poéticas de emoción verdadera. Pero esta evasión por medio del sueño o del subconsciente es, aunque muy pura, poco diáfana. Los latinos queremos perfiles y misterio visible. Forma y sensualidades. (*OC*, III, pp. 263–64)

> [This escape can be achieved in many ways. Surrealism employs dream and its logic to escape. In the world of dreams, the very real world of dreams, you can undoubtedly find poetic norms of real emotion. But this escape via dreams or the subconscious, however pure, lacks clarity. We Latins want profiles and visible mystery. Form and sensuality.]

In the spring of 1929, an opportunity arose for Lorca to make an escape of a different kind in order to try to leave his 'sentimental crisis' behind him. Fernando de los Ríos, his law professor, and a future minister in the Second Republic, invited Lorca to accompany him on a trip to New York and asked friends at Columbia University to register his former student for a course in English there. De los Ríos and Lorca left Madrid on 13 June 1929 and arrived in New York, via Paris and London, on 25 June. There Lorca would experience the Harlem Renaissance, witness the Wall Street crash and write the poems of *Poeta en Nueva York*, in which he delivers a scathing attack on the alienating consequence of modernity. While, his New York poems, written in free verse and surrealistic in character, might seem, on the surface, to be very different from his ballads, they are, nonetheless, the product of his attachment to the principles of order, beauty, harmony and form.

Lorca left the United States for Cuba in March 1930 to give a series of talks at the invitation of the Hispano-Cuban Institute of Culture. His talks were extremely well received, and he remained in Cuba until he returned to Spain that June in more buoyant mood than he had left. 'I've

Figure 4 Jorge Larco, Federico García Lorca, Manuel Fontanals and José González Caballero dressed as sailors, in Buenos Aires in 1934

become a fashionable little boy', Lorca told his parents, 'after my useful and advantageous trip to America' (Stainton, p. 268). Politically, the Spain he returned to had changed. The military dictator, General Miguel Primo de Rivera, in power since his *coup d'état* in September 1923, had resigned. Now an increasingly polarized Spain would see the exile of King Alfonso XIII and, with it, the foundation of the Second Republic following municipal elections in April 1931.[19] For Lorca, the birth of the Republic offered a new opportunity. In November, in the context of the Republic's project to foster culture and education, he accepted the invitation to become artistic director of La Barraca, a student theatre group that set out to bring Spain's classical theatre to towns and villages throughout Spain.

In 1932, Lorca completed the first in his trilogy of rural plays: *Bodas de sangre*. It premiered in Madrid in March 1933. The following September, Lorca left for Buenos Aires, where the actress Lola Membrives was due to stage his play. He remained in Argentina for six months until the end of March 1934. Feted as 'the most famous writer in the Spanish-speaking world' (Roberts, p. 163), Lorca saw several more of his plays staged in the Argentinian capital. He also gave public lectures, including, for the first time, his famous talk 'Teoría y juego del duende' ['Theory and Play of the Duende'] (OC, III, pp. 306–18), in which he describes 'a mysterious chthonic force responsible not only for inspired creation but also for the successful transmission and comprehension of works of art' (Maurer 2007, p. 35).

After the success of Argentina, Lorca returned to a Spain where the Republic had 'lurched radically to the Right' (Roberts, p. 162). For the next two years, he would divide his time between Madrid and Granada, as well as touring the country with La Barraca. In 1934, he completed the second play in his rural trilogy: *Yerma*. The play premiered in Madrid in December, with the actress Margarita Xirgu in the lead role. Earlier that year, in April, Lorca had received news of the death of Sánchez Mejías from wounds received in the bullring. In March 1935, he published his elegy to his bullfighter friend, *Llanto por Ignacio Sánchez Mejías*. He

---

19 The Republic's legitimacy, though, was not recognized by everyone either on the Left or Right. 'From the outset,' explains Roberts (p. 150), 'there were groups at either end of the political spectrum that refused to recognize its legitimacy, including the revolutionary Anarchists on the Left and more radical Monarchists, ultra-conservative Catholics and those with proto-fascist leanings on the Right.'

then spent the autumn in Barcelona where a number of his plays were due to be staged, including *Bodas de sangre* and *Yerma*. He also met with Dalí whom he had not seen since 1929. Throughout this period, Spain's political situation worsened. There were violent clashes between radical factions on the Left and the Right in the run-up to elections held in February 1936 after the collapse of the government the previous year (see Roberts, p. 190). The elections were won by the left-wing alliance, the Popular Front. Against the background of increasing political unrest, Lorca wrote the final play in his rural trilogy: *La casa de Bernarda Alba*. He completed it on 19 June and over the next few weeks read it to his circle of friends in Madrid. On 13 July, concerned by the increasing violence in the capital, he returned to his family's then summer home, the Huerta de San Vicente, in Granada.

On 18 July 1936, General Francisco Franco, from Spanish Morocco, instigated the nationalist uprising against the Republic. On 20 July, right-wing militiamen took control of Granada by force, arresting Lorca's brother-in-law, the Socialist mayor, Manuel Fernández Montesinos. Lorca took refuge in the family home of close friend and local poet, Luis Rosales, where he thought he would be safer given that Rosales's brothers were members of the Fascist Spanish Falange (see Roberts, p. 199). On Sunday 16 August, the day his brother-in-law was executed, he was arrested at Rosales's home and eventually driven by car to a building just outside the village of Víznar, a few miles from Granada. It has never been clear whether his arrest was motivated by his support for the Republic, the liberal tenor of his work, his homosexuality or personal resentment. The next day, Monday 17 August, he and three other prisoners were murdered by firing squad and his body, along with those of the other victims, buried in an unmarked grave.

THE CHAPTERS THAT follow will consider Lorca's most popular works in light of three motifs: the Gitano, the modern and the feminist. The first will explore the implications of the Gitano tag Lorca received after the popular success of his *Romancero gitano*, along with the way he represents the Gitanos in his ballads; the second, his engagement with the idea of modernity consequent to the criticism his *Romancero gitano* received and his subsequent representation of his experience of life in New York City; and the third, his feminist credentials in the context of how he treats the condition of women in rural Andalusia. Underpinning our analysis is the belief that key to the popularity of the works selected

Figure 5 Lorca with Margarita Xirgu and theatre company director, Enrique Borrás at the premiere of *Yerma*, Madrid, 1934

is Lorca's ability to combine real-life concerns with a profound interest in aesthetics and in art in and of itself. In tension with the early twentieth-century avant-garde's preference for dehumanization, autonomy and irrationality, Lorca's work resisted – challenged even – the dichotomization that set art against life.

Chapter One

Lorca, the Gitano

IN SEPTEMBER 1928, Lorca's then close friend, the famous Surrealist artist, Salvador Dalí, wrote him an oft-quoted letter about his recently published ballad book. The book had as its central motif Spain's Romani people who go by the Spanish name Gitano: a name used not only by outsiders in Spain but also by the Romani themselves and one which we prefer to use here, both in its nominal and adjectival forms, rather than the commonly used 'gypsy' in English, an exonym that has pejorative connotations. Dalí's reaction to Lorca's book, entitled *Romancero gitano* [*Gitano Ballad Book*], was a mixed one. He saw in it 'the *hugest poetic substance that ever was*, but completely bound to the norms of the old poetry, which is no longer capable of moving us or satisfying our present-day desires.'[1] And he added: 'You probably think some of your images very bold, but I can assure you that your poetry moves within the *illustration* of the commonest and most conformist of commonplaces' (Maurer 2004, pp. 101–02). Dalí was sure that it was these commonplaces rather more than the moments of poetic substance that had seduced readers and earned Lorca's ballad book its popular success. As someone in the know, Dalí distinguished his own reading from that of those he called the *putrefactos* (meaning 'putrid' or 'putrified'), a term coined by students in Madrid's Residencia de Estudiantes – the student residence where Lorca and Dalí first met – to apply to whatever or whomever 'was considered bourgeois, out-of-date or artistically fetid' (Gibson 1989, p. 140). 'I love you for what your book reveals you to be,' Dalí wrote, 'which is the complete opposite

---

[1] Christopher Maurer (ed.), *Sebastian's Arrows. Letters and Mementos of Salvador Dalí and Federico García Lorca* (Chicago: Swan Isle Press, 2004), p. 101.

of the reality the putrified of this world have made up about you – the dusky [Gitano] with black hair, childish heart, etc. etc.' (Maurer 2004, p. 104). In a letter to friend and art critic, Sebastià Gasch, which he wrote shortly after receiving Dalí's critical missal, Lorca seemed to agree with the artist on this point: 'Claro que mi libro no lo han entendido los putrefactos,' he conceded, 'aunque ellos digan que sí' ['Of course, the putrified haven't understood my book, even if they say they have'] (*EC*, p. 585).

On one level, the Gitano moniker Lorca received seemed only to reinforce the idea that his work was hackneyed and passé. For it tied it to a ballad tradition known for reproducing the trope of romantic Spain, caricatured as the land of bullfighters, bandits and, of course, Gitanos. On another, in light of the very real marginalization and denigration of Gitanos in actual life, it had implications that extended beyond matters of poetic worth or genre. Lorca himself rejected the Gitano tag, primarily, it would seem, on artistic grounds. In a letter he wrote to friend and fellow poet, Jorge Guillén, in January 1927, he complained: 'Me va molestando un poco *mi mito* de gitanería. Confunden mi vida y mi carácter. No quiero de ninguna manera. Los gitanos son un tema. Y nada más. [...] No quiero que me encasillen. Siento que me van echando cadenas' ['The Gitano myth about me is bothering me a little. They are confusing my life and my character. I don't want this at all. The Gitanos are a theme. Nothing more. I don't want them to pigeonhole me. I feel like they are throwing me in chains'] (*EC*, p. 414). And in another letter that same month, to friend and writer, Melchor Fernández Almagro, Lorca spoke enthusiastically about another of his works, *Canciones*, emphasizing its non-Gitano character: 'Ha circulado *demasiado* mi tópico de gitanismo, y este libro de *Canciones*, por ejemplo, es un esfuerzo lírico sereno, agudo, y me parece de gran poesía (en el sentido de nobleza y calidad, no de *valor*). No es un libro *gitanístico*' ['My Gitano cliché has spread too far, and this book of *Songs*, for example, is a serene, intense lyrical endeavour, and it seems to me to be great poetry (in the sense of nobility and quality, not worth). It is not a *Gitanoistic* book'] (*EC*, p. 418).

Clearly, Lorca did not want his work to be typecast, nor did he want to be categorized in narrow terms as a folkloric writer. And yet, notwithstanding the artistic rationale behind his protestations, it is difficult not to wonder whether his rejection of the Gitano tag might also have been motivated, at least in part, by a wish to defend his persona from the low esteem in which Gitanos were generally held. How else might we interpret his admission in his letter to Guillén that 'el gitanismo me da un tono de incultura, de falta de educación y de *poeta salvaje* que tú sabes bien no soy' ['Gitanoism gives me an air of ignorance, of a lack of education and of being a savage poet, which you know I am not'] (*EC*, p. 414)? From the perspective of Lorca's reputation as defender of the oppressed and the marginalized, this admission is problematic. Perhaps all it does is suggest that he, like many other people, was not free of prejudice, whether conscious or otherwise; or that, as an artist, he was tempted, at times, to put career before principle (at least in his pronouncements to his close artistic circle). Perhaps it simply reminds us that we cannot trust everything anyone, particularly an artist, says; or that it is impossible to reduce the complex motivations of human beings to a straightforward, coherent narrative. For despite his appearing to tire of the Gitano tag and his unfortunate choice of words in his letter to Guillén, *Romancero gitano* does seem to be a work in which Lorca is determined, at every opportunity, to defend the Gitanos against the denigrating views that were prevalent in the day.

Romancero gitano, arguably Lorca's most famous and best loved collection of poems, consists of Spanish ballads, known as *romances*, a narrative verse form dating back to the Middle Ages, composed of eight-syllable lines with assonance on the even lines.[2] Although it emerged from Spain's popular, oral tradition, the *romance* has been reworked by generations of Spanish poets – Lorca included – who have sought to inject it with varying degrees of lyricism in sharp tension with its original narrative emphasis. Yet, as Derek Harris (1991, p. 12) explains, while learned poets sought to develop the 'potentialities' of the form, blind balladeers continued, nonetheless, to exploit the narrative qualities of the Spanish ballad, singing tales of crime and scandal 'for pennies [...] on the street corners of Spain'.

Lorca originally entitled his collection *Primer romancero gitano* [*First Gitano Ballad Book*], though 'first' is an epithet that requires some scrutiny given that the nineteenth century had already produced 'a substantial corpus of Andalusian *romances*' on the subject of the Gitanos.[3] These *romances*, or ballads, were celebrations of a 'picturesque quaintness' encouraged by the 'steady stream of literate travellers from England and France' for whom any vignette of Spain 'had to include the [Gitano] woman, the smuggler, the bandit, and the bullfighter, all of them closely identified

---

2 Derek Harris, Introduction to Federico García Lorca, *Romancero gitano*, ed. Derek Harris, Grant & Cutler Spanish Texts (London: Grant & Cutler, 1991), pp. 7–87 (p. 11).
3 C. Brian Morris, *Son of Andalusia: The Lyrical Landscapes of Federico García Lorca* (Liverpool: Liverpool University Press, 1997), p. 310

with Andalusia' (Morris 1997, p. 329). If, therefore, Lorca thought his collection merited having 'first' in its title, it was perhaps because of the novelty of including Gitano in the title also. At a basic level, its inclusion confirms that the world of his ballads is that of the Gitanos. But, importantly, it also suggests that the voices in his ballads are Gitano too. This is a critical point when we consider the negative image of Gitanos and of Gitano culture that circulated in Spain at the time.

A decade or so earlier, in 1915, F. M. Pabanó published his *Historia y costumbres de los gitanos* [*The History and Customs of the Gitanos*]. While Pabanó might have thought he was offering an objective and balanced view of the Spanish Romani, not least because his book acknowledged the persecution suffered by this marginalized people, his descriptions are, nonetheless, indicative of society's patronising view. 'Los andares del gitano', he writes, 'son perezosos en general, y parece que camina galbanoso y *de mala gana*, con un movimiento rítmico de caderas, no saliendo de este paso descuidado, tardo y pesado, a no ser que un asunto de interés reclame mayor diligencia' ['A Gitano's gait is lazy in general, and they appear to walk lethargically and *begrudgingly*, with a rhythmic movement of the hips, never emerging from this slovenly, sluggish and heavy pace, unless a matter of interest requires greater speed'].[4] Moreover, Pabanó (p. 52) shamelessly refers to the Gitanos as 'esa banda de eternos ladrones, esa raza paria, plagada de defectos y escasa de virtudes' ['that band of eternal thieves, that pariah race, plagued with defects and lacking virtues'] whose only rule of conduct was, in his view, to act on their own desires and for their personal gain.

Against the background of such racist and patronising views, Lorca's decision to include Gitano in the title was a bold one. It is also noteworthy that his ballads should represent the Gitanos in ways that eschew the facile stereotypes prevalent both in society and the Spanish ballad tradition. By way of example, C. Brian Morris (1997, p. 312) cites two ballads by Manuel María de Santa Ana and Salvador Rueda, written in 1869 and 1911 respectively, that 'reinforce common assumptions' about Gitanos. Rueda's confirms 'the widely held belief that [the Gitano] is different because he looks different, that his physical appearance in itself is enough to set him apart from others'; Santa Ana's shows him to be 'impudent, insolent, ingenious, with a tongue as loose and as quick as his hand'. By contrast, Morris (1997, pp. 312–13) argues, Lorca models

---

[4] F. M. Pabanó, *Historia y costumbres de los gitanos* (Barcelona: Montaner y Simón, 1915), p. 50.

his Gitanos 'on a long lineage of grandly dressed ballad figures' and has them 'voice nobler thoughts in a more elevated manner befitting the new status he assigned to them.'

Bold too was Lorca's insistence, in a public lecture-recital of his ballads he delivered in April 1926, that his book, 'aunque se llama gitano, es el poema de Andalucía' ['although it is called Gitano, it is the poem of Andalusia'] (OC, III, p. 340), echoing a comment he made about his work in progress in a letter to Guillén a month earlier: 'Quedará un libro de romances y se podrá decir que es un libro de Andalucía' ['The result will be a book of ballads and we could say that it is a book about Andalusia'] (EC, p. 334). In his April lecture-recital, he added that he had called his book Gitano 'porque el gitano es lo más elevado, lo más profundo, más aristocrático de mi país, lo más representativo de su modo y el que guarda el ascua, la sangre y el alfabeto de la verdad andaluza y universal' ['because the Gitano is the highest, most profound, most aristocratic thing that my country has to offer, the most representative of its ways and that which sustains the embers, the blood and the alphabet of Andalusian and universal truth'] (OC, III, p. 340). Lorca's statement is clearly a world apart from Pabanó's derogatory descriptions, instead challenging the denigration of the Gitanos and, by association, of Andalusia, that was commonplace even in intellectual circles.

The denigration of southern Spain, its peoples and its cultures had its roots in an idea of the country that was skewed towards Castile, itself the focus of a national debate that emerged in the early twentieth century about what Spain was and what it meant to be Spanish. This moment of self-interrogation came in the wake of the country's defeat in 1898 in the Spanish-American War that resulted in the loss of Cuba – a defeat that struck the final nail in the coffin of the Spanish Empire. Moreover, as had been the case for much of the nineteenth century, when those known as the *afrancesados* (which translates as *Frenchified* in English) dared to compare Spanish social and political mores unfavourably with those of France (the Romantic essayist Mariano José de Larra is a notable example), some intellectuals looked beyond the Pyrenees to find their template for a healthy, modern, European society. It was in this context that they scrutinized the Gitanos and what they would have seen as the unfortunate conflation of Gitano and Spanish culture that had developed in the nineteenth century. And it was also in this context that the support of

Gitano culture acquired the derogatory labels of *flamenquismo* ['flamenco-ism'] and the closely related *gitanismo* ['Gitanoism'].[5]

Two chief proponents of this anti-Gitano discourse were the writers Rafael Salillas and Eugenio Noel (see Llano, pp. 983–92). For the likes of Salillas and Noel, flamenco had become a by-word for criminality, firmly associated in their minds with the poorest areas of Madrid, where Gitano communities had established themselves since the 1840s (see Llano, p. 982), as well as with the *café cantante*: music bars where flamenco was performed and cast as dens of iniquity by their detractors. Salillas and Noel made no distinction between Gitano culture more generally and its manifestation in the capital, even though the fact of extreme poverty offered a more reasonable explanation for high levels of criminality than did the peculiarity of any Gitano custom, flamenco included. Their ideas were informed by the spurious theories of racial criminality and moral degeneration propagated by Cesare Lombroso and Max Nordau (see Llano, pp. 981–82, 984, 989–92), and their pseudo-scientific view of Gitano culture and its detrimental impact on Spanish identity would inevitably extend beyond the circumstances of Madrid to be applied to the region of Andalusia also (see Llano, p. 981). This is significant given that, in the rhetoric of those intellectuals debating Spain's identity after 1898, Castile, where Madrid is situated, was regarded as having a foundational role and as being the place where the true essence of Spanishness could be found, in marked contrast, of course, to Andalusia, the region with which Gitano culture was most firmly associated. This is why Lorca's insistence on the Gitano character both of his ballads and of Andalusia was so significant. For it deliberately positioned his work in direct opposition to the current of anti-*flamenquismo* and foregrounded Andalusia's own contribution to the nation's spirit and identity. Indeed, the vitality of his representations of the Gitano 'offered', as Morris (1997, p. 363) puts it, 'an alternative cast to the dour Castilian peasants depicted by the generation of 1898', the name given to those writers and thinkers who applied themselves to the problem of Spain in the wake of the loss of Empire.

---

5 Our discussion of anti-Gitano discourse is indebted to Samuel Llano's excellent essay on the subject, entitled 'Public Enemy or National Hero? The Spanish Gypsy and the Rise of Flamenquismo, 1898–1922', *Bulletin of Hispanic Studies*, 94.6 (2017), 977–1004. For an explanation of the origins of the term *flamenquismo*, see Llano, p. 979.

The empathy Lorca felt towards the Gitanos can be traced back to his adolescence in Granada and his visits to the caves of the Sacromonte where he made friends of the singers and dancers whom he watched perform there (Gibson 1989, p. 29). This empathy led to his collaboration with the celebrated classical composer Manuel de Falla in the organisation of the *cante jondo* competition that took place in Granada in June 1922. *Cante jondo*, which translates as 'deep song', is considered the most authentic manifestation of Gitano flamenco culture, and Lorca was determined to rescue it from the associations of licentiousness and drunken behaviour that the commercial forms of flamenco performed in the *café cantantes* had acquired. 'Muy poca gente conoce el canto gitano,' Lorca would say in an interview in 1936, 'porque lo que se da frecuentemente en los tablados es el llamado flamenco, que es una degeneración de aquel' ['Few people know Gitano song, because what is often performed in venues is the so-called flamenco, which is a degenerate version of it'] (OC, III, p. 684). Thus, in the lecture he gave to Granada's Artistic and Literary Centre to promote the *cante jondo* competition, entitled 'El cante jondo. Primitivo canto andaluz' ['Deep Song. Primitive Andalusian Song'] (OC, III, pp. 195–216), Lorca emphasized the distance between deep song and commercial flamenco by tracing the former's roots, like those of the Gitanos, to a mystical Orient, approximating its music to the sounds of the mysterious, natural world: 'al trino del pájaro, al canto del gallo y a las músicas naturales del bosque y la fuente' (OC, III, p. 197) ['to the trill of birds, a cockerel's crow and the natural music of woods and freshwater springs']. As further evidence that *cante jondo* had nothing to do with the tawdry environment of the *café cantante*, Lorca explained how it had inspired the work of great classical composers such as Mikhail Glinka and Claude Debussy, and how its concise expression even struck a chord with the tendency of contemporary poets, like himself, towards a more restrained poetic style.[6] All of this in stark contrast to the exaggerated cries, gestures and clichéd motifs of flamenco performed in bars that only offered, in his words, 'el ridículo jipío' ['the ridiculous flamenco lament'] and 'la españolada' (OC, III, p. 195), a term used to denote stereotypical representations of Spain.

---

6   See Dennis Perri, 'Fulfillment and Loss: Lorca's View of Communication in the Twenties', *Hispania*, 75.3 (September 1992), 484–91, on Lorca's fascination with *cante jondo* and its connection to the avant-garde's rejection of the verbosity and sentimentality.

Musicologists will note that there are problems with Lorca's genealogy of deep song. For it does not stand up to rigorous historical examination and, moreover, offers a reductively Orientalist vision of Asia; one that, in other words, represents Asia in clichéd terms from a Western perspective. What is more, Lorca's attempt to associate deep song with classical music and contemporary poetry invites accusations that his was an elitist perspective inconsistent with the form's popular character.[7] The same might be said of his *Poema del cante jondo* [*Poem of the Deep Song*], the collection of poems he wrote in 1921 in anticipation of the competition the following year. The collection sets out to evoke the structure, content and context of different forms of deep song – namely, those known as the *siguiriya*, *soleá*, *saeta* and *petenera*. But even if it succeeds in reproducing some of deep song's characteristic mood, imagery and formal features, it cannot replicate the ardent spontaneity of the form nor, as a consequence, its popular circumstance, all of which is inevitably lost in the process of its translation into literary text and poetic conceit.

In 'Poema de la siguiriya gitana' ['Poem of the Gitano Siguiriya'], for example, simile, metaphor, synaesthesia and anthropomorphism are amongst the rhetorical devices that take pride of place in Lorca's recreation of the *siguiriya* – all accompanied by the deep sense of mystery characterizing his conceptualization of deep song.[8] Opening with a landscape likened to a dancer's fan ('El campo | de olivos | se abre y se cierra | como un abanico' ['The olive field opens and closes like a fan'] [OC, I, p. 157]), the poem moves on to introduce the guitar's lament ('Empieza el llanto | de la guitarra' [The guitar's lament begins'] [OC, I, p. 158]) before evoking a cry which it conceives figuratively as an ellipse stretching 'de monte | a monte' ['from hill to hill'] (OC, I, p. 159) and 'un arco iris negro | sobre la noche azul' ['a black rainbow over the blue night'] (OC, I, p. 159). There follows a moment of resonant silence ('un silencio ondulado' ['an undulating silence'] [OC, I, p. 160]) – a pregnant pause – after which the *siguiriya*, via the device of anthropomorphism, makes its full-bodied appearance in the shape of a dark-skinned girl. It then departs as mysteriously as it arrived ('Los candiles se apagan' ['The candles go out'] [OC, I, p. 162]), taking with it all the emotion it aroused ('El corazón | fuente del

---

[7] See, for example, Timothy Mitchell, *Flamenco Deep Song* (New Haven: Yale University Press, 1994), pp. 164–68.
[8] Federico García Lorca, *Obras completas*, I, ed. Arturo del Hoyo, 22nd edn (Madrid: Aguilar, 1986), pp. 155–63.

deseo | se desvanece' ['The heart, fountain of desire, evanesces'] [OC, I, p. 163]), the ensuing emptiness becoming the only trace of a performance that has now passed ('Solo queda el desierto. Un ondulado | desierto' [All that remains is the desert. An undulating desert'] [OC, I, p. 163]).

Poema del cante jondo also contains evocations of the accoutrements of deep song performance, though here too the rhetorical devices efface the spontaneity associated with the original music and dance. Thus, in 'Adivinanza de la guitarra' ['The Riddle of the Guitar'] (OC, I, p. 217), the intention, as the title suggests, is to reveal the musical object only at the end, the logic of the riddle privileging reason over the raw emotion of performance no matter how delightful we might regard the poem's mythological evocations to be:

En la redonda
encrucijada,
seis doncellas
bailan.
Tres de carne
y tres de plata.
Los sueños de ayer las buscan,
pero las tiene abrazadas
un Polifemo de oro.
¡La guitarra!

[At the round crossroads, six damsels dance. Three of flesh and three of silver. Yesterday's dreams seek them out, but a golden Polyphemus keeps them in his embrace. The guitar!]

And central to the poem 'Crótalo' ['Castanet'] (OC, I, p. 219) – the word *crótalo* is preferred to the more common *castañuela* – is its ingenuous observation of the onomatopoeic qualities of the percussion instrument's name. These qualities, along with the instrument's colour and shape that give rise to its figuration as a beetle, playfully recreate some of the sounds and gestures of deep song performance, but not, I hasten to add, either its passion or spontaneity:

Crótalo.
Crótalo.
Crótalo.
Escarabajo sonoro.

    En la araña
de la mano

rizas el aire
cálido,
y te ahogas en tu trino
de palo.

   Crótalo.
Crótalo.
Crótalo.
Escarabajo sonoro.

[Castanet. Castanet. Castanet. Sonorous beetle. In the spider of the hand you curl the warm air and drown in your wooden trill. Castanet. Castanet. Castanet. Sonorous beetle.]

   The poems of *Poema del cante jondo*, then, are clearly not identical in form, rationale or effect to the *cante jondo* performance that inspired them. Informed by contemporary poetic trends, they are intended only as evocations of this popular musical expression. Thus, their relation to actual *cante jondo* is metonymic, synecdochic, metaphorical or, at best, atmospheric.

   In the case of *Romancero gitano*, critics have also noted essential differences between its ballads and the popular origins of the ballad form, thus placing Lorca in the category of those learned poets who have sought to rework the *romance* and detach it from its original narrative function. Harris (1991, p. 12), for example, argues that narrative in Lorca's ballads is replaced 'by exuberant and highly ingenious imagery, by words rather than by ideas or description'. Like the poems of *Poema del cante jondo*, the ballads are informed by contemporary trends, cast in the mould of what has been termed 'pure poetry', a poetic fashion of the 1920s (in line with the tendency towards impersonality in art) that sought 'to reduce description and narrative' and emphasize 'language itself as the primary poetic element'; language as 'suggestion and allusiveness' rather than a vehicle for 'mundane meaning' (Harris 1991, p. 8).

   Such readings, in privileging the ballad book's lyricism over its storytelling and in line with the view that 'mere narrative plays little part in most of the poems',[9] serve to distinguish Lorca's work, in character

---

9 H. Ramsden, *Lorca's 'Romancero gitano': Eighteen commentaries* (Manchester: Manchester University Press, 1988), p. vi. For Ramsden (1998, p. vi), this view has had 'adverse consequences', but only because the critics' focus on individual images rather than storylines has stopped short of demonstrating the function of the former 'in the total context of the poem.' Harris (1991, p. 11) suggests that Lorca uses the ballad form 'for purposes that are far from

and function, from popular art. Lorca, for his part, apparently also felt it important to make the distinction. As Morris (1997, p. 317) notes, he chose not to give public recitals of his ballad 'La casada infiel' ['The Unfaithful Wife'] (OC, I, pp. 406–07) on the very grounds that it was 'exasperatingly popular'.[10] And remarkably, in an interview he would give in Buenos Aires in 1933, which Morris (1997, p. 318) also cites, he explained that he did not consider his *Romancero gitano*, or indeed the greater part of his poetry, to be popular. Singling out 'La casada infiel' again as an example of the very few poems that might be considered as such, he cited its visceral connection to race ('raza'), to the people ('pueblo'), and its ability to be accessible and move everyone who hears it ('puede ser accesible a todos los lectores y emocionar a todos los que lo escuchen'), as its defining, popular characteristics (OC, III, p. 558). The majority of his work, he suggested, was defined by 'una visión y una técnica que contradicen la simple espontaneidad de lo popular' ['a vision and technique that contradict the simple spontaneity of the popular'] (OC, III, p. 558). Emphasizing the importance of form over theme in categorizations of his work, he only just stopped short of describing his art as aristocratic: 'la mayor parte de mi obra no puede [ser popular], aunque lo parezca por su tema, porque es un arte, no diré aristocrático, pero sí depurado' ['most of my work cannot (be popular), even though it may seem so thematically, because it is an art, I will not say aristocratic, but definitely purified'] (OC, III, p. 558).[11]

---

popular poetry'. He argues that while Lorca 'does keep the traditional narrative function of the form', he 'handles it in a new way by compressing the anecdotal circumstances to such an extent that it is difficult on occasions to say what is the story of the poem' (Harris 1991, p. 12). Morris (1997, p. 318), too, suggests that in Lorca's ballad book 'what the poem may communicate is less important than the style of communication'. He, like others, has looked to Lorca's lecture on the Cordovan Renaissance poet, Luis de Góngora, entitled 'La imagen poética de Don Luis de Góngora' ['The Poetic Image of Don Luis de Góngora'] (OC, III, p. 223–47).

10 Morris (1997, p. 317) explains that, of all the ballads, 'La casada infiel' ['The Unfaithful Wife'] and 'Romance de la Guardia Civil española' ['Ballad of the Spanish Civil Guard'] 'are the ones that come closest to the flamboyantly melodramatic situations narrated in many nineteenth-century ballads.'

11 Morris (1997, p. 318) infers from the qualifications Lorca made in his interview that the 'vision' he referred to was 'one that transcends the obvious, devises a significance beneath the surface', and that by 'technique' he meant the ability to inject the 'unfamiliar and the enigmatic' into scenarios that

The stance Lorca takes here is surprising. His posturing, I would suggest, is a hangover from the days when he found himself having to defend his ballads against its avant-garde critics and against the romantic vision of its overzealous admirers. For there is evidence elsewhere, including in his work itself, that he actually cared little for distinctions between highbrow and popular. A case in point is the lecture he gave in Granada in 1926 on the Cordovan Renaissance poet, Luis de Góngora, entitled 'La imagen poética de Don Luis de Góngora' ['The Poetic Image of Don Luis de Góngora'] (OC, III, p. 223–47) (as mentioned above, note 9).

Although Lorca may have stopped short of characterizing his own work as aristocratic in his Buenos Aires interview, his assessment of Góngora is far more forthright as he describes the Cordovan's place in the history of Spanish poetry as being one of 'aristocrática soledad' ['aristocratic solitude'] (OC, III, p. 227). And yet, notwithstanding the preeminent position he ascribes to Góngora, he is still at pains to evoke the connections between this poet's 'aristocratic' work, renowned for its complex metaphors, and the language of ordinary Andalusians. Like Góngora's work, the vernacular of Andalusia is replete with magnificent metaphorical images. Lorca gives as examples sweets called 'tocino de cielo' ['heaven's bacon'] and 'suspiros de monja' ['nun's sighs'] (OC, III, p. 224), and the term 'buey de agua' ['water ox'] commonly used to refer to a deep channel of water moving slowly across a field (OC, III, p. 224). In emphasizing the cultural and linguistic heritage common to all Andalusians, Lorca reveals an ability to see beyond strict categorizations that keep the high and lowbrow apart. And even though, in later years, he might have sought to emphasize the less accessible aspects of his own work, the majority of his ballads, however complex they might be poetically, do, in the main, employ a vocabulary that is everyday and familiar, at least from the perspective of those with experience of the rural realities and rural lexicon of Andalusia.[12]

---

    otherwise might seem familiar and unambiguous. Thus, Morris's inferences, like those of other critics, point to Lorca as being a poet in tune with the dominant aesthetic of his day – that is, with pure poetry.

12 As Gibson (1989, p. 159) notes, Lorca's lecture on Góngora is generally considered to be a gloss of his own poetic practice. Harris (1991, p. 12) takes the connection between the work of the two men further by suggesting that Lorca's ballads were 'in part a homage to Góngora who had also replaced anecdote with metaphor and daringly incorporated conceits into folksong poems'.

In his lecture on Góngora, the high and lowbrow rub shoulders, his commentary on popular idiom serving as a prelude to observations on the Renaissance poet's classical culture. In Lorca's world view, there is no contradiction here, since what he is interested in, without preference or prejudice, is the rich complexity of Andalusia's cultural heritage that includes not only the classical legacy of Spain's Roman period but also the rich complexity of the region's vernacular. It could be argued that the high and lowbrow similarly rub shoulders in *Poema del cante jondo*, despite the criticism that has labelled Lorca's approach to deep song elitist. We might go so far as to suggest that the distinction between the high and lowbrow is suspended, if not completely erased, in the collection's playful metaphors that transform, in 'Adivinanza de la guitarra', a Spanish guitar into a golden Polyphemus, or, in 'Chumbera' ['Prickly Pear'] (OC, I, p. 220), a common cactus into a player of the Basque ball game, pelota, as well as into the classical figure of Troy's ill-fated priest, Laocoön: 'Laocoonte salvaje [...] Múltiple pelotari' ['Wild Laocoön (...) Multiple pelota player'].

In *Romancero gitano*, the popular and the classical are also in intimate proximity, the ballad book's awareness of Andalusia's cultural heritage extending beyond the influence of Gitano culture to embrace its Roman legacy too, along with its Arabic and Judeo-Christian roots.[13] In essence, Lorca's ballads are stories akin to ancient myths, the fantastical qualities of the narratives of classical mythology now transposed to an Andalusian setting. Where the gods and heroes of antiquity once walked, now walk the Gitanos. And what better way to reveal the false dichotomy between low and highbrow than to reference classical culture? For despite its association with scholarly erudition, classical mythology offers, just like the popular ballad, tales of love, conflict and personal suffering that appeal to the emotions as much as, if not more than, they do the intellect. Pitting the Gitanos against 'the forces of both fate and social repression' (Harris 1991, p. 13), the ballads render them heroes in the mould of the Ancient Greeks, all the while acknowledging the reality of their marginalised condition.

---

13 Interestingly, in an interview he gave in 1934, Lorca describes how, as a child, he witnessed a plough unearth a fragment of Roman mosaic bearing the names of Daphnis and Chloe. He describes the event as his first moment of 'asombro artístico' ['artistic wonder'] (OC, III, p. 660). How fitting, given the mixture of high and lowbrow in his work, that this moment should be one in which Andalusia's classical heritage surfaces amid its everyday, rural present.

In the end, for all their lyricism, the stories and narratives of Lorca's ballads do count for something. Yet their lyrical character also plays its part, working, as we shall see, not only to aesthetic effect, or for the purposes of mood, but rather to steer the narrative and its characters away from commonplace associations that have a prejudicial impact on the image of Gitanos. Thus, despite the tendency of critics to set one against the other, lyricism in Lorca's ballads can be seen to work not against the demands of narrative but in concert with it, as Lorca's contemporary myths set out to rescue the Gitanos, and with them the popular Spanish ballad, from denigrating stereotypes.[14]

Romancero gitano opens with 'Romance de la luna, luna' ['Ballad of the Moon, Moon'] (OC, I, p. 393–94), in which death in the form of an anthropomorphic moon comes to a blacksmith's forge to carry off a young Gitano boy who is fated, it seems, to die on this day:

> La luna vino a la fragua
> con su polisón de nardos.
> El niño la mira, mira.
> El niño la está mirando.
> En el aire conmovido
> mueve la luna sus brazos
> y enseña, lúbrica y pura,
> sus senos de duro estaño. (OC, I, p. 393)

[The moon came to the forge with her bustle of spikenards. The young boy looks at her, looks at her. The young boy keeps looking at her. In the troubled air, the moon waves her arms and shows, lubric and pure, her breasts of hard tin.]

As in the myths of antiquity, magical events are treated as real. The moon is just as able to be a character in the story as is a human being. Typically feminine, with strong erotic overtones, the moon has something of Diana, goddess of the moon and war, about her. The bustle of arrows with which Diana is usually depicted is now replaced by a bustle

---

[14] As Llano (p. 977) argues, Lorca was responding, as he had done with the organization of the Concurso del cante jondo and with his *Poema del cante jondo*, 'to a tradition of denigrating [Gitanos] and flamenco in Spanish culture'. See also William Washabaugh, *Flamenco: Passion, Politics and Popular Culture* (Oxford and Washington: Berg, 1996), p. 120, on what he describes as the attempt in the 1920s, including the Concurso del cante jondo, to 'legitimate flamenco as high art'.

of nards: white, bell-shaped flowers that reflect the moon's pale colour and reinforce her connection with nature as opposed to the world of manmade things. The scenario is charged with drama and develops along dramatic lines, the initial scene giving way to a dialogue in which the young Gitano boy vocalizes his defiant resistance. As far as we can tell from the moon's responses, he does so to no avail:

> Huye luna, luna, luna.
> Si vinieran los gitanos,
> harían con tu corazón
> collares y anillos blancos.
> Niño, déjame que baile.
> Cuando vengan los gitanos,
> te encontrarán sobre el yunque
> con los ojillos cerrados.
> Huye luna, luna, luna,
> que ya siento sus caballos.
> Niño, déjame, no pises
> mi blancor almidonado. (OC, I, p. 393)

[Run moon, moon, moon. If the Gitanos came they would make of your heart white necklaces and rings. 'Child, let me dance. When the Gitanos come, they will find you on the anvil with your little eyes shut.' 'Run moon, moon, moon, I can already hear their horses.' 'Child, let me be, don't step on my starched whiteness.']

The boy's last hope hinges, as does the drama, on the arrival of Gitanos riding to the scene and their magical ability to defy this unworldly being. The Gitano cavalry is introduced via a metaphor of sound in which drumbeats evoke the gallop of hooves:

> El jinete se acercaba
> tocando el tambor del llano.
> Dentro de la fragua el niño
> tiene los ojos cerrados.
> Por el olivar venían,
> bronce y sueño, los gitanos.
> Las cabezas levantadas
> y los ojos entornados. (OC, I, pp. 393–94)

[The horseman drew closer playing the drum of the plain. Inside the forge the young boy's eyes are shut. Through the olive groves they came, bronze and dream, the Gitanos. Their heads held high and eyes half-closed.]

The position of the young boy signals that the Gitanos have arrived too late. All that is left for them to do is mourn, a mourning that is accompanied, in moments of pathetic fallacy, by animate nature:

> ¡Cómo canta la zumaya,
> ay, cómo canta en el árbol!
> Por el cielo va la luna
> con un niño de la mano.
>
> Dentro de la fragua lloran,
> dando gritos, los gitanos.
> El aire la vela, vela.
> El aire la está velando. (OC, I, p. 394)

[How the nightjar sings! Ah, how it sings in the tree! Through the sky goes the moon with a child in her hand. Inside the forge cry, shouting, the Gitanos. The wind watches over, watches over. The wind is watching over.]

When all is said and done, 'Romance de la luna, luna' is simply a ballad about a child dying. Yet it treats its subject with dignity, seeing in death not futility but mystery; a mystery that myth is well suited to convey because of its tendency towards anthropomorphization and because of its acceptance of a magical order that renders animate the eternal struggle between the natural forces of life and death. The ballad's lyrical element serves to augment this magical order and, in so doing, complements, rather than undermines, the storytelling. It is also evidence of the fact that the poem's scenarios, despite their obvious connections to reality (human figures, the natural world, the fact of life and death), are the product of a poetic reimagining.

It is worth reflecting for a moment on the negotiation of reality and myth that takes place in 'Romance de la luna, luna' and that is characteristic of Lorca's ballads throughout. In a sense, the young boy's death belongs to the real world, inasmuch as it has the potential to have been a real event. So too, in astronomical terms, does the moon, as do the nightjar and Gitanos whose existence in the real world is undeniable. Yet just like the nards placed in the moon's bustle, all these things – the young boy's death, the moon, the nightjar and Gitanos – are set in a context that lends them an aura of unreality. In short, they belong to the world of artistic creativity; that is, to Lorca's imagination and not to documentary.

Here we are reminded that, in the early twentieth century, avant-garde production prioritized art over real life, by which we mean that it sought to put the things of the world at the service of art. 'I don't have to be your slave, Mother Nature', the Chilean poet and founder of literary Creationism, Vicente Huidobro, famously proclaimed in 1914, in his treatise on artistic autonomy; 'I will be your master. You will use me; that's fine. I don't want to, nor can I, avoid it; but I will use you also. I will have my trees, which will not be like yours, I will have my mountains, I will have my rivers and my seas, I will have my sky and my stars.'[15] Thus, Lorca was writing at the height of European Modernism, when many writers, influenced by perspectivist and subjectivist philosophies and convinced of the unreliability of mimesis – a conviction that lay at the heart of impersonal trends – sought to prioritize artistic invention over the representation of reality and, in the process, assert the autonomy of art.[16]

The emphasis on artistic autonomy, however, along with the rejection of a realist or documentarist approach, did not mean that an artist could not have real-life concerns. Lorca's own work is an example of how creative invention could be put at the service of moral, social, or political preoccupations, if an artist so wanted. Thus, in Lorca's case, there was no contradiction between his artistic priorities and his defence of the Gitanos. Quite the contrary. For his ballads, even if taken to be independent works of art, offered themselves as evidence of the aesthetic achievement and noble sentiment that the Gitanos could inspire in an artist, in stark contrast to the negative response their culture elicited from the likes of Pabanó, Noel and others. While some intellectuals belittled Gitano culture in an effort to discredit the Gitanos more generally, Lorca's esteem for the Gitanos was, conversely, rooted in his admiration for their art. For him, the Gitanos' journey from the caves of the Sacromonte to the pages of his elaborate verse was a natural one. They appeared in his ballads in

---

15 Vicente Huidobro, *Obras completas*, I (Santiago de Chile: Zig-Zag, 1964), p. 653. The original reads: 'No he de ser tu esclavo, Madre Natura, seré tu amo. Te servirás de mí; está bien. No quiero, y no puedo evitarlo; pero yo también me serviré de ti. Yo tendré mis árboles, que no serán como los tuyos, tendré mis montañas, tendré mis ríos y mis mares, tendré mi cielo y mis estrellas.'

16 Modernism is a term that covers the various isms of the avant-garde, such as Dadaism, Cubism, Ultraism, Imagism, Futurism, Surrealism and Vorticism. For an introduction to European Modernism, see Malcolm Bradbury and James Walter McFarlane, eds, *Modernism 1890–1930* (London: Penguin Books, 1991) and Michael H. Whitworth, ed., *Modernism* (Oxford: Blackwell, 2007).

flagrant disregard of the facile distinctions between high and low culture, defying the views of those who, considering their culture to be degenerate, habitually professed its negative impact on the image of Spain.

If in 'Romance de la luna, luna', the Gitanos come face to face with the irrepressible force of fate, in 'Romance de la Guardia Civil española' ['Ballad of the Spanish Civil Guard'] (OC, I, pp. 426–30) they are victims of the forces of social repression. This repression is embodied by Spain's Civil Guard, 'their traditional real-life enemies' (Ramsden 1998, p. 94), depicted sacking and burning an encampment where the Gitanos had been preparing for religious festivities. As Ramsden (1998, p. 94) explains, the Civil Guard was 'popularly seen in Spain as the most disciplined and incorruptible of the country's forces of law and order', but was also 'associated with over-rigorous methods, especially in the treatment of those involved in petty crime'. Lorca's own impressions of the Civil Guard are captured in a letter he wrote to his brother, Francisco, in late January or early February 1926. In his letter he recounts details of an excursion he had made to the Alpujarra. He notes how the region, on the slopes of the Sierra Nevada, was totally under the control of the Civil Guard. He cites two horrific episodes a young boy had recounted to him during his trip there, each of which illustrated the cruelty the Civil Guard was capable of. First, in the village of Carataunas, an officer who had wanted to rid the vicinity of its Gitanos summoned them one day to his barracks. There he used a pair of fire tongs to extract a tooth from each of the Gitanos, warning that unless they left the area immediately they would each lose another tooth the very next day. Then, in the village of Cañar, at Easter, the Civil Guard punished a fourteen-year-old Gitano for stealing a chicken from the mayor by parading him around the village with his arms tied to a log and making him sing at the top of his voice while the Guardsmen beat him with a belt (EC, p. 330).

Given these tales of cruelty, it is little wonder that Lorca's ballad should introduce the Civil Guard as a dark, menacing, deathly force. Their menace is conveyed by the utter blackness of their horses and attire and by the association of their personas with inanimate materials like leather and lead, as well as with the night:

Los caballos negros son.
Las herraduras son negras.
Sobre las capas relucen
manchas de tinta y de cera.
Tienen, por eso no lloran,
de plomo las calaveras.

Con el alma de charol
vienen por la carretera.
Jorobados y nocturnos,
por donde animan ordenan
silencios de goma oscura
y miedos de fina arena.
Pasan, si quieren pasar,
y ocultan en la cabeza
una vaga astronomía
de pistolas inconcretas. (OC, I, p. 426)

[Black are the horses. The horseshoes are black. On their capes gleam stains of ink and wax. They do not cry because their skulls are cast in lead. With their patent leather souls, they ride the roads. Hunchbacked and nocturnal, wherever they appear, they command dark rubber silence and fears of fine sand. They go wherever they please and hide in their heads a vague astronomy of abstract pistols.]

The Guardsmen are headed for the Gitano encampment, which the ballad, in subsequent verses, associates with the Holy Family and the feast of the Nativity. The figures of the Virgin Mary and St Joseph are rendered Gitano or, at the very least, Andalusian (see Harris 1991, p. 67). In addition, a typically Andalusian figure, Pedro Domecq, the maker of sherry in the province of Jerez, is pictured accompanying the Magi who are referred to in the ballad as three Persian sultans:

La Virgen y San José
perdieron sus castañuelas,
y buscan a los gitanos
para ver si las encuentran.
La Virgen viene vestida
con un traje de alcaldesa
de papel de chocolate
con los collares de almendras.
San José mueve los brazos
bajo una capa de seda.
Detrás va Pedro Domecq
con tres sultanes de Persia. (OC, I, p. 427)

[The Virgin and St Joseph lost their castanets and are looking for the Gitanos to see if they can find them. The Virgin is wearing a mayoress's dress of chocolate wrappers and necklaces of almonds. St Joseph swings his arms beneath a silk cape. Behind them comes Pedro Domecq with three Persian sultans.]

The encampment's inhabitants are unaware of the coming onslaught, despite premonitory warnings that lurk mysteriously amidst the festive preparations, like the reflection of sobbing dancers in mirrors or the mysterious evocation of water and shadow:

> La media luna soñaba
> un éxtasis de cigüeña.
> Estandartes y faroles
> invaden las azoteas.
> Por los espejos sollozan
> bailarinas sin caderas.
> Agua y sombra, sombra y agua
> por Jerez de la Frontera. (OC, I, pp. 427–28)

[The half moon was dreaming up a stork's ecstasy. Banners and lamps take over the rooftops. In every mirror, there sob dancers with no hips. Water and shadow, shadow and water in Jerez de la Frontera.]

The atmosphere in these lines, despite the stork's traditional connotations of birth and despite water's normally positive associations, is strangely unsettling and tense. But then, the reader knows what is coming, as does the narrator who sends a warning to the Gitanos which he, as the storyteller, must already know is in vain:

> ¡Oh ciudad de los gitanos!
> En las esquinas banderas.
> Apaga tus verdes luces
> que viene la benemérita.
> ¡Oh ciudad de los gitanos!
> ¿Quién te vio y no te recuerda?
> Dejadla lejos del mar
> sin peines para sus crenchas. (OC, I, p. 428)

[Oh city of the Gitanos! Flags flying on every corner. Put out your green lights, the Civil Guard is coming. Oh city of the Gitanos! Who has seen you and does not remember? Leave her far from the sea without a comb to part her hair.]

Against the background of biblical allusion, the Civil Guardsmen, advancing two abreast towards the festive scene ('Avanzan de dos en fondo | a la ciudad de la fiesta' [OC, I, p. 428]), have an air of Roman centurions about them. Lorca said as much in a letter he wrote to fellow poet Guillén in November 1926: 'A veces, sin que se sepa por qué, se convertían en centuriones romanos' ['At times, without it being known why, they turned into Roman centurions'] (*EC*, p. 394). This letter contains several stanzas from the ballads, but Lorca had yet to finish those devoted to the scenes of the Civil Guard's attack on the encampment. For this reason, he only summarizes these scenes, including details of the Civil Guardsmen's celebrations which, as it turned out, did not actually make it into the final version: 'Ahora llega la Guardia Civil y destruye la ciudad. Luego se van los guardias al cuartel y allí brindan con anís Cazalla por la muerte de los gitanos' ['Now the Civil Guard arrives and destroys the city. Then the guardsmen return to their barracks where they toast the death of the Gitanos with aniseed liqueur'] (*EC*, p. 394). But it is Lorca's subsequent comments that are most telling since they bring into sharp relief his aesthetic priorities in his treatment of even the most violent of social realities: 'Las escenas del saqueo serán preciosas [...] La apoteosis final de la Guardia Civil es emocionante' ['The scenes of the sacking are beautiful' (...) The Civil Guard's grand finale is moving'] (*EC*, p. 394).

The scenes Lorca most likely had in mind here include those depicted in the following stanza:

> La ciudad, libre de miedo,
> multiplicaba sus puertas.
> Cuarenta guardias civiles
> entran a saco por ellas.
> Los relojes se pararon,
> y el coñac de las botellas
> se disfrazó de noviembre
> para no infundir sospechas.
> Un vuelo de gritos largos
> se levantó en las veletas.
> Los sables cortan las brisas
> que los cascos atropellan.
> Por las calles de penumbra
> huyen las gitanas viejas
> con los caballos dormidos
> y las orzas de monedas.
> Por las calles empinadas
> suben las capas siniestras,
> dejando detrás fugaces
> remolinos de tijeras. (*OC*, I, pp. 428–29)

[The city, free of fear, multiplied its doors. Forty Civil Guardsmen rush through them. The clocks stopped and bottles of cognac disguise themselves as November so as not to arouse suspicion. A flight of long screams rose from the weathervanes. Sabres cut the breezes trampled by the hooves. Through the dimly lit streets the old Gitano women flee on sleepy horses and with jars of coins. Up the steep streets climb the sinister capes, leaving behind sudden whirlwinds of shears.]

Such lines epitomize the way in which Lorca is able to transform social realities into artistic moments. The encampment's vulnerability and its inhabitants' ignorance of what is about to happen are conveyed figuratively by the augmentative 'multiplication of doors' ('multiplicaba las puertas') through which the guardsmen will enter unresisted. As in 'Romance de la luna, luna', an animate nature accompanies the scene; here, manmade objects – the clocks and brandy bottles – share in the Gitanos' shock and fear by stopping and hiding, respectively. But perhaps most notable is the way in which 'breezes' ('brisas') stand in for people as the recipients of violence, while the guardsmen are conveyed metonymically by 'sabres' ('sables') and 'hooves' ('cascos') and their violence, metaphorically by 'whirlwinds' ('remolinos').

The next stanza, for which the frame of reference is still the Nativity, presents the victims and perpetrators of violence in ever more physical terms, even though it is no less preoccupied with the aesthetics of the scene:

> En el Portal de Belén
> los gitanos se congregan.
> San José, lleno de heridas,
> amortaja a una doncella.
> Tercos fusiles agudos
> por toda la noche suenan.
> La Virgen cura a los niños
> con salivilla de estrella.
> Pero la Guardia Civil
> avanza sembrando hogueras,
> donde joven y desnuda
> la imaginación se quema.
> Rosa la de los Camborios,
> gime sentada en su puerta
> con sus dos pechos cortados
> puestos en una bandeja.
> Y otras muchachas corrían
> perseguidas por sus trenzas,
> en un aire donde estallan
> rosas de pólvora negra.
> Cuando todos los tejados
> eran surcos en la tierra,
> el alba meció sus hombros
> en largo perfil de piedra. (OC, I, pp. 429–30)

[In the stable of Bethlehem the Gitanos gather. St Joseph, badly wounded, lays a maiden in a shroud. Stubborn pointed rifles fire through the night. The Virgin tends to children with saliva from a star. But the Civil Guard advances sowing fires, where young and naked imagination burns. Rosa of the Camborios sits moaning at her door with her severed breasts upon a tray. And other girls ran around chased by their braids, in a wind where roses of black powder explode. When all the tile rooves were furrows in the earth, dawn moved its shoulders, a long silhouette of stone.]

The Nativity scene is a mutilated one, death usurping the miracle birth. Violence has physical presence in the form of St Joseph's wounds, the maiden's dead body and the Civil Guard's rifles, as well as the fires they light (the fact that it is the 'imagination' burning in these fires implies that the violence extends beyond the physical realm to impact on mental freedoms too). Rosa Camborio's mutilated body has connotations of Christian martyrdom, and this, along with the savaging of the Nativity more generally, makes clear which group belongs to the wicked and which to the righteous. Poetic flourishes are ever present in the shape of the rose form given to gunpowder explosions ('estallan | rosas de pólvora negra' ['roses of black powder explode'], in the images of girls seemingly chased by their own braids as they run, as well as in the apparition of the dawn which, rather than bringing light, looms over the catastrophe like some ponderous stone giant. If the mythic scenario of 'Romance de la luna, luna' served to cast death as a mysterious rather than futile event, the Christian allusions and poeticization of violence in 'Romance de la Guardia Civil española' render the Gitanos' struggle an epic one. In the process, it elicits sympathies in the reader on a par, say, with those they might feel regarding Herod's massacre of the innocents in the New Testament. In this way, the poem's metaphorical ingenuity, which enabled Lorca to think of its violent scenes, in aesthetic terms, as beautiful, serves a social agenda. The effect is not only to remind readers of the persecution which Gitanos have been subjected to, but also, in order to bring about a broader, cultural shift, have them accept the Gitanos as fellow human beings who inhabit a shared history, provided here by their insertion into a common, biblical frame of reference.

The final stanzas of the poem leave us with both the image of the Gitano encampment in flames and a moment of self-reference by the narrator:

¡Oh ciudad de los gitanos!
La Guardia Civil se aleja
por un túnel de silencio
mientras las llamas te cercan.

¡Oh ciudad de los gitanos!
¿Quién te vio y no te recuerda?
Que te busquen en mi frente.
Juego de luna y arena. (OC, I, p. 430)

[Oh city of the Gitanos! The Civil Guard leaves through a tunnel of silence as the flames encircle you. Oh city of the Gitanos! Who has seen you and does not remember? Let them find you in my brow. Play of moon and sand.]

Some have seen the switch to the first-person voice in this last stanza as enabling us to identify the voice as being that of the poet rather than of a fictional Gitano storyteller. But ultimately the distinction is immaterial. For the perspective is, in either case, necessarily Gitano, whether it is delivered by a fellow Gitano or a poet who sees himself as fellow to them. What the insistence that others look for the Gitanos' city in the speaker's brow seems to be suggesting is that the memory of the Gitanos' plight can only be preserved by a mind that engages with them as equals across the full gamut of human experience.

In a few of Lorca's ballads, Gitanos are the perpetrators as well as the victims of violence. One of these is 'Reyerta' ['Feud'] (OC, I, pp. 398–99);

En la mitad del barranco
las navajas de Albacete,
bellas de sangre contraria,
relucen como los peces.
Una dura luz de naipe
recorta en el agrio verde,
caballos enfurecidos
y perfiles de jinetes.
En la copa de un olivo
lloran dos viejas mujeres.
El toro de la reyerta
se sube por las paredes.
Ángeles negros traían
pañuelos y agua de nieve.
Ángeles con grandes alas
de navajas de Albacete.
Juan Antonio el de Montilla
rueda muerto la pendiente,
su cuerpo lleno de lirios
y una granada en las sienes.
Ahora monta cruz de fuego
carretera de la muerte.

*

El juez, con guardia civil,
por los olivares viene.
Sangre resbalada gime
muda canción de serpiente.
Señores guardias civiles:
aquí pasó lo de siempre.
Han muerto cuatro romanos
y cinco cartagineses. (OC, I, pp. 398–99)

[Half-way down the ravine, the knives of Albacete, beautiful with rival blood, gleam like fishes. The hard light of a card cuts out, in the bitter green, furious horses and horsemen's silhouettes. In the crown of an olive tree two old women cry. The bull of the feud climbs the walls. Black angels brought handkerchiefs and snow water. Angels with big wings of Albacete knives. Juan Antonio de Montilla rolls dead on the slope, his body full of irises and a pomegranate in his temples. Now he rides a fiery cross on the road of death. The judge, with the Civil Guard, comes through the olive groves. Spilling blood moans a mute, serpent's song. Gentleman of the Civil Guard: here has happened what always happens. Four Romans and five Carthaginians have died.]

Lorca's choice of a knife fight as the subject of this poem was a bold one given the very common and frequent associations of Gitanos with violence. Newspaper headlines, for example, functioned as a 'formulaic stigmatization' (Morris 1997, p. 335) of the Gitanos by constantly emphasizing the race of those involved in acts of violence. But Lorca counters, or at least problematizes, such associations via the processes of poeticization. The knives in the opening lines are disconnected from those who wield them and are instead associated only with Albacete, the place where they were crafted. Although they may have been used to stab a rival, the brutality of the act is displaced by an aesthetic consideration that conceives of blood as a beautifying element and that compares gleaming blades to fishes. Until the introduction of Juan Antonio de Montilla, the combatants remain indistinct figures; instead, their fury and the feud itself are embodied by horses and a bull, respectively. What the combatants' apparent lack of agency does is lend the ballad an air of inevitability, as it tells of a tragedy that has played itself out since time immemorial. The accompanying angels – 'Ángeles con grandes alas'('Angels with big wings') – add to this sense of timeless foreboding. When Juan Antonio is finally introduced, his fatal wounds are transformed into images of flowers and fruit, and his death, into a metaphorical journey astride a burning cross. The lack of agency is reinforced in the final stanza, where blood is detached from any bleeding body and is instead given its own voice as it moans a 'muda canción de serpiente' ('mute, serpent's song').

When the narrator eventually steps in to address the Civil Guard, their conclusion, that what has happened is what always happens, lays emphasis on the universal character of an event that Lorca, had he wanted to, might have cast in far more specific terms. But, as he makes clear in his lecture-recital of his ballads, his preference was for a universal reading of 'Reyerta'. Explaining its violence in terms that are as poetic as the ballad itself, he attributes to it a meaning that extends well beyond the Gitano context to involve not only Andalusia but the country as a whole:

> En el romance *Reyerta* de mozos está expresada esa lucha latente en Andalucía y en toda España de grupos que se atacan sin saber por qué, por causas misteriosas, por una mirada, por una rosa, porque un hombre de pronto siente un insecto sobre la mejilla, por un amor de hace dos siglos. (OC, IIII, p. 343).

> [In the ballad 'Feud' between young boys, is expressed the struggle latent in Andalusia and in all of Spain, of groups that attack one another without knowing why, for some mysterious reason, on account of a look, a rose, because a man all of a sudden feels an insect on his cheek, because of a love two centuries before.]

Naturally, the universalization (and poeticization) of violence, and indeed of the Gitano world more generally, incurs the risk of de-historicizing real-life circumstances. Yet Lorca's intention was not in any way to diminish their historical importance. Instead, by connecting a Gitano's knife fight to the Punic Wars (as occurs in the final two lines of 'Reyerta' with its reference to Romans and Carthaginians) or the Gitanos to the protagonists of the Nativity (as is the case in 'Romance de la Guardia Civil española'), Lorca sought, as Morris (1997, p. 363) argues, to make the Gitanos 'actors on the world stage, protagonists or victims of life's great tragedies'. In effect, by opting for epic scenarios over historical specificity, Lorca finds a way of countering discriminatory views that are fed on a diet of prejudicial accounts. For such accounts, by contrast, habitually centre on local events and on a parochial view of the Gitano race and its culture. His poeticization of Gitano realities, including the violence, also works to counter such discriminatory views by abstracting the Gitanos from the mundane and denigrating settings to which common narratives habitually consign them.

Commenting on another ballad, 'Prendimiento de Antoñito el Camborio en el camino de Sevilla' ['The Arrest of Antoñito el Camborio on the Road to Seville'] (OC, I, pp. 417–18), Lorca declared that he wanted it to possess 'una gran solidaridad y *gitanismo*' ['a great solidarity and *Gitanoism*'] (EC, p. 325). This is solidarity, I would suggest, in face of the negative view of Gitanos that circulated at the time, views that attached the patronising and derogatory term *gitanismo* to their culture and to the work of its enthusiasts. That Lorca should want to instil one of his own ballads with *gitanismo* – even the mere fact of voluntarily using the term to describe his own work – becomes, in this context, an act of defiance and reappropriation that seeks, in a spirit of solidarity, to counter *gitanismo*'s negative associations. How significant, then, that, in 'Prendimiento de Antoñito el Camborio', the taunts directed at Antonio by the Civil Guardsmen should connect their prisoner's (dis)honour and that of his fellow Gitanos to their prowess (or lack of it) as fighters. For their taunts betray a double standard, their machoistic insistence on measuring Antoñito's masculinity in terms of his capacity for violence in contradiction with the common tendency among *payos* (non-Gitanos) to associate violence with the Gitanos only in order to stigmatize them:

> Antonio, ¿Quién eres tú?
> Si te llamaras Camborio,
> hubieras hecho une fuente
> de sangre con cinco chorros.
> Ni tú eres hijo de nadie,
> ni legítimo Camborio.
> ¡Se acabaron los gitanos
> que iban por el monte solos!
> Están los viejos cuchillos
> tiritando bajo el polvo. (OC, I, p. 418)

['Antonio, who are you? If you were really a Camborio, you would have made a fountain of blood with five spouts. You are neither anyone's son or a true Camborio. Gone are the Gitanos who wandered the hills alone! Their old knives are trembling beneath the dust.']

Antonio el Camborio's demise is told in the related ballad, 'Muerte de Antoñito el Camborio' ['Death of Antoñito Camborio'] (OC, I, pp. 419–20), and comes not, as it turns out, at the hands of the Civil Guard but instead those of his cousins. 'Muerte de Antoñito el Camborio' has a mythic aura about it, initiated by disembodied voices that 'anticipate the fatal outcome' (Ramsden 1998, p. 79):

> Voces de muerte sonaron
> cerca del Guadalquivir.
> Voces antiguas que cercan
> voz de clavel varonil.
> Les clavó sobre las botas
> mordiscos de jabalí.
> En la lucha daba saltos
> jabonados de delfín.
> Bañó con sangre enemiga
> su corbata carmesí,
> pero eran cuatro puñales
> y tuvo que sucumbir.
> Cuando las estrellas clavan
> rejones al agua gris,
> cuando los erales sueñan
> verónicas de alhelí,
> voces de muerte sonaron
> cerca del Guadalquivir. (OC, I, p. 419)

[Voices of death were heard near the Guadalquivir. Ancient voices surround the voice of virile carnation. He cut into their boots with the bites of wild boar. In the fight he made lathered dolphin leaps. He bathed his red silk tie in enemy blood, but there were four knife blows and he had to succumb. When the stars drive lances into grey water, when young bulls dream veronicas of gillyflowers, voices of death were heard near the Guadalquivir.]

Here the sense of the event's timelessness is augmented by the references to the age-old ritual of the bullfight, which is rendered unworldly by virtue of the stars' transformation into *rejoneros* (mounted bullfighters with lances) and by having the bulls themselves dream of veronicas (passes with the cape). Additionally, Antonio's metamorphoses into a boar and dolphin – in metaphors that capture his movements in the fight – reinforce the ballad's mythical qualities.

Surprisingly, the next stanza takes the form of a dialogue between Antonio and Lorca himself, the poet stepping out from behind the figure of the Gitano narrator to incorporate himself directly into the scene:

> Antonio Torres Heredia,
> Camborio de dura crin,
> moreno de verde luna,
> voz de clavel varonil:
> ¿quién te ha quitado la vida
> cerca del Guadalquivir?

Mis cuatro primos Heredias,
hijos de Benamejí.
Lo que en otros no envidiaban,
ya lo envidiaban en mí.
Zapatos color corinto,
medallones de marfil,
y este cutis amasado
con aceituna y jazmín.
¡Ay Antonio el Camborio
digno de una Emperatriz!
Acuérdate de la Virgen
porque te vas a morir.
¡Ay Federico García,
llama a la Guardia Civil!
Ya mi talle se ha quebrado
como caña de maíz. (OC, I, pp. 419–20)

['Antonio Torres Heredia, Camborio of tough mane, dark skinned of green moon, voice of virile Carnation: who took your life near the Guadalquivir?' 'My four Heredia cousins, sons of Benajemí. What they did not envy in others, they envied in me. Maroon-coloured shoes, ivory medallions, and this skin mixed in with olive and jasmine.' 'Ay, Antonio el Camborio, worthy of an Empress! Think of the Virgin because you are about to die.' 'Ay, Federico García, call the Civil Guard! My waist has snapped like a stalk of corn.']

In this exchange, the poet's compliments to Antonio – the references to the qualities of his skin, of his voice, to the fact that he is worthy of an empress – make clear his solidarity with the Gitano as does the fact that he accompanies him in the last moments before death. In the final stanza, we see that angels accompany Antonio also:

Tres golpes de sangre tuvo,
y se murió de perfil.
Viva moneda que nunca
se volverá a repetir.
Un ángel marchoso pone
su cabeza en un cojín.
Otro de rubor cansado,
encendieron un candil.
Y cuando los cuatro primos
llegan a Benamejí,
voces de muerte cesaron
cerca del Guadalquivir. (OC, I, p. 420)

[Three times his blood spilled out and he died in silhouette. A live coin the like of which we shall never see again. A spirited angel sets his head on a cushion. Others, of weary colour, lit a lamp. And when the four cousins arrive back in Benamejí, voices of death were no longer heard near the Guadalquivir.]

This scene, like the whole poem, is shrouded in an air of saintly death: Antonio laid to rest on a cushion, angels keeping vigil. The voices of death, like a Greek chorus, cease once the drama has come to an end ('voces de muerte cesaron' ['voices of death were no longer heard']), a parenthetical device that at once brings the episode to its conclusion and publicly confirms the hero's death. Throughout, the ballad marks Antonio as special, poetry transforming the gruesome character of his death into an epic encounter between the forces of life and death.

In all the ballads we have looked at so far, the poetic qualities do not work, I would suggest, to undermine the storytelling. The stories of the death of a young boy at the forge, or of the assault on the Gitano encampment, or of feuding clans and the arrest and murder of Antonio Camborio, are all accessible and clear whatever their lyrical qualities. The ballad 'Romance sonámbulo' ['Sleepwalking Ballad'] (OC, I, pp. 400–03), on the other hand, along with the more cryptic 'Muerto de amor' ['Dead from Love'] (OC, I, pp. 421–22), is generally considered to be an exception in this respect. Indeed, its most famous line, the refrain 'Verde que te quiero verde' [Green I want you green'], is possibly the most lyrical and mysterious in all of the Gitano ballads. As Ramsden (1998, p. 24) notes, the refrain was taken from the opening of a popular ballad in which green is associated with the colour of olives. In Lorca's ballad, however, the colour green 'takes on wider and less contoured resonances and these radiate increasingly as the poem progresses', from 'freshness, freedom and life' to death and 'putrefaction' (Ramsden 1998, p. 24). Typically, 'Romance sonámbulo' also contains an animate landscape – a staple of Lorca's ballads – here creating tension and mood, as in the following lines in which the ballad's female figure is illuminated by the moon:

Bajo la luna gitana,
las cosas la están mirando
y ella no puede mirarlas. (OC, I, p. 400)

[Beneath the Gitano moon, things are looking at her and she cannot look at them.]

Or as in these:

Grandes estrellas de escarcha
vienen con el pez de sombra
que abre el camino del alba.
La higuera frota su viento
con la lija de sus ramas,
y el monte, gato garduño,
eriza sus pitas agrias. (OC, I, p. 400)

[Large stars of frost come with the shadowy fish that opens the road for dawn. The fig tree rubs its wind with the sandpaper of its boughs, and the hill, a sly cat, bristles with bitter agaves.]

Or even in these:

Temblaban en los tejados
farolillos de hojalata.
Mil panderos de cristal,
herían la madrugada. (OC, I, p. 402)

[There trembled on the tiled rooves little tinplate lamps. One thousand tambourines wounded the dawn.]

Typically too, the human figures of this ballad are abstracted from the real world by poetic descriptions which, for example, turn the hair and skin of a young Gitano woman – possibly the poem's somnambulist – green ('verde carne, pelo verde' [green flesh, hair green'] [OC, I, p. 400]) and a man's wounds into 'Three hundred brown roses' ('Trescientas rosas morenas' [OC, I, p. 401]). There are three protagonists in the ballad, though the connection between them is not immediately clear. Nor, indeed, is their identity completely stable: 'Pero yo ya no soy yo, ni mi casa es ya mi casa' ['I am no longer myself, nor is my house my house'] (OC, I, p. 401). In this respect, the state of sleeping or dreaming alluded to in the title might apply as much to the ballad's atmosphere as to the figure of the young woman who is depicted dreaming at her railing ('sueña en su baranda' ['she dreams at her railing'] [OC, I, p. 400]). During his lecture-recital of his ballads, Lorca explained that 'El romance típico había sido siempre una narración y era lo narrativo lo que daba encanto a su fisonomía, porque, cuando se hacía lírico, sin eco de anécdota, se convertía en canción' ['The typical *romance* had always been a narration and it was its narrative character that gave it its charm; because, whenever it became too lyrical, without even an echo of anecdote, it turned into song'] (OC, III, p. 341). He declared that what he wanted to do with his Gitano ballads was 'fundir el romance narrativo con el lírico sin que perdieran ninguna calidad' ['fuse the narrative ballad with the lyrical without it losing either quality'] (OC, III, p. 341). He added that he had succeeded in doing just this in his 'Romance sonámbulo', 'donde hay una gran sensación de anécdota, un agudo ambiente dramático y nadie sabe lo que pasa ni aun yo, porque el misterio poético es también misterio para el poeta que lo comunica, pero que muchas veces lo ignora' ['where there is a great sense of anecdote, an acutely dramatic atmosphere and nobody knows what is happening, me included, since poetic mystery is a mystery also for the poet communicating it, though often without knowing it'] (OC, III, p. 341).

We can take Lorca's suggestion that he does not know what is happening in his ballad with a pinch of salt. His suggestion, made no doubt in front of a captivated audience, was intended to deepen the mystique surrounding the poem. For its mystery did not come about by accident, but is, after all, a consequence of a deliberate strategy on the part of the poet who, to put it simply, purposely left the events of his ballad vague. In doing so, he also left it open to multiple interpretations, something to which poetry, especially lyrical poetry is, in any case, always prone. And yet, notwithstanding the uncertainties and the deeply lyrical character of sections of 'Romance sonámbulo', the narrative thread – its storyline – is still not impossible to discern. Far from it. There is enough there to enable us to presume that what we have before us is a tale of a young Gitano woman desperately awaiting the object of her affection, who is most likely a Gitano too. We can infer that there is a romantic connection between her and the wounded man in the ballad from the details of the exchange the latter has with her father in the penultimate stanza, where both men use the colloquial term for friend, *compadre*, in order to refer to one another:

> ¡Compadre! ¿Dónde está, dime?
> ¿Dónde está tu niña amarga?
> ¡Cuántas veces te esperó!
> ¡Cuántas veces te esperara,
> cara fresca, negro pelo,
> en esta verde baranda! (OC, I, p. 401)

['Compadre! Tell me, where is she? Where is your bitter girl?' 'How often she waited for you! How often she waited for you, fresh face, black hair, at these green railings!']

In a prior exchange between them, the wounded man reveals his fatal condition. But what are the circumstances of his wounding? While today we can only hazard a guess, for a contemporary readership, the assumption may well have been that he suffered his wounds exercising the profession of smuggler or bandit, not least because he has just arrived from the mountain passes of Cabra, an area traditionally associated with smuggling and banditry (see Morris 1997, p. 351):

> Compadre, quiero cambiar
> mi caballo por su casa,
> mi montura por su espejo,
> mi cuchillo por su manta.
> Compadre, vengo sangrando,
> desde los puertos de Cabra.
> Si yo pudiera, mocito,
> este trato se cerraba.
> Pero yo ya no soy yo.
> Ni mi casa es ya mi casa.
> Compadre, quiero morir
> decentemente en mi cama.
> De acero, si puede ser,
> con las sábanas de holanda.
> ¿No veis la herida que tengo
> desde el pecho a la garganta?
> Trescientas rosas morenas
> lleva tu pechera blanca.
> Tu sangre rezuma y huele
> alrededor de tu faja.
> Pero yo ya no soy yo.
> Ni mi casa es ya mi casa.
> Dejadme subir al menos
> hasta las altas barandas,
> ¡dejadme subir!, dejadme
> hasta las verdes barandas.
> Barandales de la luna
> por donde retumba el agua. (OC, I, p. 401)

['Compadre, I want to exchange my horse for your house, my saddle for your mirror, my knife for your blanket. Compadre, I come bleeding from the passes of Cabra.' 'If I could, lad, this would be a done deal. But I am no longer myself, nor is my home my home.' 'Compadre, I want to die decently in my bed. Of steel, if possible, with sheets of Dutch linen. Can you not see the wound I have from my chest to my throat?' 'Three hundred brown roses your shirt front bears. Your blood oozes and smells around your sash. But I am no longer myself, nor is my house my house.'

'Let me climb at least up to the green railings. Railings of the moon where the water resounds.']

As in a dream, certain details in the ballad remain unclear and are open to interpretation, like the father's confession that he is neither himself nor the owner of his own house. And as we have already suggested, while we may assume the wounded man to be a Gitano and a smuggler or bandit, we cannot be absolutely certain. Consequently, this, along with the poeticization of the man's wounds – 'Trescientas rosas morenas' ['Three hundred brown roses'] – shifts the emphasis away from the real-life context, which stands to reinforce prejudices connecting Gitanos to criminality, onto the drama of personal misfortune, desire and human relations converging on his last wish to die under the roof of the woman he loves.

In the final stanza, it appears the wounded man has arrived too late to avert the young woman's death, the circumstances of which – mysterious to the last – we may surmise to be connected to her desperate wait for him. Whereas elsewhere in the ballad, including in an early description of the woman, the colour green seems to have positive connotations, here it takes on a deathly hue as it describes her skin and hair as she floats in the well:

> Sobre el rostro del aljibe,
> se mecía la gitana.
> Verde carne, pelo verde,
> con ojos de fría plata.
> Un carámbano de luna
> la sostiene sobre el agua.
> La noche se puso íntima
> como una pequeña plaza.
> Guardias civiles borrachos
> en la puerta golpeaban.
> Verde que te quiero verde.
> Verde viento. Verdes ramas.
> El barco sobre la mar.
> Y el caballo en la montaña. (OC, I, pp. 402-3)

[On the face of the well swayed the Gitano girl. Green flesh, hair green, with eyes of cold silver. An icicle of the moon holds her on the water. The night became intimate like a small square. Drunk Civil Guardsmen pounded on the door. Green I want you green. Green wind. Green boughs. The boat on the sea. And the horse on the mountain.]

Irrespective of how the woman died (if this is indeed what happened), the drunk Civil Guardsmen's appearance is an unwelcome intrusion into an otherwise intimate scene. Despite its mystery, the ballad is consistent with other ballads of the *Romancero gitano* in terms of its negative portrayal of the Civil Guard. The lyrical ending, which reprises the ballad's start, adds pathos to the scene, leaving us with a mysterious evocation of desire – 'Verde que te quiero verde' ['Green I want you green'] (OC, I, p. 403) – and the simplest of topographical arrangements: 'El barco sobre la mar. | Y el caballo en la montaña' ['The boat on the sea. The horse on the mountain'] (OC, I, p. 403). These, because they are so generic, lend the ballad a timeless, mythical quality that runs counter to any inclination we might have had to want to situate its account historically.

The character of 'Romance sonámbulo' and Lorca's statements about it seem to place it in that category of those ballads by learned poets who sought to revise the form. But formal experimentation is perhaps less important, in the end, than the fact of extracting the Gitano people from the commonplaces that shore up prejudice. Lorca offers us storylines in 'Romance sonámbulo' and in his other ballads but injects them with a lyricism that curtails conventional readings, however tempting these may be. As Morris (1997, p. 313) puts it, the settings and protagonists of Lorca's ballads 'appear to promise a reassuring familiarity which turns out to be illusory and elusive' and 'readers are caught between reminiscence and striking novelty, between echo and variation, between stereotype and stylish remodelling'. If, for a moment, we consider 'La casada infiel' in this light, it is not difficult to see why Lorca might have been reticent to read it in public. For while 'La casada infiel', inspired by a muleteer's song (see Morris 1997, p. 342), displays the stylization typical of Lorca's collection as a whole, this in itself is insufficient, despite the 'ironic distancing' detected by some (see Harris 1991, p. 37), to make the tale anything more than a stereotypical account of an illicit, sexual conquest told by an archetypal male, lacking, it would seem, any sense of ironic self-awareness:

Pasadas las zarzamoras,
los juncos y los espinos,
bajo su mata de pelo
hice un hoyo sobre el limo.
Yo me quité la corbata.
Ella se quitó el vestido.
Yo el cinturón con revólver.
Ella sus cuatro corpiños.
Ni nardos ni caracolas

tienen el cutis tan fino,
ni los cristales con luna
relumbran con ese brillo.
Sus muslos se me escapaban
como peces sorprendidos,
la mitad llenos de lumbre,
la mitad llenos de frío.
Aquella noche corrí
el major de los caminos,
montado en potra de nácar
sin bridas y sin estribos.
No quiero decir, por hombre,
las cosas que ella me dijo.
La luz del entendimiento
me hace ser muy comedido.
Sucia de besos y arena
yo me la llevé del río.
Con el aire se batían
las espadas de los lirios.
Me porté como quien soy.
Como un gitano legítimo.
La regalé un costurero
grande de raso pajizo,
y no quise enamorarme
porque teniendo marido
me dijo que era mozuela
cuando la llevaba al río. (OC, I, pp. 406–07)

[Past the brambles, reeds and hawthorns, beneath her mane of hair, I made a hollow in the sand. I took off my tie. She took off her dress. I, my belt and pistol. She, her four-boned corset. Neither spikenards nor shells have a skin as fine, nor do moonlit panes shine with the same sparkle. Her thighs slipped from me like startled fish, half filled with fire, the other half with cold. That night I rode the finest of roads on a filly of nacre, without bridle or stirrups. I do not want to tell, as a man, the things she told me. The light of understanding requires I be discreet. Dirty with kisses and sand I took her from the river. Against the wind were thrashing the swords of lilies. I behaved as the man I am. As a trueborn Gitano. I gave her a large sewing basket as a gift, of straw-coloured satin, and I did not want to fall in love because, though she had a husband, she told me she was not married when I took her to the river.]

Elsewhere, however, sexuality is approached with a greater degree of nuance and complexity in ballads whose plotlines are akin to psychodramas, thus revealing Lorca's familiarity with Freudian psychology.[17] The allusion to the inner narratives of the mind represents a challenge to the commonplace narratives of nineteenth-century ballads by involving Gitanos in sexual dilemmas that are in tension with the flagrant bravado apparently on show in 'La casada infiel'. 'Preciosa y el aire' ['Preciosa and the Wind'] (OC, I, pp. 395–97), for example, has its sources in, amongst other things, Ovid's account of the rape of Orithyia by Boreas.[18] Lorca's contemporary version of the myth presents us with the story of the wind's pursuit of a Gitano girl called Preciosa. The chase, though, may also be understood as an allegory of a young woman's unconscious resistance to the forces of sexual awakening.

The initial stanza introduces an innocent Preciosa playing a tambourine amidst an idyllic, animate landscape. It is significant, in terms of the psychosexual possibilities of the narrative, that the wind's pursuit of Preciosa will take place while the armed guards – the moralising super-ego in this drama – are sleeping and thus disarmed, their association with the English quite possibly an allusion to the national stereotype of extreme, repressive self-discipline and reserve:

Su luna de pergamino
Preciosa tocando viene
por un anfibio sendero
de cristales y laureles.
El silencio sin estrellas,
huyendo del sonsonete,
cae donde el mar bate y canta
su noche llena de peces.
En los picos de la sierra
los carabineros duermen
guardando las blancas torres
donde viven los ingleses.
Y los gitanos del agua
levantan por distraerse,

---

17 For an account of Freud's influence on Lorca, see Julio Huélamo Kosma, 'La influencia de Freud en Federico García Lorca', *Boletín de la Fundación Federico García Lorca*, 6 (1989), 59–83.
18 See David Loughran, 'Myth, the Gypsy, and Two "Romances históricos"', *Modern Language Notes*, 87.2 (1972), 253–71 (p. 257). On the various sources of the ballad, see Harris 1991, p. 20 and Ramsden 1998, pp. 8–9.

glorietas de caracolas
y ramas de pino verde. (OC, I, p. 395)

[Her moon of parchment Preciosa comes playing along an amphibious path of crystals and laurels. Silence without stars, fleeing the rhythmic beat, falls where the sea crashes and sings its night filled with fish. On the peaks of the sierra the carabineers sleep as they guard the white towers where the English live. And the Gitanos of the water raise, to pass the time, arbours of shells and branches of green pine.]

Although the animate landscape is apparently unaware of the peril lying in wait, silence's flight from the sound of Preciosa's tambourine-playing seems somehow to presage the imminent chase. The connection between the tambourine and the moon underscores the feminine principle in face of the masculine threat that the wind represents in the next stanza:

Su luna de pergamino
Preciosa tocando viene.
Al verla se ha levantado
el viento, que nunca duerme.
San Cristobalón desnudo,
lleno de lenguas celestes,
mira a la niña tocando
una dulce gaita ausente. (OC, I, pp. 395–96)

[Her parchment moon Preciosa comes playing. On seeing her, the wind, which never sleeps, has risen up. A naked giant St Christopher full of heavenly tongues, watches the young girl as he plays his sweet absent flute.]

As in 'Romance de la luna, luna', Lorca's myth borrows from classical culture the familiar mechanism of anthropomorphism. Here the wind is a satyr of the elements. The whistling air is conveyed by a 'gaita ausente' ('absent flute') [OC, I, p. 396], an object associated with satyrs that may also have, in this ballad, phallic connotations. The association of the wind-satyr with St Christopher is possibly a reference to size. For the saint is traditionally represented as 'a giant of a man' (Harris 1991, p. 19), a point driven home by the addition of the augmentative suffix '-ón' to his Spanish name: San Cristóbal becoming 'San Cristobalón' (OC, I, p. 395). The association may also be a reference to the Mr Punch of Spanish puppet theatre, also called Cristóbal; a figure who 'carries the usual enormous cudgel with clear phallic intent' (Harris 1991, p. 19). Above all, the fact that the wind never sleeps confirms its equation in the psychodrama with the forces of the id: the instinctual desires in the domain of the unconscious (hence the invisibility implied by the 'absent flute') that are ever-present even though morality acts to try to keep them at bay.

In keeping with the treatment of sex and violence throughout the collection, the menace and intrusiveness of the wind's words give rise to a highly stylized, poetic image:

> Niña, deja que levante
> tu vestido para verte.
> Abre en mis dedos antiguos
> la rosa azul de tu vientre. (OC, I, p. 396)

> [Girl, let me lift your dress to see you. Open in my ancient fingers the blue rose of your belly.]

The wind's insistence frightens Preciosa and instigates her flight against the backdrop of an increasingly animated landscape:

> Preciosa tira el pandero
> y corre sin detenerse.
> El viento-hombrón la persigue
> con una espada caliente.
> Frunce su rumor el mar.
> Los olivos palidecen.
> Cantan las flautas de umbría
> y el liso gong de la nieve.
>
> ¡Preciosa, corre, Preciosa,
> que te coge el viento verde!
> ¡Preciosa, corre, Preciosa!
> ¡Míralo por donde viene!
> Sátiro de estrellas bajas
> con sus lenguas relucientes. (OC, I, p. 396)

> [Preciosa throws down her tambourine and runs away. The wind-giant pursues her with a hot sword. The sea frowns its murmurs. Olive trees turn pale. The flutes of shadow and the snow's smooth gong sing. Preciosa, run, Preciosa, or the bawdy wind will get you! Preciosa, run, Preciosa! See how close he is! Satyr of low stars with his shining tongues.]

Unlike other myths, it is not a metamorphosis that comes to the rescue of the escapee. Instead, Preciosa finds refuge in the house of the English. Once again, the stereotype of English reserve comes into play:

> Preciosa, llena de miedo,
> entra en la casa que tiene,
> más arriba de los pinos,
> el cónsul de los ingleses.
>
> Asustados por los gritos
> tres carabineros vienen,
> sus negras capas ceñidas
> y los gorros en las sienes.
>
> El inglés da a la gitana
> un vaso de tibia leche,
> y una copa de ginebra
> que Preciosa no se bebe.
>
> Y mientras cuenta, llorando,
> su aventura a aquella gente,
> en las tejas de pizarra
> el viento, furioso, muerde. (OC, I, pp. 396–97)

[Preciosa, fearful, enters the house beyond the pines owned by the English consul. Frightened by the shouting come three carabineers, their black capes wrapped around them, their caps pulled over their temples. The Englishman gives the Gitano girl a glass of warm milk, and another of gin which Preciosa does not drink. And while, in tears, she tells these people her adventure, on the tiles of the slate roof the wind, furious, keeps biting.]

In Lorca's modern myth, Preciosa's fears are contained within the walls of the house where the young girl, crying, relates her story. She accepts a glass of warm milk but not gin, a distinction that is symbolic of her abstemiousness. The phlegmatic, albeit clichéd, connotations of Englishness connect her refuge with discretion, control and restraint. And yet the wind-satyr continues to howl across the rooftops. His presence is constant, despite his being kept outside, as constant as the desires that call to us from the seemingly absent place of our unconscious.

Whereas 'Preciosa y el aire' may be read as an allegory of sexual repression, 'La monja gitana' ['The Gitano Nun'] (OC, I, pp. 404–05) offers an account of the displacement of sexual desire onto a creative act. The central figure of the poem is not frightened by her sexuality, nor is she constrained by any morality she may have internalized. But, as a nun, she is bound by her vows of chastity and by the rules of the order she belongs to:

Silencio de cal y mirto.
Malvas en las hierbas finas.
La monja borda alhelíes
sobre una tela pajiza.
Vuelan en la araña gris,
siete pájaros de prisma.
La iglesia gruñe a lo lejos
como un oso panza arriba.
¡Qué bien borda! ¡Con qué gracia!
Sobre la tela pajiza,
ella quisiera bordar
flores de su fantasía.
¡Qué girasol! ¡Qué magnolia
de lentejuelas y cintas!
¡Qué azafranes y qué lunas,
en el mantel de la misa!
Cinco toronjas se endulzan
en la cercana cocina.
Las cinco llagas de Cristo
cortadas en Almería.
Por los ojos de la monja
galopan dos caballistas.
Un rumor último y sordo
le despega la camisa,
y al mirar nubes y montes
en las yertas lejanías,
se quiebra su corazón
de azúcar y yerbaluisa.
¡Oh!, qué llanura empinada
con veinte soles arriba.
¡Qué ríos puestos de pie
vislumbra su fantasía!
Pero sigue con sus flores,
mientras que de pie, en la brisa,
la luz juega el ajedrez
alto de la celosía.

[Silence of lime and myrtle. Mallows in the fine grasses. The nun embroiders gillyflowers on a straw-coloured cloth. In the grey chandelier fly the prism's seven birds. The church growls in the distance like a bear on its back. How well she embroiders! With what grace! On the straw-coloured cloth she would like to embroider flowers of her fantasy. What a sunflower! What magnolias of sequins and ribbons! What crocuses and moons, on the altar cloth! Five grapefruit sweeten in the nearby kitchen. The five wounds of Christ cut in Almería. Across the nun's eyes two horsemen gallop. A final and dull noise detaches her shirt, and as she watches the clouds and hills in the rigid distance, her heart of sugar and lemon verbena breaks. Oh what a steep plain with twenty suns above! What rivers on their feet her fantasy glimpses! But she continues with her flowers, while standing, in the breeze, the light plays its latticework chess on high.]

Stirring the nun's imagination are sexual thoughts, referred to obliquely via the 'horsemen' ('caballistas' [OC, I, p. 404]) glimpsed by her mind's eye, via the mysterious 'noise' ('rumor' [OC, I, p. 404]) that detaches her clothing from her skin, and via the peculiar details of an imaginary landscape – the 'rigid distance' ('yertas lejanías' [OC, I, p. 405]), the impossibly 'steep plane' ('llanura empinada' [OC, I, p. 405]) and the equally impossible 'rivers on their feet' ('ríos puestos de pie' [OC, I, p. 405]) – with all their phallic innuendo. Yet her desires are channelled into a creative act, the varied and colourful flowers she embroiders on the straw-coloured altar cloth standing as a metaphor for the displacement of sexual desire in this most religious of settings.[19] The reference to Christ's five wounds – 'Las cinco llagas de Cristo' (OC, I, p. 404) – is perhaps an allusion to the nun's self-sacrifice in giving up the things of the world and accepting a vow of chastity. The church, transformed into a growling bear, is possibly a reminder of the strictures of her order, although by being on its back and thus revealing its belly ('panza' [OC, I, p. 404]) it seems, at least for the moment, to be exposed and vulnerable. The spectrum of colours produced by the contrastingly grey, prismatic chandelier and the light filtering through latticework that is at once a 'chessboard' of white and black – 'la luz juega el ajedrez | alto de la celosia' ['the light plays its latticework chess on high'] (OC, I, p. 405) – all confirm that, even in seclusion, the colours of desire will inevitably show through.

---

19 The symbolic potential of embroidery in Lorca's poetry, as well as his theatre, is explored by Manuel Delgado Morales in 'Embroiderers of Freedom and Desire in Lorca's Poetry and Theater', in *Lorca, Buñuel, Dalí: Art and Theory*, ed. by Manuel Delgado Morales and Alice J. Poust (London and Toronto: Associated University Presses, 2001), pp. 37–51. Delgado Morales (p. 37) notes how for Buñuel and Dalí, as well as Lorca, the 'richness and complexity of this symbol was to increase significantly under the influence of Freudian and surrealist ideas'. As we see in 'La monja gitana', Lorca would transform the embroiderer's instruments 'into symbols (= voices) of desire and sexual liberation' (Delgado Morales, p. 39).

This irrepressibility of desire is also conveyed by the oxymoron of the poem's title – oxymoronic because it was extremely unlikely that a *gitana* would ever become a nun. Thus, 'monja gitana' appears to be a contradiction in terms that requires a symbolic rather than literal interpretation. With this in mind, 'gitana' may be interpreted here as an epithet evoking the desire that is present in everyone, even in the seemingly most devout and abstemious of personalities. If this is the case, Lorca's choice of terminology is provocative given the common associations of Gitano women and, indeed, Gitano culture more generally with sexual permissiveness, just as his treatment of violence in the Camborio poems was provocative given the common associations of Gitanos with criminal violence. In the *café cantante*, for example, flamenco had become associated with licentiousness, as it 'involved or connoted some degree of eroticism, ranging from sexually suggestive dancing by fascinating dark-skinned girls to the evocation of jealousy and passion in song lyrics to sexual commerce, whether paid or voluntary in nature' (Mitchell, p. 43). Lorca's provocation was to challenge conventional morality and prejudice by injecting sexuality into a religious setting and seeing sexual desire as something wondrous and natural – hence its connection in the poem to creativity via the imagination and via the embroidering of colourful flowers.

Just as provocative as his association of Gitano women with the sacred place of the convent is Lorca's camp treatment of Antonio el Camborio which, given the common hyper-masculine and chauvinist associations of the Gitano male, was designed to test the limits of convention. After all, what was it his murderers envied in him in the ballad 'Muerte de Antoñito Camborio'? Not his manly prowess, but his 'Maroon-coloured shoes, ivory medallions, and this skin mixed in with olive and jasmine' ('Zapatos color corinto, | medallones de marfil, | y este cutis amasado | con aceituna y jazmín' [OC, I, p. 420]). As Jonathan Mayhew points out, Antonio is depicted as something of a dandy.[20] We can see here, and elsewhere in Lorca's ballad book, detail delivered with such flamboyance and relish that its effect is to undercut conventional, macho associations and instead enter the aesthetic realm of camp. As Susan Sontag writes in her seminal essay on the subject, 'Camp taste draws on a mostly unacknowledged truth of taste: the most refined form of sexual attractiveness [...] consists in going

---

20 Jonathan Mayhew, in his *Lorca's Legacy: Essays in Interpretation* (New York: Routledge, 2018), eBook, writes: 'In both poems, Antonito is a dandy, physically beautiful and ostentatiously dressed' (344.2/586).

against the grain of one's sex.'[21] In other words, if 'what is most beautiful in feminine women is something masculine', in the case of virile men, what is most beautiful 'is something feminine' (Sontag, p. 279). It is thus in the spirit of camp that we ought understand the attention to Antonio Camborio's dress and complexion; so too the description of the effigy of St Michael in the ballad 'San Miguel (Granada)' ['St Michael (Granada)'] (OC, I, pp. 41–11). Here the tone seems more than vaguely desirous as the speaker remarks on the saint's attire and bodily charm:

> San Miguel, lleno de encajes
> en la alcoba de su torre,
> enseña sus bellos muslos
> ceñidos por los faroles. (OC, I, p. 410)

> [St Michael, covered in lace,
> in the alcove of his tower,
> reveals his handsome thighs
> hugged by the lanterns' light.]

Similarly, in the opening verses of 'San Gabriel' ['St Gabriel'] (OC, I, pp. 414–16), it is a young boy's physical splendour that is brought to the fore in an image combining masculine robustness with feminine lines:

> Un bello niño de junco,
> anchos hombros, fino talle,
> piel de nocturna manzana,
> boca triste y ojos grandes,
> nervio de plata caliente,
> ronda la desierta calle. (OC, I, p. 414)

> [A handsome reed of a boy,
> shoulders wide, tight waist,
> skin of an apple at night,
> sad mouth and big eyes,
> a nerve of hot silver,
> walks the empty streets.]

Camp sensibility in Lorca's ballads extends beyond the way men are described. 'The hallmark of Camp', wrote Sontag (p. 283), 'is the spirit of extravagance'. Such a spirit is evident not only in many of the characters of Lorca's ballads but also in the elaborate metaphors and images he uses;

---

21 Susan Sontag, 'Notes on "Camp"', *Against Interpretation and other essays* (London: Penguin Classics, 2009), pp. 275–92 (p. 279).

or, to put it another way, in the balladeer's way of telling. For Mayhew (2018: 335.5/586), it is because Lorca's work 'anticipates the camp aesthetic' of the mid-twentieth century that his legacy 'lends itself readily to *kitsch* treatment'; in other words, to readings that are all too ready to exaggerate his work's sentimentality and offer an ironic appreciation of its folkloric aspects. As Mayhew (2018: 339.0/586) also points out, Lorca was aware of the danger that his ballads might be susceptible to such readings, hence his vigorous 'preemptive defense' of his ballad book in his lecture-recital (see OC, III, p. 340). His book, Lorca conceded, 'es un retablo de Andalucía con gitanos, caballos, arcángeles, planetas, con su brisa judía, con su brisa romana, con ríos, con crímenes, con la nota vulgar del contrabandista, y la nota celeste de los niños desnudos de Córdoba que burlan a San Rafael' ['a tableau of Andalusia with Gitanos, horses, archangels, planets, with its Jewish breeze, its Roman breeze, its rivers, its crimes, with the common touch of smugglers, and the heavenly touch of Cordoba's naked boys making fun of St Raphael'] (OC, III, p. 340). And yet, in the same breath he argued that it was 'Un libro donde apenas si está expresada la Andalucía que se ve, pero donde está temblando la que no se ve. Y ahora lo voy a decir. Un libro anti-pintoresco, anti-folklórico, anti-flamenco. Donde no hay ni una chaquetilla corta ni un traje de torero, ni un sombrero plano ni una pandereta' ['A book in which the Andalusia you can see is barely expressed, but where trembles instead that which you cannot see. And now I'll say it. A book that is anti-picturesque, anti-folkloric, anti-flamenco. Where there is not a single short jacket or bullfighter's costume, nor a wide-brimmed hat or tambourine'] (OC, III, p. 340). Despite its array of figures, ultimately there was only one character in his book, 'grande y oscuro como un cielo de estío, un solo personaje que es la Pena que se filtra en el tuétano de los huesos y en la savia de los árboles' ['dark and large as a summer sky, a single character in the shape of Sorrow, who sinks into bone marrow and the sap of trees'] (OC, III, p. 340). And in order to fend off associations with trite sentimentality and point to deeper meanings, he insisted that the character of sorrow 'no tiene nada que ver con la melancolía ni con la nostalgia ni con ninguna aflicción o dolencia del ánimo, que es un sentimiento más celeste que terrestre; pena andaluza que es una lucha de la inteligencia amorosa con el misterio que la rodea y no puede comprender' ['has nothing to do with melancholy or nostalgia or with any affliction or ailment of the soul, but is an emotion more heavenly than earthly; Andalusian sorrow that is the struggle between loving intelligence and the incomprehensible mystery surrounding it'] (OC, III, p. 340).

Whatever Lorca may have said, however, we know that the figures in his ballads have strong connections with folklore and that there is more than one rattle of the tambourine amid his ballad book's pages. Yet, notwithstanding the moments of disingenuity in his lecture-recital, Lorca's final point on the character of sorrow is an important one. For it marks an important divergence with the camp aesthetic which is, Sontag (p. 287) argues, antithetical to tragedy: 'There is seriousness in Camp [...] and, often, pathos. [...] But there is never, never tragedy.' The sincerity that tragedy necessarily involves is not a feature of camp. Camp is 'wholly aesthetic' and, as such, 'incarnates a victory of "style" over "content," "aesthetics" over "morality," of irony over tragedy' (Sontag, p. 287). So it is not insignificant that tragedy should be a feature of Lorca's ballads, as we saw in the unavoidable death of the young Gitano boy in 'Romance de la luna, luna' or the unstoppable sacking by the Civil Guard of the Gitano encampment in 'Romance de la guardia civil española'. For despite its aesthetic priorities, Lorca's ballads have a social and moral agenda. Style, therefore, camp or otherwise, is not an end in itself but is put at the service of this agenda, helping, as Llano (p. 1001) argues, 'to disassociate [Gitanos] from the bigoted attacks to which they had been subjected'.

Inevitably, by straddling high and low culture, by seeking to preserve both moral and aesthetic concerns, and, indeed, by approaching a subject as steeped in prejudice and bound up with stereotype as the world of Spain's Gitanos, Lorca left his work exposed to readings that might prioritize one facet over the other rather than see the full picture. He was clearly aware of the risk when, in his lecture-recital, he put the picturesque readings of his work down to the vagaries of interpretation: 'Pero un hecho poético, como un hecho criminal, o un hecho jurídico, son tales hechos cuando viven en el mundo y son llevados y traídos, en suma, interpretados' ['But a poetic fact, like a criminal fact, or a judicial fact, are such facts when they live in the world and are traded back and forth, in short, interpreted' (OC III, p. 340). For this reason, he was able to concede in his lecture-recital that he could not complain of 'la falsa visión andaluza que se tiene de este poema a causa de recitadores sensuales de bajo tono, o criaturas ignorantes' ['the false Andalusian vision that there is of this collection thanks to the unabashedly lurid readings of reciters and ignorant beings'], although he still made a point of insisting that 'la pureza de su construcción y el noble tono con que me esforcé al crearlo, lo defenderán de sus actuales amantes excesivos, que a veces lo llenan de baba' ['the purity of its construction and the noble tone, which I made every effort to maintain when I created it, will defend it from its present over-the-top admirers who tend to drool over it'] (OC, III, p. 340).

It is important to remember that at the same time as Lorca was presenting his Gitano version of Andalusia, the region itself was the object of characterizations that were as prejudiced and clichéd as those of the Gitanos disseminated by Noel, Salillas or Pabanó. In April 1927, José Ortega y Gasset published his *Teoría de Andalucía* [Theory of Andalusia] in the national newspaper *Sol*.[22] In it, he argued that laziness was a deeply rooted element of Andalusian culture that corresponded directly to an Andalusian's lack of ambition: 'en vez de esforzarse para vivir, vive para no esforzarse, hace de la evitación del esfuerzo principio de su existencia' ['instead of making an effort to live, he lives in such a way as to not to make an effort, he makes the avoidance of effort the principle of his existence'] (Ortega y Gasset 1961, p. 116). Commenting on a renewed interest in Andalusia, Ortega y Gasset (1961, p. 112) suggests that 'No hay probabilidad de que nos vuelva a conmover el cante hondo, ni el contrabandista, ni la presunta alegría del andaluz. Toda esta quincalla meridional nos enoja y fastidia' ['It is improbable that we will be moved again by deep song, or smugglers, or the supposed cheerfulness of Andalusians. All these southern knick-knacks infuriate and bother us']. While there is no indication that Ortega y Gasset specifically had Lorca in mind, he might just as well have had. In face of such animosity, the importance of Lorca's focus on Andalusia and on Gitanos in particular is clear and all the more courageous for it. Interestingly, Ortega y Gasset, at one point in his *Teoría de Andalucía*, refers to 'el gesto frívolo, casi femenil, del andaluz' ['the frivolous, almost feminine, mannerisms of the Andalusian'] (Ortega y Gasset 1961, p. 113). How appropriate, then, that Lorca's male figures should have something of the feminine about them also. Their femininity is an example of how the camp aesthetic in his work can have social import.

Lorca has been accused of being 'no purist: he embraced romantic conceptions of Andalusia and celebrated popular art even as he stylized it' (Mayhew 2018, 335.5/586). But against the background of its denigration,

---

22 See José Ortega y Gasset, *Teoría de Andalucía, Obras Completas*, VI (1941–1946), 5th edn (Madrid: Revista de Occidente, 1961), pp. 111–20. Originally published in *El Sol*, April 1927. Mayhew (2018, 335.5/586) notes that 'Lorca certainly would have been unsympathetic to the negative views about his native region that Ortega set forth in *Teoría de Andalucía*', even though he published his *Primer romancero gitano* with Ortega y Gasset's *Revista de Occidente* in 1928.

revisiting Andalusian culture, particularly with all its romantic apparel, is a statement of resistance. At the heart of this resistance is pleasure. This is what the ballads bring, in keeping (dare we say it) with 'Camp taste [which] is, above all, a mode of enjoyment, of appreciation – not judgment' (Sontag, p. 291). It has been said too that Lorca 'sees the [Gitanos] not as the socially marginal group they were (and are), but as the representatives of a kind of spiritual aristocracy' (Mayhew 2018, 335.5/586). Yet the two perspectives, I would argue, are not incompatible. In the end, Lorca's idealized representation of Gitanos can only be understood against the background of their marginalization and, indeed, against the background of the vilification of Andalusia more generally. For however literary his treatment of Gitanos in his ballads, or indeed of deep song in *Poema del cante jondo*, his decision to treat the subject at all was a decision to promote Gitano culture and its centrality in Andalusian culture at a time when the denigration of Gitanos, and indeed of Andalusia, was commonplace.

Chapter Two

Lorca, the Modern

IN THE FIRST decades of the twentieth century, despite having a largely rural economy, Spain's towns and cities, like towns and cities in other parts of Europe, bustled with cars and tramways. The country had its own airline, its own telecommunications companies, as well as a thriving film industry. And yet we would be forgiven for presuming that Lorca did not move about in this modern Spain at all – or at least not very much – if we based our view purely on the reading of his work alone. For sure, he presents a contemporary appearance in photographs that show him wearing the fashionable suits, blazers, ties, and sweaters of the day; or sitting in the rear of a four-door convertible; or posing behind a fairground cut-out of a biplane or motorcycle sidecar with then friend and future film director, Luis Buñuel. But despite images like these that exist of him, the epithet 'modern' somehow sits uneasily with the man and, indeed, with much of his work. So much so that it comes across as quite a novelty when, in Paula Ortiz's 2015 *La novia* [*The Bride*], a film version of *Bodas de sangre* [*Blood Wedding*], the eponymous Bride and her lover Leonardo flee the wedding reception not on a horse, as Lorca had it in his play, but rather on that most modern of contraptions: a motorbike.

In his letter to Guillén on the subject of his Gitano tag, Lorca claimed that he was just as able to write about 'hydraulic landscapes' ('paisajes hidráulicos') as he was about 'sewing needles' ('agujas de coser') (*EC*, p. 414), the former serving as shorthand for modernity in contrast to the traditional associations of manual needlework and of the Gitano culture with which he and his work had become connected. Yet, despite this claim, nothing really approaching a 'hydraulic landscape' appears

Figure 6 Lorca and Buñuel in a paper biplane cut-out, at the festivities of San Antonio de la Florida, Madrid, in 1923

Figure 7 Lorca seated in the back of an automobile in Guadix, Granada, in 1926

in his work until 1929 when, during a period of residence in New York, he finally set about engaging with what we would most usually think of as the modern world.

Until then, Lorca could only make a claim to modernity on the grounds that he was au fait with the literary and artistic trends of the day and, thus, a 'modern' writer. Indeed, we see his desire to keep apace with literary modernity even in his early poetry, in which he progressively abandoned the effusive style and earnest self-expression imitative of nineteenth-century Romantic lyricism. In its place, he adopted a style and approach more in keeping with the avant-garde's abatement of emotion that had become fashionable in the early twentieth century. All this was consistent with the general tendency of writers and artists to turn their back on the representation of external reality and the very real people who moved within it – emotions and all – and focus instead on the internal logic of their artistic work. Thus, Lorca's first collection of poems, *Libro de poemas*, and subsequent collections such as his *Poema del cante jondo*, *Suites* and *Canciones*, bear, to varying degrees, the hallmarks of what we might call impersonal, autonomous art.

Yet even on this basis, Lorca's modern credentials were not unquestionable. For, as I suggest in my introduction, Lorca only ever engaged with 'impersonality' – what Ortega y Gasset called 'dehumanized' art – reluctantly. We can see this in *Romancero gitano*. On the one hand, it is shaped by the principle of impersonality, inasmuch as its emotions are tied neither directly nor personally to the poet himself but belong instead to the seemingly independent figures populating his ballads. On the other hand, the very narrative character of the ballads does itself mean, somewhat paradoxically, that Lorca never quite cuts loose from real-life, which takes the form, in this case, of the Gitanos' real-life dilemmas.

Lorca, it would seem, felt unable to turn his back completely on the things or, indeed, on the people of the world. Apart from anything else, he was possibly all too aware that reality is always the starting point even for art that seeks to shun or deform it. This is the implication of his insistence, in his famous lecture on Góngora, on a poet's reliance on the five senses in the creation of images. Yet, while he concedes that poets need to remain in touch with their senses in order to create their most beautiful images, he also suggests that it is often necessary for them to 'superponer sus sensaciones' ['superimpose one sensation over another'] and 'aun de disfrazar sus naturalezas' ['even disguise their true nature'] (OC, III, p. 229). Here, no doubt aware of the contradictions inherent in the project to create impersonal and autonomous art, Lorca was obliged to resort to the metaphor of 'disguise' in order to square his ambition to construct purely poetic (as opposed to actual) realities with his inevitable reliance on the senses – sight (foremost), as well as touch, hearing, smell and taste (OC, III, p. 229) – all of which connected him to the real world.

Lorca's difficulty in abandoning human reality in art is apparent also in his forays first into the world of Cubism and then Surrealism. Lorca's interest in both coincided with his own ambitions as a pictorial artist, the idea of the 'image' providing a fundamental link between his poetry and drawing. 'Todas las imágenes', he explained in his lecture on Góngora, 'se abren [...] en el campo visual' ['All images reveal themselves in the field of vision'] (OC, III, p. 230). But, importantly, it also coincided with his friendship with Dalí, whom he first met in 1923. The first four or five years of this friendship, right up to the publication of Romancero gitano, had a deep impact on Lorca's artistic thinking and are sometimes referred to as the poet's 'época daliniana' ('Dalí epoch'). But although the two men exchanged countless letters, drawings and poems in what was an intense period of personal and professional contact, there were signs even then that they disagreed on fundamental aesthetic principles; a disagreement which, ultimately, would lead to Dalí's criticism of Lorca's Romancero gitano and a rupture in their friendship.

In April of 1926, in the literary magazine Revista de Occidente, Lorca published an ode to his friend, entitled quite simply 'Oda a Salvador Dalí' ['Ode to Salvador Dalí'] (OC, I, pp. 953–57). In it, he praised his friend's art which was still in its pre-Surrealist, Cubist phase. He lauded what he called Dalí's 'ansias de eterno limitado' ['yearning for eternity with limits'] (OC, I, p. 954) and held the cubists up to be 'pintores modernos' ['modern painters'] (OC, I, p. 953), seeming also to count himself amongst their ranks, as the use of the first-person plural suggests: 'Un deseo de forma y límites nos gana' ['a desire for form and limits wins us over'] (OC, I, p. 953). And yet, despite the laudatory tones of his ode, Lorca took the opportunity as well to note his own divergence from Dalí's approach. Unlike Dalí, he was concerned not to lose sight of human reality which, in Cubism, was subordinated to a concern with geometric form. In the end, Lorca concluded, what united the two men was not art but rather the human bonds of love and friendship, including (paradoxically) the disagreements they shared, conveyed in the following stanza by the pithy metaphor of crossing swords:

> Pero ante todo canto un común pensamiento
> que nos une en las horas oscuras y doradas.

Figure 8 Lorca and Dalí standing on the shore at Cadaqués in 1927

> No es el Arte la luz que nos ciega los ojos.
> Es primero el amor, la amistad o la esgrima. (OC, I, p. 956)

[But above all I sing of a common thought that unites us in dark and golden times. The light that dazzles us is not art. Rather it is love, friendship and fencing.]

Writing to friend and Catalan art critic Sebastiá Gasch in September of the following year, Lorca, as Cecilia Castro Lee has noted,[1] restated this inability to ignore the human even in the most abstract of his own creations:

> Yo nunca me aventuro en terrenos que no son del hombre, porque vuelvo tierras atrás en seguida y *rompo* casi siempre el producto de mi viaje. Cuando hago una cosa de pura abstracción, siempre tiene (creo yo) como un salvoconducto de sonrisas y un equilibrio bastante humano. (*EC*, p. 518)

[I never venture out onto lands that are not the lands of men, because I'm compelled to turn back immediately and *tear up* almost everything my journey has produced. When I do something that is entirely abstract, it always retains (I believe) a safe conduct that secures a smile and an equilibrium that is rather human.]

It is for this reason, no doubt, that, as Castro (p. 71) also notes, Lorca's ode to Dalí ends with a plea to his friend never to lose sight of the things and people of the world: 'Viste y desnuda siempre tu pincel en el aire, | frente a la mar poblada con barcos y marinos' ['Always dress and undress your brush in the air, before a sea peopled by sailors and boats'] (OC, I, p. 957).

As Dalí moved ever closer to Surrealism, Lorca continued to shadow him. But far from abandon himself to the irrational processes of Surrealist production, he adopted a rational, critical stance and continued to enquire into the limits of what good art could and ought to be. Surrealism's focus was on art that emerged unconsciously via dreams or by chance, producing images and texts that were often difficult to fathom, at least via the conventional processes of rational interpretation. Lorca, by contrast, never seemed able or willing to relinquish control over his art, however intrigued he might have been by the unfettered character of Surrealist production.

---

[1] See Cecilia Castro Lee, 'La "Oda a Salvador Dalí": significación y trascendencia en la vida y creación de Lorca y Dalí', *Anales de Literatura Española Contemporánea*, 11 (1986), 61–78 (pp. 71–72).

In an unfinished dialogue that he composed in late 1927 or early 1928, and whose title, 'Corazón bleu y Coeur azul' (*PP*, pp. 91–92), at once combines and opposes the Spanish and French words for 'blue' and 'heart', Lorca puts control at the very heart of the exchange.[2] The dialogue takes place between two figures, named simply 'POETA' ['POET'] and 'MI AMIGO' ['MY FRIEND'], who almost certainly represent Lorca and Dalí respectively. In defence of the irrational, the friend insists that poets have 'un miedo horrible a perder la cabeza y un amor incomprensible a [...] la calidad lógica' ['a terrible fear of losing their heads and an incomprehensible love for the quality of logic'] (*PP*, p. 91). 'Es absurdo,' MI AMIGO tells POETA, 'que te conformes a que el zapato no sirva nada más que de zapato y la cuchara de cuchara. El zapato y la cuchara son dos formas de una extrema belleza y de una vida propia tan intensa como la tuya' ['It's absurd that you are prepared to accept that a shoe should serve as nothing but a shoe or a spoon, as nothing but a spoon. Shoes and spoons are forms of extreme beauty and have a life as intense as your own'] (*PP*, p. 91). To which POETA responds by exulting the possibilities of metaphor – '¡Ay vamos! Yo puedo convertir el zapato en un barquito o ...' ['Oh come on! I can transform a shoe into a boat or ...'] (*PP*, p. 92) – only to be interrupted by MI AMIGO's insistence that he ought to allow shoes quite simply to be shoes, 'sin inventarle nueva personalidad' ['and not invent for them a new personality'] (*PP*, p. 92). For MI AMIGO would rather conjure up new and surprising (and indeed irrational) combinations and place a shoe 'con una aceituna o con una nariz, por el mar del Sur, en medio de una simple emoción de brisa' ['with an olive or a nose, across the Southern seas, in the midst of a simple sentiment of the breeze'] (*PP*, p. 92). Although POETA does not disagree with MI AMIGO, there is a fundamental difference in their views. For POETA believes that such surprising combinations are a product of a poetic process – 'un hecho poético más' ['just another poetic fact'] (*PP*, p. 92). On the other hand, MI AMIGO sees them as being an actual fact of life – 'real, realísimo, vivo ' ['real, very real, alive'] (*PP*, p. 92), as if they had a life of their own and had simply been stumbled upon rather than conceived via a rational, creative process.

We can suppose, given the subject of his unfinished dialogue and the enquiry on which he had already embarked, that Lorca may not have been totally surprised by Dalí's criticism of his *Romancero gitano*. If anything,

---

2   Federico García Lorca, *Poemas en prosa*, ed. by Andrew A. Anderson (Comares / La Veleta, 2000), pp. 91–92. Abbreviated henceforth to *PP*.

we can see in Lorca's reaction to the criticism at least an attempt to take a view that was as balanced as that which comes across in the albeit incomplete dialogue 'Corazón bleu y Coeur azul'. So it was that Lorca wrote to Gasch in September 1928 that he considered Dalí's criticism 'un pleito poético interesante' ['an interesting poetic complaint'] (*EC*, p. 585). Still, the signals Lorca was sending were mixed, to say the least, just as they had been from the time that he first became involved with Dalí and the artist's work. In a letter Lorca wrote to Gasch in September 1927, Lorca must have had Surrealism in his sights when he stated 'abomino del arte de los sueños' ['I loathe the art of dreams'] (*EC*, p. 519). Yet, just a year later, in October 1928, in a lecture he gave to Granada's Athenaeum, entitled 'Sketch de la nueva pintua' ['Sketch of the New Painting'] (*OC*, III, pp. 272–81), he actually hailed Surrealism's apparent spontaneity, bemoaning the way art had otherwise become cerebral and intellectualized: '¿A dónde vamos? Vamos al instinto, vamos al acaso, a la inspiración pura, a la fragancia de lo directo' ['Where are we heading? We are heading towards instinct, towards chance, pure inspiration, the fragrance of the direct'] (*OC*, III, p. 278).

In another letter he wrote to Gasch, in September that year, he sent the art critic two poems that belonged to what he called his new spiritualist tendency. He characterized this tendency as 'emoción pura descarnada, desligada del control lógico' ['pure, stark emotion, untied from logical control'], all the while insisting that his poems retained 'una tremenda *lógica poética*' ['a tremendous poetic logic'] (*EC*, p. 588). This point is echoed in his lecture, 'Imaginación, inspiración, evasión' ['Imagination, Inspiration, Escape'] (*OC*, III, pp. 258–71), which he first delivered in Granada only a couple of weeks before 'Sketch de la nueva pintura'. In 'Imaginación, inspiración, evasión', Lorca distinguishes between, on the one hand, poetry that is the product of the imagination, tied to reality (since reality is the starting point for the imagination, as you cannot imagine what does not exist) and thus possesses a 'human logic' ('lógica humana') (*OC*, III, p. 259); and, on the other hand, poetry that is born of inspiration, manages to escape the realm of reality, and thus possesses a 'poetic logic' ('lógica poética') (*OC*, III, p. 261). But while we can see here how Lorca was moving towards the aesthetic terrain occupied by Surrealism, his movement was by no means complete. In his letter to Gasch, he is also quick to add that what he was doing was absolutely not Surrealism: '¡ojo!' ['Be careful!'], he warned his friend, his poems were illuminated by 'la *conciencia* más clara' ['the clearest consciousness'] (*EC*, p. 588).

Whatever concessions, then, Lorca may have made to Dalí on personal or professional grounds, he clearly stopped short of embracing Surrealism, which is why it is all the more remarkable that his next major collection of poems after *Romancero gitano*, entitled *Poeta en Nueva York* [*Poet in New York*], should, on the face of it, appear Surrealist in character. The surprising and seemingly irrational combinations of images and words, the dreamscapes and the verbosity akin to uncontrolled streams of consciousness, and the scant attention paid by its poems in free verse to the qualities of beauty, harmony or form, all point to the collection's Surrealist influence. It is, though, significant that this Surrealist experiment (if we can properly call it that) should have taken place during Lorca's time in New York, a city that, by any standards, was the epitome of modernity. And it is significant also that, for all their surrealistic veneer, the poems retain a logic that, notwithstanding their frequently complex and elusive images, succeeds in communicating their critical intent. Inevitably, the targets of this criticism are modernity, epitomized by the modern city, as well as, at a less explicit level, Surrealism itself. And as we shall see, even in the most modern of modern cities, Lorca seemed unable, or even unwilling, to put his *Romancero gitano* behind him. For his New York poems acquire their full force and significance, I would argue, when we keep in mind the images offered by the Gitano ballads of an animate, spirited nature and of colourful characters and religious tableaux.

In a letter dated 28 June 1929, two days after his arrival in New York, Lorca wrote to his family about the city in the most positive terms. 'A mí,' he explained, 'me levantó el espíritu ver cómo el hombre con ciencia y con técnica logra impresionar como un elemento de naturaleza pura' ['It raised my spirits to see how mankind can, with science and technology, make an impression as great as an element of pure nature'] (*EC*, p. 614). He marvelled at the unique spectacle offered by the lights of New York's harbour and towering buildings, declaring Paris and London (where he had stopped off en route to America) to be but little towns when compared with this 'Babilonia trepidante y enloquecedora' ['frenetic and maddening Babylon'] (*EC*, p. 615). He suggested that it was easier to move around New York's numbered street blocks than it was Paris, or most certainly London, and he reassured his family that he felt good and had acclimatized. Moreover, New York was 'alegrísimo y acogedor' ['very cheerful and welcoming'] and the people, 'ingenua y encantadora' ['naïve and charming'] (*EC*, p. 616). He felt happier there than he had in Paris, which seemed to him to be 'un poco podrido y viejo' ['a little run down and old'] (*EC*, p. 616). He recounted an evening he had spent out

Figure 9 Lorca seated with friends at the granite ball at Columbia University in 1929

with friends 'al corazón del inmenso Broadway' ['at the heart of immense Broadway'] (*EC*, p. 616). There, the spectacle of Broadway, in all its brash modernity, simply took his breath away:

> El espectáculo del Broadway de noche me cortó la respiración. Los inmensos rascacielos se visten de arriba a abajo de anuncios luminosos de colores que cambian y se transforman con un ritmo insospechado y estupendo, chorros de luces azules, verdes, amarillas, rojas, cambian y saltan hasta el cielo. Más altos que la luna, se apagan y se encienden los nombres de bancos, hoteles, automóviles y casas de películas, la multitud abigarrada de jerseys de colores y pañuelos atrevidos sube y baja en cinco ríos distintos, las bocinas de los autos se confunden con los gritos y músicas de las radios, y los aeroplanos encendidos pasan anunciando sombreros, trajes, dentífricos, cambiando sus letras y tocando grandes trompetas y campanas. Es un espectáculo soberbio, emocionante, de la ciudad más atrevida y moderna del mundo. (*EC*, pp. 616–17)

> [The spectacle of Broadway at night took my breath away. The immense skyscrapers are dressed from top to toe in luminous adverts of all colours that change and transform with unexpected and astonishing speed. Streams of blue, green, yellow and red lights, revolve and shoot into the sky. Higher than the moon, the names of banks, hotels, cars and film studios flicker on and off, crowds of motley-coloured jerseys and striking kerchiefs flow one way and the other along five or six different streams, the sound of car horns mixes with shouts and music from radios, and airplanes, lit-up, fly by advertising hats, suits and toothpaste, their letters changing to the fanfare of trumpets and ringing bells. It's a magnificent, moving spectacle, in one of the most daring and modern cities in the world.]

Clearly, on the evidence of this letter alone, and indeed subsequent letters to his family, we might never have guessed how negatively his New York poems would portray the city. But that's precisely what they did, from the very start. The opening poem of *Poeta en Nueva York*, 'Vuelta de paseo' ['Back from a Walk'] (*OC*, I, p. 447), sets the tone for a journey into apparent oppression and isolation. In 'Vuelta de paseo', as is the case elsewhere in the collection, alienation and loss are marked by personal disorientation and the absence or deformation of nature, which is cast here and throughout the collection as a victim of the insensitivity, immorality and inhumanity of modern urban living.

> Asesinado por le cielo,
> entre las formas que van al sierpe,

    y las formas que buscan el cristal,
dejaré crecer mis cabellos.

    Con el árbol de muñones que no canta
y el niño con el blanco rostro de huevo.

    Con los animalitos de cabeza rota
y el agua harapienta de los pies secos.

    Con todo lo que tiene cansancio sordomudo
y mariposa ahogada en el tintero.

    Tropezando con mi rostro de cada día.
¡Asesinado por el cielo! (OC, I, p. 447)

[Murdered by the sky, between the forms that head to the serpent and the forms that look for glass, I will let my hair grow. With the tree of stumps that does not sing and the child with its white, egg face. With little animals with their heads broken and the ragged water of dry feet. With all that is deaf-dumb tired, and a butterfly drowned in the inkwell. Bumping into my face, different each day. Murdered by the sky!]

In light of the collection's title, which foregrounds the figure of the poet and locates him in the city, the presumption must be that the first-person voice of 'Vuelta de paseo' is Lorca's own. Words are not put in the mouths of characters, as is the case in *Romancero gitano*, but instead the poet speaks to us directly. This alignment of the first-person voice with its author's personality is confirmed in other poems in which the speaker specifically refers to himself as the poet. This is the case, for example, in 'Paisaje de la multitud que vomita' ['Landscape of the Vomiting Crowd (Nightfall at Coney Island)'] (OC, I, pp. 473–74) and 'Poema doble del lago Edén' ['Double Poem of Lake Eden'] (OC, I, pp. 489–90).

    Although 'Vuelta de paseo' is, relatively speaking, one of the most straightforward and intelligible poems of the collection, it shares formal processes with other, more verbose poems that are structurally less compact and altogether denser. These processes are principally 'destructive adjectivisation', the suppression of simile, condensing and displacing 'imagistic statements', and personification, together leading frequently to bewildering combinations of words and harrowing imagery.[3] Although

---

3 See Derek Harris, *Federico García Lorca. 'Poeta en Nueva York'*, Critical Guides to Spanish Studies (London: Grant & Cutler / Tamesis, 1978), pp. 15–16.

the poet's source material would have been the very real things and people he encountered in the city, by subjecting them to these processes he renders them deformed and other-worldly, and endows his poetry with a hallucinatory and nightmarish quality.[4] Thus, the personification that is at work in the opening statement and concluding exclamation of 'Vuelta de paseo' casts the sky as the poet's murderer. Condensation and displacement are also at work here since there is no explanation as to why the sky might harbour a murderous instinct or what in real terms this murder might mean.[5]

We cannot, most certainly, take this murder at face value. So what might it mean? Does it point to the emotional turmoil the poet feels as he looks up at a dark, foreboding sky, or a sky crowded out by tall buildings? Or rather than the sky, ought we understand 'cielo' to mean 'heaven', another meaning of the word in Spanish? In which case, is the poet pointing to the prospect of divine condemnation in a world devoid of spiritual life? The answer is not clear, and, in the end, all the poem provides us with is an idea that victimizes the speaker and frames a nightmarish scene. The poet comes across as a lost figure, despite his claim that he will let his hair grow ('dejaré crecer mis cabellos'), possibly in some bohemian, but ultimately pathetic, act of defiance. Are the forms 'heading for the serpent' ('que van al sierpe') or 'looking for the glass' ('que buscan el cristal') actually people? And might the uncanny reference to a serpent be the product of the suppression of a simile which would have, in explicit terms, likened rows of traffic or perhaps the tunnels of the New York subway to the form of a snake? If so, all that is now left of the snakelike, once the simile has been suppressed, is the perilous presence of the snake itself, just as all that is left of New York's glass towers is the glass. In the image of the unsinging tree stump ('el árbol de muñones que no canta'), we see condensed the idea of a tree that has been mutilated by having been cut back, as well as

---

4   See Derek Harris (ed.), *Metal Butterflies and Poisonous Lights: Language of Surrealism in Lorca, Alberti, Cernuda and Aleixandre* (Arncroach, Scotland: La Sirena, 1998), p. 87. Harris writes: 'Much of the imagery of the New York poems can be seen to derive from detailed specific experience.' 'The city and the whole American experience', Harris (1998, p. 85) also explains, 'is subjected to a process of hallucination in *Poeta en Nueva York*.' 'In the New York of the roaring twenties of prohibition Lorca began to "see" some very strange things' (Harris 1998, p. 86)]. See also Harris (1978, p. 19) on the 'state of hypersensitivity' and the 'hallucinated gaze'.
5   For an explanation of the processes of condensation and displacement, see Harris 1998, p. 86.

the idea of a tree bereft of birds: creatures that, in real terms, would have been the source of the tree's song. The elimination of simile means that a boy's face is not described as being white like an egg but instead becomes the white egg itself ('blanco rostro de huevo').[6] And destructive adjectivisation means that animals' heads are broken ('animalitos de cabeza rota') and water is rendered ragged ('agua harapienta') and, in an impossible paradox, connected to dry feet ('pies secos').

We could debate whether Lorca's approach in 'Vuelta de paseo', and in poems throughout the collection, is Expressionist or Surrealist. The distinction turns on the fact that in Expressionism the deformation of reality is a wilful expression of a subjective state, whereas in Surrealism it is the product of a process that by-passes the will altogether, as in the case of so-called automatic writing or creativity that is based on games of pure chance. Surrealist art is, as a result, characterized by arbitrary ideas and images with seemingly little or no logical connection, while Expressionist art offers patterns that allow us to come to some tangible, logical, overarching interpretation. 'Vuelta de paseo', despite its surprising images and the questions it raises – despite, in other words, its surrealistic veneer – seems to fall into the category of Expressionism. For it is possible for us, notwithstanding the lack of fixity of certain meanings (as in the case, for example, of 'cielo'), to arrive at an interpretation that brings together its various parts.[7] On one level, the modern city, far from the spirited world of *Romancero gitano* and Andalusia, is presented as an enemy of nature and humanity. Indeed, the penultimate line of the poem, with its reference to the speaker's many faces, conveys the disorientating and dehumanizing impact on the poet himself. But just as importantly, the city is also presented as an enemy of poetry. The idea, in the penultimate couplet, of 'deaf-dumb tiredness' ('cansancio sordomudo') and the image

---

6 As Harris (1998, p. 86) explains, 'The strangeness of the image comes from the condensation and emotional intensification which suppress a series of implied similes.'

7 Harris (1998, p. 86) argues that 'This is the distorted and intensified emotionalism of Expressionism not the bringing together of widely separate realities in the Surrealist abolition of contradiction.' In respect of the collection as a whole, he explains that 'Expressionist intensification is consistently present [...] and is often the cause of the hermeneutic difficulty of the text. However, textual clues or external information can permit the compression to be expanded and the associative links revealed as conscious and concordant, obeying both the concept of "poetic logic" and forming part of the overarching symbol system that runs throughout Lorca's work' (Harris 1998, p. 88).

of 'a butterfly drowned in the inkwell' ('mariposa ahogada en el tintero') allude both to the city's assault on the poet's senses and to the resulting catastrophe of the writing process. In this self-conscious moment, the poet offers us an explanation as to why his poem's images are so strange. It is because, to put it simply, beautiful poetry is incompatible with the ugliness of modern life. The poetry spawned in the city, then, is as much about the challenge modernity poses to a poet's creativity as it is about the challenge it poses to lives of human beings.

The challenge to poetic creativity is central also to the poem 'Paisaje de la multitud que vomita (Anochecer de Coney Island)' (OC, I, pp. 473–74), inspired by Lorca's trip to New York's famous amusement park. It is not insignificant that in a letter to his family, dated 6 July 1929, Lorca, though he judged the park to be 'monstruoso' ['monstrous'] (EC, p. 621) because of its size and the vast crowds that thronged there, offered a picture of his excursion that emphasized the fun and spectacle of the place over any feelings of horror. He mentions its 'montañas rusas increíbles, lagos encantados, grutas, músicas, monstruos humanos, grandes bailes, colecciones de fieras, ruedas y columpios gigantescos, las mujeres más gruesas del mundo, el hombre que tiene cuatro ojos' ['incredible roller coasters, enchanted lakes, grottos, music, human monsters, dancing, menageries, gigantic Ferris wheels and swings, the world's fattest women, the man with four eyes'] (EC, p. 621), as well as its 'miles de puestos de helados, salchichas, frituras, panecillos, dulces, en una variedad fantástica' ['thousands of stalls selling a fantastic variety of ice cream, hot dogs, fried food, rolls and sweets'] (EC, p. 621). At night, the place lit up, 'y fue cosa de prodigio infantil, las grandes ruedas de oro y las torres de madera y cristales, brillantes sobre las músicas y tatachines' ['and it was like a child's dream, the great golden Ferris wheels, the wood and glass towers, sparkling above the music and chatter'] (EC, p. 621). His friends made him order things so that he could practice his English, and although this put him in all sorts of difficulty, he triumphed in the end 'entre las risas de todos ellos' ['amidst the laughter of one and all'] (EC, p. 621). And yet, for all his enthusiasm, the contrast between his letter and his poem on the subject of Coney Island could not be greater.

Although Lorca conceded in his letter to his family that Coney Island was a wonderful spectacle, he also noted that it was excessive, advising that a single visit to the park was more than enough. The wonder he speaks of, however, is completing missing from 'Paisaje de la multitud que vomita' which, instead, emphasizes only the excess and does so in the most exaggerated and, indeed, excessive of terms:

La mujer gorda venía delante
arrancando las raíces y mojando el pergamino de los tambores;
la mujer gorda
que vuelve del revés los pulpos agonizantes.
La mujer gorda, enemiga de la luna,
corría por las calles y los pisos deshabitados
y dejaba por los rincones pequeñas calaveras de paloma
y levantaba las furias de los banquetes de los siglos últimos
y llamaba al demonio del pan por las colinas del cielo barrido
y filtraba un ansia de luz en las circulaciones subterráneas.
Son los cementerios, lo sé, son los cementerios
y el dolor de las cocinas enterradas bajo la arena;
son los muertos, los faisanes y las manzanas de otra hora
los que nos empujan en la garganta.

   Llegaban los rumores de la selva del vómito
con las mujeres vacías, con niños de cera caliente,
con árboles fermentados y camareros incansables
que sirven platos de sal bajo las arpas de la saliva.
Sin remedio, hijo mío, ¡vomita! No hay remedio.
No es el vómito de los húsares sobre los pechos de la prostituta,
ni el vómito del gato que se tragó una rana por descuido.
Son los muertos que arañan con sus manos de tierra
las puertas de pedernal donde se pudren nublos y postres.

   La mujer gorda venía delante
con las gentes de los barcos y de las tabernas y de los jardines.
El vómito agitaba delicadamente sus tambores
entre algunas niñas de sangre
que pedían protección a la luna.
¡Ay de mí! ¡Ay de mí! ¡Ay de mí!
Esta mirada mía fue mía, pero ya no es mía,
esta mirada que tiembla desnuda por el alcohol
y despide barcos increíbles
por las anémonas de los muelles.
Me defiendo con esta mirada
que mana de las ondas por donde el alba no se atreve,
yo, poeta sin brazos, perdido
entre la multitud que vomita,
sin caballo efusivo que corte
los espesos musgos de mis sienes.

   Pero la mujer gorda seguía delante
y la gente buscaba las farmacias

donde el amargo trópico se fija.
Sólo cuando izaron la bandera y llegaron los primeros canes
la ciudad entera se agolpó en las barandillas del embarcadero. (OC, I, pp. 473–74)

[The fat lady came forth tearing out roots and wetting the parchment of drums. The fat lady, who turns agonizing octopuses inside out. The fat lady, enemy of the moon, ran through the streets and deserted apartment blocks and left the tiny skulls of pigeons in the corners and stirred up the furies of the banquets of the last centuries and summoned the demon of bread across the hills of the sweeping sky and filtered a longing for light in subterranean flows. It's the cemeteries. I know. It's the cemeteries and the pain of kitchens buried beneath the sand. It's the dead, the pheasants and apples of another time that push into our throats. The murmurs from the jungle of vomit came with the empty women, with children of hot wax, with fermented trees and tireless waiters serving plates of salt beneath saliva harps. There's nothing doing, my son. Vomit! There's nothing doing. It's not the vomit of hussars on a prostitute's breasts, nor the vomit of a cat that carelessly swallowed a frog. It's the dead who scratch with their dirt hands at the stone gates where storm clouds and desserts rot. The fat lady came forth with the crowds from the boats, from the taverns and from the parks. Vomit delicately shook its drums among some girls of blood begging protection from the moon. Oh my! Oh my! Oh my! This look was once mine but is no more. This look that shivers naked from the alcohol and sees off incredible boats through the anemones of the piers. I defend myself with this look that flows from the waves where the dawn dares not go. I, poet without arms, lost among the vomiting crowd, without an effusive horse to cut the thick moss on my temples. But the fat lady kept coming and the people looked for pharmacies where the bitter tropic is set. Only when the flag was raised, and the first dogs arrived, did the entire city rush to the railings of the pier.]

In a recital of his New York poems in Madrid in 1932, Lorca would also dwell heavily on Coney Island's excesses:

Coney Island es una gran feria a la cual los domingos de verano acuden más de un millón de criaturas. Beben, gritan, comen, se revuelcan y dejan el mar lleno de periódicos y las calles abarrotadas de latas, de cigarros apagados, de mordiscos, de zapatos sin tacón. Vuelve la muchedumbre de la feria cantando, y vomita en grupos de cien personas apoyadas sobre las barandillas de los embarcaderos, y orina en grupos de mil en los rincones, sobre los barcos abandonados y sobre los monumentos de Garibaldi o el soldado desconocido. (OC, III, p. 353)

[Coney Island is a huge fair visited every Sunday by more than a million creatures. They drink, shout, eat, thrash about and leave the sea covered in newspapers and the streets littered with tin cans, cigarette butts, half-eaten food, heelless shoes. The crowds return from the fair in song; they vomit in groups of one hundred people, leaning over the railings of the piers; they urinate in groups of one thousand on street corners, over abandoned boats and the monuments of Garibaldi and the unknown soldier.]

This prelude to his recital of his poem was, as Derek Harris (1978, p. 19) points out, 'a calculated exaggeration, an exaggeration that is greatly increased in the poem derived from the experience'. How else, if not as a 'calculated exaggeration', ought we to understand Lorca's claim, in the very same introduction to his recital, that 'Nadie puede darse idea de la soledad que siente allí un español, y más todavía si éste es hombre del sur. Porque si te caes, serás atropellado, y si resbalas al agua, arrojarán sobre ti los papeles de las meriendas' ['No one has the faintest idea how lonely a Spaniard feels there, and more so if he's from the south. Because if you fall, you'll be trampled on, and if you slip and fall into the water, they'll chuck their sweet wrappers all over you'] (OC, III, p. 353)?

While on the surface, the images of 'Paisaje de la multitud que vomita' might seem as close as any in the collection to the arbitrary character of Surrealist production (see Harris 1998, p. 96), a logic does run through the poem, initiated by the figure of the fat lady, and consolidated, as we shall see, by the poet's self-involvement in his text. The fat lady, possibly one of those 'world's fattest women' that Lorca mentions in his letter, is a kind of grotesque reworking of Preciosa from the Gitano ballad 'Preciosa y el aire', the young girl's tambourine now substituted by the drums. If Preciosa, who threw her tambourine away in fright, epitomized naivety, the fat woman is her corrupt opposite, even corrupting the sound of drums by wetting their skeins with vomit. The fat lady does not flee from sexual menace, as the young girl did, but is a debauched figure who herself orchestrates the excesses in the amusement park. Preciosa, in a sense, was fleeing from nature, but the fat lady is altogether the nemesis of the natural world, 'tearing out roots' ('arrancando las raíces' [OC, I, p. 473]), turning 'agonizing octopuses inside out' ('vuelve del revés los pulpos agonizantes' [OC, I, p. 473]), an 'enemy of the moon' ('enemiga de la luna' [OC, I, p. 473]), leaving 'tiny skulls of pigeons' ('pequeñas calaveras de paloma' [OC, I, p. 473]) in her wake. It is she who incites the vomiting, depicted by the poet in the most exaggerated and excessive terms. For what is thrown up is 'the furies of the banquets of the last centuries' ('las furias de los banquetes de los siglos últimos' [OC, I, p. 473]), 'the demon of bread' ('demonio del pan' [OC, I, p. 473]), 'the cemeteries and the pain of kitchens' ('los cementerios | y el dolor de las cocinas' [OC, I, p. 473]) and 'the dead, the pheasants and apples of another time' ('los faisanes y las manzanas de otra hora' [OC, I, p. 473]). The vomit flows from subterranean depths, 'longing for light' ('ansia de luz' [OC, I, p. 473]), it emerges from 'beneath the sand' ('bajo la arena' [OC, I, p. 473]), its contents 'push into our throats' ('nos empujan en la garganta' [OC, I, p. 473]). The process of vomiting is aided by 'tireless waiters serving plates of salt' ('camareros incansables | que sirven platos de sal' [OC, I, p. 473]), whose customers are denoted, synecdochally, only by their open mouths – by the strings of saliva conveyed in the image of 'saliva harps' ('arpas de saliva' [OC, I, p. 473]). The vomiting is the result of excesses so profound that it exceeds even the idea of a hussar vomiting 'on a prostitute's breasts' ('sobre los pechos de la prostituta' [OC, I, p. 473]) or a cat vomiting up a frog that it has swallowed by mistake. It is, instead, more accurately conveyed by the idea of the dead scratching at 'stone gates' ('puertas de pedernal' [OC, I, p. 473]). Throw into the mix 'empty women' ('las mujeres vacías' [OC, I, p. 473]), 'children of hot wax' ('niños de cera caliente' [OC, I, p. 473]), 'fermented trees' ('árboles fermentados' [OC, I, p. 473]), 'storm clouds' ('nublos' [OC, I, p. 473]) and 'desserts' ('postres' [OC, I, p. 473]), and we have a powerful concoction that makes the vomiting irrepressible.

'Paisaje de la multitude que vomita' clearly offers a critique of consumerist excess. Its approach is highly selective, retaining none of the wonder Lorca expressed when he wrote to his family about the 'fantastic variety' available at Coney Island's 'thousands of stalls'. It is this very selective approach, along with the poet's direct self-involvement in the poem, that offers an additional, though not incompatible, reading. For when the poet does appear, it is, as was the case in 'Vuelta de paseo', in order to testify in person to the creative difficulties he is experiencing in an environment that is emblematic of the mass consumerist culture associated with modernity. He shouts out 'Oh my! Oh my! Oh my!' ('¡Ay de mí! ¡Ay de mí! ¡Ay de mí!' [OC, I, p. 474]), because the scene is so overwhelming that it undermines his agency as an observer – 'This look was once mine but is no more' ('Esta mirada mía fue mía, pero ya no es mía' [OC, I, p. 474]) – and it requires that he take up a defensive position: 'I defend myself with this look that flows from the waves where the dawn dares not go' ('Me defiendo con esta mirada | que mana de las ondas por donde el alba no se atreve' [OC, I, p. 474]). Most telling is his admission that he, as a poet, 'lost among the vomiting crowd' ('perdido | entre la multitud que vomita'

[OC, I, p. 474]), has been rendered powerless through the (figurative) loss of his arms: 'I, poet without arms' ('yo, poeta sin brazos' [OC, I, p. 474]). Perhaps unsurprisingly, he has recourse to a natural image in order to convey his fall from the poet he once was (for example, in *Romancero gitano*) to the poet he is now: one who has been left 'without an effusive horse to cut the thick moss on [his] temples' ('sin caballo efusivo que corte | los espesos musgos de mis sienes' [OC, I, p. 474]). This line is a self-conscious reflection on his lack of mental clarity and the resulting disorder of a poem which, formally, via its hyperbole and long lists, seems to want to replicate the vomiting it sets out to describe. But his is a lack of clarity and his poem's a disorder in appearance only. When all is said and done, 'Paisaje de la multitude que vomita' is a controlled poem about losing control, and its surrealistic veneer suggests that the target of the poet's criticism is not only consumerist excess but also the loss of control and disorder associated with Surrealist art. Whether or not in reality it was a battle for him to remain in control in New York, Lorca is determined to show what he considered to be the ugly side of modernity, both in modern life and in modern art.

Lorca's critique of Surrealism's abandonment of control and, with it, its specific claim to modernity is inseparable in *Poeta en Nueva York* from his condemnation of the alienating character of modern life. The title of the collection and the constant use of the first person assure the connection even when, as is often the case, the figure of the poet is not mentioned directly as it is in 'Paisaje de la multitud que vomita'. We cannot help, for that matter, comparing its surrealistic (if not properly Surrealist) depictions of deformed nature with the vibrant and often animate representations of Andalusia's natural world that we find in *Romancero gitano*. The comparison is clearly unfavourable and throws into sharp relief Lorca's association of Surrealism with the excesses of modernity. Compare, for example, the dawn image at the start of 'San Miguel (Granada)', from *Romancero gitano*, with the depiction of the sunrise in the New York poem 'La aurora' ['The Dawn'] (OC, I, p. 485). 'San Miguel (Granada)' opens with a delightful conceit in which mules laden with baskets of sunflowers come to evoke the sun rising from the darkness as the working animals climb the hill:

Se ven desde las barandas,
por el monte, monte, monte,
mulos y sombras de mulos
cargados de girasoles.

Sus ojos en las umbrías
se empañan de inmensa noche.
En los recodos del aire
cruje la aurora salobre. (OC, I, p. 410)

[You can see from the railings on the hill, hill, hill, mules and shadows of mules carrying sunflowers. Their eyes in the shadows cloud over with immense night. In the bends of the breeze the salty dawn rustles.]

By contrast, in 'La aurora', the dawn is not woven into a brilliant image but is put to rather more prosaic use. A far cry from the picturesque scene revealed in 'San Miguel (Granada)', daylight serves only to reveal the city's grime, inhumanity and desolation:

La aurora de Nueva York tiene
cuatro columnas de cieno
y un huracán de negras palomas
que chapotean las aguas podridas.

La aurora de Nueva York gime
por las inmensas escaleras
buscando entre las aristas
nardos de angustia dibujada.

La aurora llega y nadie la recibe en su boca
porque allí no hay mañana ni esperanza posible.
A veces las monedas en enjambres furiosos
taladran y devoran abandonados niños.

Los primeros que salen comprenden con sus huesos
que no habrá paraíso ni amores deshojados;
saben que van al cieno de números y leyes,
a los juegos sin arte, a sudores sin frutos.

La luz es sepultada por cadenas y ruidos
en impúdico reto de ciencia sin raíces.
Por los barrios hay gentes que vacilan insomnes
como recién salidas de un naufragio de sangre.

[The dawn in New York has four columns of mire and a hurricane of black pigeons splashing in the putrid waters. The dawn in New York moans along immense stairways looking amongst the edges for spikenards of sketched anguish. The dawn arrives and no one receives it in their mouth because there neither morning nor hope are possible: sometimes coins, in furious swarms, drill into and devour abandoned children. The first who go out feel in their bones that there will be neither paradise nor loves depetalled: they know that they're going to the mire of numbers and laws, to artless games, to fruitless labours. The light is buried by chains and noise under the shameless challenge of rootless science. Through the neighbourhoods there are people staggering sleeplessly as if they had just emerged from a shipwreck of blood.]

Dark towers, like 'columns of mire' ('columnas de cieno'); dirty pigeons in even dirtier water; unnerving angles, corners, and stairways; a lust for money over any concern for children; a loveless world in which love-me-nots is not a game worth playing; city workers whose efforts will come to nothing; people staggering about, exhausted from lack of sleep. It is all this that is revealed by the dawn, now bereft of its common connotations of light, hope and new beginnings. For in New York, 'neither morning nor hope are possible' ('no hay mañana ni esperanza posible'). Instead, its light 'is buried by chains and noise' ('La luz es sepultada por cadenas y ruidos') and the city, with its science, technology, numbers and laws, inevitably wins out over the natural world. It wins out over poetry too because the dawn-motif, a staple of the poetic tradition, has itself succumbed to the ugliness and brutality of modern city life.

Poetry faces a struggle also in 'Panorama ciego de Nueva York' ['Blind Landscape of New York'] (OC, I, pp. 482–83), a poem whose images, in keeping with its title, are often obscure, to say the least:

Si no son los pájaros
cubiertos de ceniza,
si no son los gemidos que golpean las ventanas de la boda,
serán las delicadas criaturas del aire
que manan sangre nueva por la oscuridad inextinguible.
Pero no, no son los pájaros,
porque los pájaros están a punto de ser bueyes;
pueden ser rocas blancas con la ayuda de la luna
y son siempre muchachos heridos
antes de que los jueces levanten la tela.

   Todos comprenden el dolor que se relaciona con la muerte,
pero el verdadero dolor no está presente en el espíritu.
No está en al aire ni en nuestra vida,
ni en estas terrazas llenas de humo.
El verdadero dolor que mantiene despiertas las cosas
es una pequeña quemadura infinita
en los ojos inocentes de los otros sistemas.

Lorca, the Modern   91

   Un traje abandonado pesa tanto en los hombros
que muchas veces el cielo los agrupa en ásperas manadas.
Y las que mueren de parto saben en la última hora
que todo rumor será piedra y toda huella latido.
Nosotros ignoramos que el pensamiento tiene arrabales
donde el filósofo es devorado por los chinos y las orugas.
Y algunos niños idiotas han encontrado por las cocinas
pequeñas golondrinas con muletas
que sabían pronunciar la palabra amor.

   No, no son los pájaros.
No es un pájaro el que expresa la turbia fiebre de laguna,
ni el ansia de asesinato que nos oprime cada momento,
ni el metálico rumor de suicidio que nos anima cada madrugada.
Es una cápsula de aire donde nos duele todo el mundo,
es un pequeño espacio vivo al loco unisón de la luz,
es una escala indefinible donde las nubes y rosas olvidan
el griterío chino que bulle por el desembarcadero de la sangre.
Yo muchas veces me he perdido
para buscar la quemadura que mantiene despiertas las cosas
y sólo he encontrado marineros echados sobre las barandillas
y pequeñas criaturas del cielo enterradas bajo la nieve.
Pero el verdadero dolor estaba en otras plazas
donde los peces cristalizados agonizaban dentro de los troncos;
plazas del cielo extraño para las antiguas estatuas ilesas
y para la tierna intimidad de los volcanes.

   No hay dolor en la voz. Sólo existen los dientes,
pero dientes que callarán aislados por el rasgo negro.
No hay dolor en la voz. Aquí solo existe la tierra.
La tierra con sus puertas de siempre
que llevan al rubor de los frutos.

[If it isn't the birds covered in ash, if it's not the cries beating against the windows of the wedding, it must be the delicate creatures of the air that gush new blood into the inextinguishable darkness. But no, it's not the birds, because the birds are about to become oxen. They can become white rocks with the moon's help, and they are always wounded boys before the judges lift the cloth. Everyone understands the pain related to death, but true pain lives not in the spirit. It's not in the air, nor in our lives, nor in the terraces filled with smoke. The true pain that keeps things awake is a small, infinite burn on the innocent eyes of the other systems. An abandoned suit weighs so heavily on the shoulders that the sky often groups them into ragged herds; and those who die in childbirth know in their final hour that every murmur will be stone and every step a heartbeat. We do not know that thought has boroughs where the philosopher is devoured by the Chinese and the caterpillars, and where some idiot children have found, in the kitchens, small swallows on crutches able to pronounce the word love.[8] No, it's not the birds. A bird can't express the turbid fever of a lagoon, nor the thirst for murder that oppresses us every moment, nor the metallic murmur of suicide inspiring us each morning. It's a capsule of air where we suffer all the world, a small space alive to the mad unison of the light, an indefinable scale where the clouds and roses forget the Chinese shouts seething on the pier of the blood. I've often lost myself looking for the burn that keeps things awake and I've only found sailors leaning over railings and small creatures of the sky buried beneath the snow. But the true pain was in other plazas where crystallized fish were dying inside tree trunks; plazas of a sky unfamiliar to the ancient statues unscathed and to the tender intimacy of volcanoes. There is no pain in the voice. All that exists is teeth, but teeth that will fall silent, isolated by black satin. There is no pain in the voice. Here all that exists is the Earth. The Earth with its timeless doors leading to blush of fruit.]

The difficulty of 'Panorama ciego de Nueva York' arises, in part, from its use of negative structures: 'Si no son los pájaros' ['If it isn't the birds'] (OC, I, p. 482), 'si no son los gemidos' ['if it's not the cries'] (OC, I, p. 482), 'Pero no, no son los pájaros' ['But no, it's not the birds'] (OC, I, p. 482), 'No está en el aire, ni en nuestra vida, | ni en estas terrazas' ['It's not in the air, nor in our lives, nor in the terraces'] (OC, I, p. 482), 'No, no son los pájaros' ['No, it's not the birds'] (OC, I, p. 483), 'No es el pájaro el que expresa' ['A bird can't express'] (OC, I, p. 483), 'No hay dolor en la voz' ['There is no pain in the voice'] (OC, I, p. 483). After the idea of the 'thing-that-it-is-not' is presented to our mind's eye, the 'thing-that-it-is'

---

8 As Pablo Medina and Mark Statman point out, in the introduction to their translation of the collection, the use of the word *chino* is common in *Poeta en Nueva York*. As well as referring literally to a Chinese person – further testament to Lorca's awareness of New York's ethnic diversity – it can also have pejorative connotations and 'refer to someone who is deceitful, a trickster'. This might be an allusion intended by the image, in 'Panorama ciego de Nueva York', of *chinos* devouring philosophers. Medina and Statman also note that *chino* can refer to 'a kind of aural cacophony', which may make sense of its qualification of *'griterío'* [shouts] in the next stanza. See Federico García Lorca, *Poet in New York* [*Poeta en Nueva York*], trans. by Pablo Medina and Mark Statman (New York: Grove Press, 2008), p. xxi.

is then presented in terms often so arcane that it is difficult to make sense of what we see, if indeed we see anything at all. Perhaps this is a perspective, or lack of it, shared by the poet-speaker who is depicting this 'blind' panorama for us. The poet-speaker himself declares that he has often got lost in his search for 'la quemadura que mantiene despiertas las cosas' ['the burn that keeps things awake'] (OC, I, p. 483), admitting that he has only found 'marineros echados sobre las barandillas | y pequeñas criaturas del cielo enterradas bajo la nieve' ['sailors leaning over railings and small creatures of the sky buried beneath the snow'] (OC, I, p. 483). These images – the former reminiscent of the crowds at the railings of the pier in 'Paisaje de la multitud que vomita', the latter cohering with the collection's motif of nature corrupted and defiled (as do, for example, 'pequeñas golondrinas con muletas' ['small swallows on crutches'] (OC, I, p. 482) and 'plazas | donde los peces cristalizados agonizaban dentro de los troncos' ['plazas where crystallized fish were dying inside tree trunks'] (OC, I, p. 483) – are a stark reminder of the limits on the poet's creative quest in the city. Ultimately, all the poet can muster in this environment are images of despair and mutilation.

That the poet-speaker should be concerned with 'keeping things awake' is telling because it reminds us of Lorca's attachment to art that is produced in a state of wakefulness, of his rejection of the abandonment of consciousness in favour of retaining control. The metamorphoses of the opening stanza – birds 'a punto de ser bueyes' ['about to become oxen'], able to 'ser rocas blancas' ['become white rocks'] and 'siempre muchachos heridos' ['always wounded boys'] – also call to mind the discussion between POETA and MI AMIGO in 'Corazón bleu y Coeur azul', in which the former's insistence that he can transform a shoe into a boat is rebuffed as the latter states his preference for irrational combinations. In 'Panorama ciego de Nueva York', the poet-speaker seems not to have control over these transformations. Fixity and, consequently, reason are undone as the image of birds shifts between being 'about to become' ('a punto de'), being 'able to become' ('pueden') and 'always being' ('son siempre'). This state of affairs is, I would suggest, closer to MI AMIGO's conception of irrationality in life than it is to POETA's attachment to poetic order. 'Nadie diga esto es oscuro, porque la poesía es clara' ['No one should say [of a poem] that this is obscure, because poetry is clear'] (OC, III, p. 258), said Lorca in the opening remarks to his lecture, 'Imaginación, inspiración, evasión'. And he added: 'Es decir, necesitamos buscar, "con esfuerzo y virtud, a la poesía, para que esta se nos entregue"' ['That is, we need to search "for poetry, with effort and virtue, for it to give itself up to us"'] (OC, III, p.

258). By contrast, despite Lorca's admonishment of those who are loath to take up the challenge of poetry, the lack of clarity in the verses of many of his New York poems, 'Panorama ciego de Nueva York' included, seems not to be a virtue but is rather a sign (however deliberate) of a poet who has become overwhelmed – or who at least wants to convey the idea of having become overwhelmed – despite his best efforts to ply his trade.

In 'Romance de la Guardia Civil española', the nativity provided the backdrop for the Civil Guard's sacking of the gypsy encampment. With its strong echoes of the massacre of the innocents, its biblical frame of reference made clear whose side the reader should be on. This is also the case in the New York poem 'Nacimiento de Cristo' ['The Birth of Christ'] (OC, I, p. 484), though here the assault is now on the meaning of the nativity itself as it is emptied of any positive connotation and, in keeping with the deformations of the collection, is conveyed in a language that renders it almost unrecognizable:

> Un pastor pide teta por la nieve que ondula
> blancos perros tendidos entre linternas sordas.
> El Cristito de barro se ha partido los dedos
> en los filos eternos de la madera rota.
>
> ¡Ya vienen las hormigas y los pies ateridos!
> Dos hilillos de sangre quiebran el cielo duro.
> Los vientres del demonio resuenan por los valles
> golpes y resonancias de carne de molusco.
>
> Lobos y sapos cantan en las hogueras verdes
> coronadas por vivos hormigueros del alba.
> La mula tiene un sueño de grandes abanicos
> y el toro sueña un toro de agujeros y de agua.
>
> El niño llora y mira con un tres en la frente.
> San José ve en el heno tres espinas de bronce.
> Los pañales exhalan un rumor de desierto
> con cítaras sin cuerdas y degolladas voces.
>
> La nieve de Manhattan empuja los anuncios
> y lleva gracia pura por las falsas ojivas.
> Sacerdotes idiotas y querubes de pluma
> van detrás de Lutero por las altas esquinas.

[A shepherd begs to be suckled in the snow that ripples with white dogs stretched out between muffled lanterns. The little clay Christ has split its fingers on the eternal edges of the broken wood. Here come the ants and the feet frozen cold. Two small threads of blood fracture the hard sky. The devil's entrails fill the valleys with thudding sounds and the echoes of the flesh of molluscs. Wolves and toads sing in green bonfires crowned by the fiery anthills of the dawn. The mule has a dream of large fans and the bull dreams a bull of holes and water. The child cries and watches with a three on its forehead. St Joseph sees in the hay three bronze thorns. The swaddling clothes exhale a desert's murmur with unstrung zithers and voices with slit throats. The snow of Manhattan drives against the billboards and carries pure grace through the fake Gothic arches. Idiot priests and cherubim in feathers follow Luther along the high corners.]

Several elements are familiar to the nativity: the shepherd, the little Christ, St Joseph, the hay, and possibly the mule and the bull, if these can be considered to be barn animals. But this familiarity is immediately undone by the intrusion of elements completely foreign to the traditional scene of the birth of Christ: the devil, wolves and toads, bonfires and anthills, Manhattan's billboards and Gothic arches, not to mention the troubling images of a shepherd begging to be 'suckled' ('pide teta') or 'a little clay Christ with split fingers' ('El Cristito de barro se ha partido los dedos'). That the arches should be 'fake Gothic' conveys an out-of-placeness and artificiality that extend beyond architecture to raise questions about the depth and integrity of religious belief. Strange too are the snow and cold that pervade the scene, even though they are possibly the most faithful reflection of Lorca's time in New York where he witnessed record snowfalls for the city in the month of December 1929. In the penultimate stanza, the complex metaphor of 'swaddling clothes' ('pañales') exhaling 'a desert's murmur' is qualified by subsequent images of 'unstrung zithers' ('cítaras sin cuerdas') and 'voices with slit throats' ('degolladas voces'). These now useless instruments and maimed voice are emblematic of the creative difficulties the poet experiences in the city.

The reference in the final lines of 'Nacimiento de Cristo' to 'idiot priests' ('Sacerdotes idiotas') following Luther is a direct criticism of Protestantism from the standpoint of Lorca's Catholic upbringing. Lorca made his views of Protestantism quite clear in a letter he wrote to his family, dated 14 July 1929. He explained that, after attending the services of different religions since his arrival in the city, he had come out 'dando vivas al portentoso, bellísimo, sin igual catolicismo español' ['cheering for marvellous, beautiful and unrivalled Spanish Catholicism'] (*EC*, p. 626). In fact, he could not understand how people could be Protestant at all. 'Es lo más ridículo,' he declared, 'y lo más odioso' ['It's the most ridiculous and odious thing'] (*EC*, p. 626). Commenting on a Protestant service in which, he noted, an organ was placed where the altar should be and the pastor talked and the congregation did little more than sing, he suggested that what was lacking was 'todo lo que es humano y consolador y bello' ['everything that is human and comforting and beautiful'] (*EC*, p. 626). Protestantism had even, in his view, had a negative effect on Catholicism in America: 'tiene esa misma frialdad' ['it's just as cold'] (*EC*, pp. 626–27). But while American Catholics lacked 'calor humano' ['human warmth'], he did at least acknowledge their extraordinary devotion. In the same letter, he also acknowledged the impressively beautiful singing he heard when he attended a synagogue for Spanish Jews. He thought the ceremony beautiful and solemn but also 'vacío de sentido' ['empty of meaning'] (*EC*, p. 628). Rather tellingly, it was the absence of Christ that irked him. 'Me parece demasiado fuerte la figura de Cristo para negarla' ['The figure of Christ is too important to be denied'] (*EC*, p. 628), he explained.

The lack of warmth Lorca associates with Protestantism may, as well as the snow, explain the cold motif running through 'Nacimiento de Cristo'. Lorca missed the kind of religiosity to which he had been accustomed in Spain, and this may also explain, at least in part, his depiction of Christmas in 'Navidad en el Hudson' ['Christmas on the Hudson'] (*OC*, I, pp. 478–79), dated 27 December 1929. Once again, the depiction of the festivities in his poem is far removed from the manner in which he wrote to his family on the subject. In a letter he wrote around the same time as 'Navidad en el Hudson' and, most likely, 'Nacimiento de Cristo', Lorca enthuses about the many Christmas Eve invitations he had received – all from American households insisting that he not spend Christmas alone. 'Esta gente', he explains, 'tendrá muchos defectos, pero en cambio es cordialísima en extremo y cariñosa con verdad' ['The American people may have many defects, but on the other hand they are extremely friendly and truly affectionate'] (*EC*, p. 670). While it did not compare, in his view, to Christmas in Granada 'cuyo ambiente poético y popular es único en el mundo' ['whose poetic and popular atmosphere is unique in the world'], he does concede that Christmas in New York 'es de una alegría extraordinaria' ['is extraordinarily joyful'] (*EC*, p. 670). The following extract from his letter illustrates how, when he wanted, Lorca was able to appreciate the energy of the modern city and write about it in the most positive terms, albeit in the very specific context of Christmas:

> el espectáculo popular es también vivísimo en esta gran ciudad. Todas las tiendas, teatros, cafés, fachadas, escaparates y casas particulares están llenas de coronas de muérdago con cintas rojas, en espera de la buena

suerte. En todos sitios están puestos los arbolitos de Noël, en las estaciones, en las librerías, en las farmacias, en el metro. Y por si no fuera poco, en Times Square, que es el centro de la ciudad, donde se reúnen todas las locuras eléctricas y todos los ritmos mecánicos y todos los ruidos de metal y temblores increíbles, allí, en medio de la calle, han puesto un gran pino cubierto de luces eléctricas y letreros dando las felices pascuas a todos los vecinos de New York y *extranjeros*. El pino está lleno por las ramas de bocinas que transmiten música de baile de las mejores orquestas. Es un rasgo de buena delicadeza este de poner un árbol de Noël que sólo expresa hogar y tono íntimo, en medio de la gran urbe, para los que no tienen casa, ni tierra, ni nada. (*EC*, p. 670)

[the popular spectacle is also very lively in this big city. All the shops, theatres, cafes, facades, shop windows and private homes are covered in garlands of mistletoe with red ribbons, awaiting good fortune. There are little Christmas trees everywhere, in stations, bookshops, pharmacies, the subway. And if that wasn't enough, in Times Square, in the centre of town, where you can find all sorts of crazy electric things and mechanical rhythms and metallic noises and incredible judders, there, in the middle of the street, they've placed a large pine covered in electric lights and signs wishing festive joy to all New York's residents and foreigners. The pine's branches are full of loudspeakers emitting dance music by the very best orchestras. It's such a nice touch to place a Christmas tree, the expression of homeliness and intimacy, in the middle of this big metropolis for the benefit of those who do not have a home, a land or anything of their own.]

'Éstos son los contrastes de New York', explained Lorca. 'Desde luego, el movimiento es mayor y se nota que es la Pascua' ['These are the contrasts in New York. And of course, there is more movement, so you notice it's Christmas'] (*EC*, pp. 670–71). Yet what he wrote next is indicative of his general reluctance, more evident in his poems than in his letters, to cast New York in a good light. For no sooner had he alluded to the festive spirit of New York than he set about explaining it away in sweeping terms that reveal a cynicism that does him little credit: 'Yo creo que la gente cristiana celebra con esta alegría el nacimiento de Cristo para expresar su desprecio a los judíos. Aquí en New York hay *dos millones y medio* de judíos, que son los que llevan el peso de los negocios pero que los americanos odian hondamente' ['I believe that Christian folk celebrate the birth of Christ so joyfully in order to express their contempt for Jews. Here in New York there are *two and a half million* Jews; they bear the burden of business and yet the Americans hate them intensely'] (*EC*, p. 671).

Given his apparently begrudging compliments to the American people at Christmas time, it comes as no surprise that, in 'Navidad en el Hudson', the joy of Christmas is totally expunged. In its place there is an overriding sense of lifelessness, loneliness, and desperation:

¡Esa esponja gris!
Ese marinero recién degollado.
Ese río grande.
Esa brisa de límites oscuros.
Ese filo, amor, ese filo.
Estaban los cuatro marineros luchando con el mundo,
con el mundo que no se puede recorrer sin caballos.
Estaban uno, cien, mil marineros,
luchando con el mundo de las agudas velocidades,
sin enterarse de que el mundo
estaba solo por el cielo.

El mundo solo por el cielo solo.
Son las colinas de martillos y el triunfo de la hierba espesa.
Son los vivísimos hormigueros y las monedas en el fango.
El mundo solo por el cielo solo
y el aire a la salida de todas las aldeas.

Cantaba la lombriz el terror de la rueda
y el marinero degollado
cantaba al oso de agua que lo había de estrechar;
y todos cantaban aleluya,
aleluya. Cielo desierto.
Es lo mismo, ¡lo mismo!, aleluya.

He pasado toda la noche en los andamios de los arrabales
dejándome la sangre por la escayola de los proyectos,
ayudando a los marineros a recoger las velas desgarradas.
Y estoy con las manos vacías en el rumor de la desembocadura.
No importa que cada minuto
un niño nuevo agite sus ramitos de venas,
ni que el parto de la víbora, desatado bajo las ramas,
calme la sed de sangre de los que miran el desnudo.
Lo que importa es esto: hueco. Mundo solo. Desembocadura.
Alba no. Fábula inerte.
Sólo esto: desembocadura.
¡Oh esponja mía gris!
¡Oh cuello mío recién degollado!
¡Oh río grande mío!

¡Oh brisa mía de límites que no son míos!
¡Oh filo de mi amor, oh hiriente filo!

[That grey sponge! That sailor, throat just cut. That great river. That breeze of dark limits. That blade, love, that blade. The four sailors were battling [against] the world. The world of sharp edges that all eyes see. The world that cannot be traversed without horses. There were one, a hundred, a thousand sailors battling the world of acute velocities, not knowing that the world was alone in the sky. The world alone in the sky. It's the hills of hammers and the triumph of thick grass. It's the oh so alive anthills and coins in the mire. The world alone in the sky and the air at the edge of every village. The earthworm sang its terror of the wheel and the sailor, throat cut, sang to the water-bear that held him in a hug; and everyone sang hallelujah, hallelujah. Deserted sky. It's all the same – the same! – hallelujah. I've spent the night on the scaffolds in the boroughs, leaving my blood on the plaster of projects, helping the sailors to take in their torn sails. And I stand with my hands empty amidst the murmur of the river's mouth. It doesn't matter that each minute a new child waves its branches of veins, or that a viper's giving birth, unravelling beneath the branches, should quench the bloodlust of those who gaze on nudes. What matters is this: the emptiness. Lonely world. River's mouth. Not dawn. Lifeless fable. Only this: river's mouth. Oh, my grey sponge! Oh, my throat just cut! Oh, my great river! Oh, my breeze of dark limits that aren't mine! Oh, blade of my love, oh, the wounding blade!]

The logic of the apparently irrational images is by now familiar. In this godless world – a world 'alone in the sky' ('solo por el cielo') (OC, I, p. 478) – the river has become a lifeless 'grey sponge' ('esponja gris') [OC, I, p. 478), an object possibly connoting the Holy Sponge that was dipped in vinegar and offered to Christ on the cross (see Harris 1978, p. 49). As such, it is an all too premature reminder of the Crucifixion at a time that ought to be associated with birth rather than death. The idea of birth itself is sullied in the poem by its connection to a viper. The snake brings to mind the serpent in the Garden of Eden and the original sin, an association compounded by the lustful gazes upon the viper as it gives birth: 'No importa que cada minuto | un niño nuevo agite sus ramitos de venas, | ni que el parto de la víbora, desatado bajo las ramas, | calme la sed de sangre de los que miran el desnudo' ['It doesn't matter that each minute a new child waves its branches of veins, or that a viper's giving birth, unravelling beneath the branches, should quench the bloodlust of those who gaze on nudes'] (OC, I, p. 479).

Beyond the Crucifixion, there are other, more explicit references to sacrifice that frame the battle between nature and the worlds of speed ('el mundo de las agudas velocidades' ['the world of acute velocities'] [OC, I, p. 478]), industry ('las colinas de martillos' ['the hills of hammers'] [OC, I, p. 478]) and capital ('las monedas en el fango' ['coins in the mire'] [OC, I, p. 478]). This sacrifice is represented first by the sailor with his throat recently cut ('Ese marinero recién degollado' [OC, I, p. 478]). He is at the centre of the battle as he navigates the river, a battle which, with 'torn sails' ('velas desgarradas' [OC, I, p. 478]), he seems doomed to lose no matter how augmented his numbers are: 'Estaban uno, cien, mil marineros, | luchando' ['There were one, a hundred, a thousand sailors battling'] (OC, I, p. 478). The poet-speaker is himself closely associated with the sailor of the poem. In fact, Lorca, who put his hand to the pictorial arts, often drew sailors, associating these figures, in some of his drawings, with love.[9] It is possibly love, therefore, in the form of the sailor, that is locked in the deathly struggle with the city depicted in 'Navidad en el Hudson'. The poet-speaker is clearly on the side of love. Not only does he help the sailor take in his sails, but he also bears the same sacrificial wounds, exclaiming in the final lines of the poem both that the river's 'sponge' is his own and that his throat, like the sailor's, is also cut: '¡Oh esponja mía gris! | ¡Oh cuello mío recién degollado!' ['Oh, my grey sponge! Oh, my throat just cut!'] (OC, I, p. 479). The poet, like the sailor and nature too, is a witness to the desolation of New York at Christmas time, and it is their collective testimony, characterized in the poem as song, that offers some form of resistance, however futile: 'Cantaba la lombriz el terror de la rueda | y el marinero degollado | cantaba al oso de agua que lo había de estrechar; | y todos cantaban aleluya, | aleluya' ['The earthworm sang its terror of the wheel and the sailor, throat cut, sang to the water-bear that held him in a hug; and everyone sang hallelujah, hallelujah'] (OC, I, p. 478).

The motif of sacrifice reappears in 'New York. Oficina y denuncia' ['New York: Office and Denunciation'] (OC, I, pp. 517–19) in the figure of the bleeding sailor and, on a vaster scale, in the slaughter of countless animals offered to the gods of unbridled consumption:

Debajo de las multiplicaciones
hay una gota de sangre de pato.
Debajo de las divisiones
hay una gota de sangre de marinero.

---

9   On sailors as victims of love and as symbols of homosexuality, see Ángel Sahuquillo, *Federico García Lorca and the Culture of Male Homosexuality* (Jefferson, N.C.: McFarland & Co., 2007), pp. 76–80.

Debajo de las sumas, un río de sangre tierna;
un río que viene cantando
por los dormitorios de los arrabales,
y es plata, cemento o brisa
en el alba mentida de New York.
Existen las montañas, lo sé.
Y los anteojos para la sabiduría,
lo sé. Pero yo no he venido a ver el cielo.
He venido para ver la turbia sangre,
la sangre que lleva las máquinas a las cataratas
y el espíritu a la lengua de la cobra.
Todos los días se matan en New York
cuatro millones de patos,
cinco millones de cerdos,
dos mil palomas para el gusto de los agonizantes,
un millón de vacas,
un millón de corderos
y dos millones de gallos,
que dejan los cielos hechos añicos.
Más vale sollozar afilando la navaja
o asesinar a los perros en las alucinantes cacerías,
que resistir en la madrugada
los interminables trenes de leche,
los interminables trenes de sangre
y los trenes de rosa maniatadas
por los comerciantes de perfumes.
Los patos y las palomas,
y los cerdos y los corderos
ponen sus gotas de sangre
debajo de las multiplicaciones
y los terribles alaridos de las vacas estrujadas
llenan de dolor el valle
donde el Hudson se emborracha con aceite.
Yo denuncio a toda la gente
que ignora la otra mitad,
la mitad irredimible
que levanta sus montes de cemento
donde laten los corazones
de los animalitos que se olvidan
y donde caeremos todos
en la última fiesta de los taladros.
Os escupo en la cara.
La otra mitad me escucha
devorando, cantando, volando en su pureza,

como los niños de las porterías
que llevan frágiles palitos
a los huecos donde se oxidan
las antenas de los insectos.
No es el infierno, es la calle.
No es la muerte, es la tienda de frutas.
Hay un mundo de ríos quebrados y distancias inasibles
en la patita de ese gato quebrada por el automóvil,
y yo oigo el canto de la lombriz
en el corazón de muchas niñas.
Oxido, fermento, tierra estremecida.
Tierra tú mismo que nadas por los números de la oficina.
¿Qué voy a hacer, ordenar los paisajes?
¿Ordenar los amores que luego son fotografías,
que luego son pedazos de madera y bocanadas de sangre?
No, no; yo denuncio.
Yo denuncio la conjura
de estas desiertas oficinas
que no radian agonías,
que borran los programas de la selva,
y me ofrezco a ser comido por las vacas estrujadas
cuando sus gritos llenan el valle
donde el Hudson se emborracha con aceite.

[Beneath the multiplications there's a drop of duck's blood; beneath the divisions there's a drop of sailor's blood; beneath the additions, a river of tender blood. A river that sings its way through the bedrooms of the boroughs, and is silver, concrete and breeze in New York's fake dawn. Mountains exist. I know this. As do eyeglasses for the wise. I know this. But I haven't come to see the sky. I've come to see the turbid blood, the blood that carries machines towards cataracts and the spirit towards the cobra's tongue. Every day in New York, they slaughter four million ducks, five million pigs, two thousand doves to please the dying, one million cows, one million lambs and two million cockerels, smashing the skies to pieces. It's better to sob while sharpening the knife or to kill dogs on hallucinatory hunts rather than resist at dawn the endless trains of milk, the endless trains of blood, and the trains of roses shackled by the traders of perfumes. The ducks and doves and pigs and lambs lay their drops of blood beneath the multiplications, and the terrible shrieks of wrung and mangled cows fills with sorrow the valley where the Hudson gets drunk on oil. I denounce everyone who ignores the other half, the irredeemable half that raises its mountains of concrete there where beat the hearts of forgotten little animals and there where all of us will fall in the final feast of electric drills. I spit in your faces. The other half listens to me, devouring, urinating, flying in their purity, like the children in lobbies who carry brittle sticks to the empty spaces where insects' antennae rust. It's not hell, it's the street. It's not death. It's the fruit stores. There's a world of broken rivers and distances beyond our grasp in the paw of that cat broken by an automobile, and I hear the earthworm's song in the hearts of many girls. Rust, fermentation, trembling earth. You yourself are the earth, you who are swimming in the numbers of the office. What shall I do? Set the landscapes in order? Set in order the loves that thence become photographs, that thence become pieces of wood and mouthfuls of blood? No, no: I denounce it all. I denounce the conspiracy of these deserted offices that do not broadcast the agonies, that erase the forest's plans, and I offer myself up to be eaten by the wrung and mangled cows when their cries fill the valley where the Hudson gets drunk on oil.]

The poet is defiant in his condemnation of the slaughter in a poem that reprises elements from 'Navidad en el Hudson', such as the figure of the sailor, the song of the earthworm and the Hudson itself, now 'drunk on oil' ('se emborracha con aceite' [OC, I, pp. 518 and 519]). As in 'Navidad en el Hudson', being defiant means bearing witness. As the poet-speaker explains, 'yo no he venido a ver el cielo | He venido para ver la turbia sangre' ['I haven't come to see the sky. I've come to see the turbid blood'] (OC, I, p. 517). It is by recounting what he sees, as well as what he hears, that he is able to voice his condemnation. And, importantly, what he hears is not only 'the terrible shrieks of wrung and mangled cows' ('los terribles alaridos de las vacas estrujadas' [OC, I, p. 518]), but also the songs of resistance offered by the river of blood as it 'sings its way through the bedrooms of the boroughs' ('viene cantando | por los dormitorios de los arrabales' [OC, I, p. 517]) and by the earthworm he can hear singing 'in the hearts of many girls' ('en el corazón de muchas niñas' [OC, I, p. 518]). The poet-speaker also offers himself in sacrifice, 'to be eaten by the wrung and mangled cows when their cries fill the valley' ('a ser comido por las vacas estrujadas | cuando sus gritos llenan el valle' [OC, I, p. 518]). This offer of self-sacrifice is a gesture of solidarity with nature against the machinery of mass slaughter and mass consumption; and yet, for all the defiance, it is difficult to banish the sense of futility in the poem given the numbers involved, 'the endless trains of milk, the endless trains of blood' ('los interminables trenes de leche, | los interminables trenes de sangre' [OC, I, p. 518]), and the collusion of New York's consumers who ignore the beating hearts of 'forgotten little animals' ('los animalitos que se olvidan' [OC, I, p. 518]) and thus make inevitable 'the final feast of electric drills' ('la última fiesta de los taladros' [OC, I, p. 518]), an image recalling the mechanical slaughter that puts food on consumers' plates.

The poet's self-sacrifice here can also be understood as a surrender of his poetic principles, where these correspond to his preference for control over any abandonment to the unconscious or to irrationality. Significantly, 'New York. Oficina y denuncia' is dedicated to the writer Fernando Vela. Vela, in an essay he wrote in 1924 for the *Revista de Occidente*, the literary journal that he co-founded, revealed his irritation with Surrealism's 'advocacy of disorder'.[10] Thus, when Lorca writes '¿Qué voy a hacer, ordenar los paisajes?' ['What shall I do? Set the landscapes in order?'] (OC, I, p. 518), it is not difficult to see how Vela's criticism of Surrealism is relevant. Faced by the overwhelming multiplications of slaughter and distress, the poet has little recourse but to give in to the disorder. As was the case in 'Paisaje de la multitud que vomita', the poet 'sin brazos' ['without arms'] (OC, I, p. 474) must inevitably compromise his aesthetic principles so that he can properly bear witness. More important than art is the poet's denunciation of what he sees: '¿Ordenar los amores que luego son fotografías, | que luego son pedazos de madera y bocanadas de sangre? | No, no; yo denuncio' ['Set in order the loves that thence become photographs, that thence become pieces of wood and mouthfuls of blood? No, no: I denounce it all'] (OC, I, pp. 518–19). The result, inevitably, is the surreal confusion of images that characterize this and other poems which, though they may seem to be thoroughly modern (at least at an aesthetic level), constitute a deeply rooted critique of both modern living and the unruly products of Surrealism (those of his former friends, Dalí and Buñuel, included).

In the ballads of his *Romancero gitano*, Lorca had the Gitanos as the heroes of his modern-day myths, as the 'protagonists or victims of life's great tragedies' (Morris 1997, p. 363). In *Poeta en Nueva York*, the site of life's tragedies has changed and thus Lorca chooses another marginalized group, New York's African American population, to play the heroic role, most prominently in his poems 'Norma y paraíso de los negros' ['Norm and Paradise of the Blacks'] (OC, I, pp. 457–58) and 'El rey de Harlem' ['The King of Harlem'] (OC, I, pp. 459–63), both written in August 1929. Just as he took the side of the Gitanos in *Romancero gitano*, he now takes

---

10 Andrew P. Debicki, *Spanish Poetry of the Twentieth Century: Modernity and Beyond* (University Press of Kentucky, 1994), p. 40. Gibson (1989, p. 149) tells us that Lorca would have read the December 1924 issue of the journal.

the side of the blacks of Harlem, victims, like the Gitanos before them, of racial prejudice and social repression.[11]

Lorca experienced Harlem at the height of the social and cultural phenomenon known as the Harlem Renaissance that saw the emergence of notable African American writers, artists and musicians.[12] Among these was the author Nelly Larsen who took Lorca to visit Harlem and invited him to musical gatherings. In a letter to his family, Lorca wrote enthusiastically about these gatherings, exclaiming that the songs he heard there were comparable only to *cante jondo* (EC, p. 625) – high praise indeed from such an aficionado of flamenco deep song. During the few months he spent in such company, Lorca would almost certainly have been exposed to the ideas of the New Negro Movement and the black community's rediscovered pride for its African ancestry (see Llera, pp. 51–52). This would explain the prominence of African motifs in both 'Norma y paraíso de los negros' and 'El rey de Harlem'. Yet, however well-intended, Lorca's treatment of New York's African Americans is naively primitivist and stereotypical. Indeed, primitivist stereotypes abound as the Africa he connects Harlem to lacks historicity and is often little more than the idea of Africa constructed by the Western imaginary.

The problem, in great part, stems from Lorca's constant enthralment to the negative idea of modernity, meaning that New York's black population also has to be enlisted to carry out his condemnation of the city and, in being so, becomes associated with the world of nature and instinct. The rationale of this approach is clear in Lorca's 1932 recital of his New York poems in Madrid. There he declared that he had wanted to write 'el poema de la raza negra en Norteamérica' ['the poem of the Black race in North America'] and underscore 'el dolor que tienen los negros de ser negros en un mundo contrario, esclavos de todos los inventos del hombre blanco y de todas sus máquinas' ['the pain that the blacks feel for being black in an opposite world, slaves of every one of the white man's inventions and of all his machines'] (OC, III, p. 351). It is precisely within this binary logic, where the African American represents pristine nature in conflict with machine society, as well as with capitalism and the urban

---

11 Interestingly, the famous black poet and social activist, Langston Hughes, closely associated with the Harlem Renaissance, produced an English translation of *Romancero gitano* in 1951.
12 See José Antonio Llera, 'Federico García Lorca en Harlem', in Luis Bagué Quílez (ed.), *Cosas que el dinero puede comprar: Del eslogan al poema* (Madrid: Iberoamericana-Vervuert, 2018), pp. 51–79.

environment, that Lorca feels able to talk of the perpetual fear that African Americans have 'que se les olvide un día encender la estufa de gas o guiar el automóvil o abrocharse el cuello almidonado, o [de] clavarse el tenedor en un ojo' ['of one day forgetting to light their gas stoves or being able to steer their cars or fasten their starched shirt collars, or of sticking their knives into one of their own eyes'] (OC, III, p. 351). And it is the same binary logic that leads him to express surprise that a black girl should even be able to ride a bike:

> vi a una niña negrita montada en bicicleta. Nada más enternecedor. [...] Miré fijamente y ella me miró. Pero mi mirada decía: «Niña, ¿por qué vas en bicicleta? ¿Puede una negrita montar en ese aparato? ¿Es tuyo? ¿Dónde lo has robado? ¿Crees que saber guiarlo?» Y efectivamente dio una voltereta y se cayó con piernas y ruedas por una suave pendiente. (OC, III, p. 351)

> [I saw a little black girl riding a bicycle. Nothing more endearing. I looked at her intently and she looked back. But my look said: 'Little girl, why are you riding a bike? Can a little black girl ride such a contraption? Is it yours? Did you steal it? Do you think you know how to steer it?' And, wouldn't you know it, she tipped over and fell legs and wheels down a gentle slope.]

In Lorca's mind, within the binary logic that pits nature against modernity, it is the black population's saving grace that they are absolutely not suited to, nor indeed responsible for, the things of the modern world: 'los inventos no son suyos, viven de prestado' ['the inventions are not theirs, they're living on something borrowed'] (OC, III, p. 351).

Blacks versus whites, nature versus modernity. Lorca's polarized thinking meant that he could envisage no place in the modern city for New York's black citizens. Instead, theirs is a place in some paradisiacal alternative to the hell represented by New York – the very polar opposites that structure his poem 'Norma y paraíso de los negros':

> Odian la sombra del pájaro
> sobre el pleamar de la blanca mejilla
> y el conflicto de luz y viento
> en el salón de la nieve fría.
>
> Odian la flecha sin cuerpo,
> el pañuelo exacto de la despedida,
> la aguja que mantiene presión y rosa
> en el gramíneo rubor de la sonrisa.

    Aman el azul desierto,
las vacilantes expresiones bovinas,
la mentirosa luna de los polos,
la danza curva del agua en la orilla.

    Con la ciencia del tronco y el rastro
llenan de nervios luminosos la arcilla
y patinan lúbricos por aguas y arenas
gustando la amarga frescura de su milenaria saliva.

    Es por el azul crujiente,
azul sin un gusano ni una huella dormida,
donde los huevos de avestruz quedan eternos
y deambulan intactas las lluvias bailarinas.

    Es por el azul sin historia,
azul de una noche sin temor de día,
azul donde el desnudo del viento va quebrando
los camellos sonámbulos de las nubes vacías.

    Es allí donde sueñan los torsos bajo la gula de la hierba.
Allí los corales empapan la desesperación de la tinta,
los durmientes borran sus perfiles bajo la madeja de los caracoles
y queda el hueco de la danza sobre las últimas cenizas. (OC, I, pp. 457–58)

[They hate the bird's shadow on the high tide of white cheeks and the conflict of light and wind in the hall of cold snow. They hate the arrow without a body, the exact handkerchief of farewells, the needle that maintains pressure and pink in the gramineous blush of its smile. They love the desert blue, the hesitant bovine faces, the deceptive moon of the poles, the water's curved dance on the shore. With the science of tree trunks and tracks they cover the clay in luminous nerves and slip and slide across water and sand tasting the bitter freshness of millenary spit. It's in the crisp blue, blue without a single worm or sleeping footprint, where ostrich eggs stay forever, and dancing rains wander intact. It's in the blue without a history, the blue of a night without fear of day, the blue where the wind's nude breaks up the sleepwalking camels of empty clouds. It's there where the torsos dream beneath the gluttony of the grass. There the corals soak up the ink's desperation, the sleepers efface their profiles beneath the skein of shells and the space left by the dance lingers over the last of the ashes.]

    'Norma y paraíso de los negros' establishes an opposition between what the blacks hate and what they love. While precise meanings are elusive (as is so often the case with Lorca's New York poems), the binary logic pits elements belonging to the city of the whites, in the first two stanzas, against elements, in subsequent stanzas, that are evocative of a paradisiacal, natural world to which the blacks properly belong. In the former, it is a sense of unease, discomfort and dislocation that predominates, as in the image of a 'bird's shadow' ('la sombra del pájaro' [OC, I, p. 457]) upon 'white cheeks' ('blanca mejilla' [OC, I, p. 457]), the 'conflict of light and wind' ('conflicto de luz y viento' [OC, I, p. 457]), the 'cold snow' ('nieve fría' [OC, I, p. 457]), the 'arrow without a body' ('flecha sin cuerpo' [OC, I, p. 457]) to shoot or aim at, the 'handkerchief' ('pañuelo' [OC, I, p. 457]) to say one's goodbyes ('despedida' [OC, I, p. 457]), and the pressure of needles ('la aguja que mantiene presión' [OC, I, p. 457]). By contrast, the things that the blacks love belong to nature. The references to 'desert blue' ('azul desierto' [OC, I, p. 457]), to 'hesitant bovine faces' ('vacilantes expresiones bovinas' [OC, I, p. 457]), to a 'deceptive moon' ('mentirosa luna' [OC, I, p. 457]), to the dancing water's curve against the shore ('la danza curva del agua en la orilla' [OC, I, p. 457]) all evoke the mysteries of nature as opposed to the anxieties associated with the city. Far removed from the science of capital and industry, the blacks' sphere of knowledge is that of the 'science of tree trunks' ('ciencia del tronco' [OC, I, p. 457]) and 'tracks' ('rastro' [OC, I, p. 457]) in the earth. Theirs is a land of 'water and sand' ('aguas y arenas' [OC, I, p. 457]), of 'ostrich eggs' ('huevos de avestruz' [OC, I, p. 457]) and 'dancing rains' ('lluvias bailarinas' [OC, I, p. 457]), and of 'sleepwalking camels' ('camellos sonámbulos' [OC, I, p. 458]). It is a land where the blue of the sky has no history ('azul sin historia' [OC, I, p. 458]) – a statement that possibly lets slip Lorca's reductively ahistorical approach – and where the 'blue of a night' ('azul de una noche' [OC, I, p. 458]) has no 'fear of day' ('sin temor de día' [OC, I, p. 458]), presumably because daybreak will not reveal the horrors that are lit up by New York's grim dawn, as in the poem 'La aurora'. In the final stanza, there is possibly a self-conscious reference to the poet's craft, although in this paradisiacal land, and in contrast to other poems, the connotations are positive as the 'corals' have the potentially soothing ability to 'soak up the ink's desperation' ('los corales empapan la desesperación del tinto' [OC, I, p. 458]).

The poem ends with a reference to ashes, possibly an allusion to the vestiges of a fireside tribal dance. If so, then the ritual has ended and what we are left with is the space the dancers have vacated ('queda el hueco de la danza' ['the space left by the dance'] [OC, I, p. 458]) and the fire's dying embers ('the last of the ashes' ['las últimas cenizas'] [OC, I, p. 458]). In this case, the absence evoked by the poem's final image might be suggestive of

African Americans' estrangement from the land of their forefathers. Yet there is a more sinister interpretation of the scene that recalls not Africa but the United States and the horrors of public lynching and mutilation, burning and mockery of its victims. As Llera (p. 54) reminds us, in an early draft of the poem the title appeared as 'Negro quemado' ['Burnt Black']. The same title was also given to a photograph Lorca had intended to use as an illustration. In the end, Lorca was dissuaded from including any illustrations in *Poeta en Nueva York*, apparently on aesthetic grounds (see Llera, p. 54), and when, after his death, the collection was finally published, 'Negro quemado' and the many photographs and postcards he had collected in New York were omitted. This and the change of title are examples of how artistic choices can obscure the source of a poem's images and ideas. In 'Norma y paraíso de los negros', the brutal reality underpinning Lorca's social critique is ultimately diminished in favour of poetic nuance and ambiguity.

The binary logic pitting nature against modernity is evident again in 'El rey de Harlem'. Whereas 'Norma y paraíso de los negros' alludes to a lost paradise, 'El rey de Harlem', as Llera (p. 65) points out, offers the promise of a 'redeeming utopia' in what is, in effect, a passionate call to arms. The poem is thus shot through with a revolutionary spirit as it exhorts Harlem's black population to defy the economic and social injustices synonymous with the whites' mechanized world. Yet significantly, the emphasis on undermining modern values and on pointing to the dissonance of modern life means that revolution is inevitably cast in terms of securing the dominion of nature, instinct and innocence over the dehumanizing principles of mechanization and capital, rather, that is, than claiming an equal share of the benefits of modernity and modern living for New York's black population.

The poem is divided into four sections, the first of which introduces us to the poem's central figure, the king of Harlem:

Con una cuchara,
arrancaba los ojos a los cocodrilos
y golpeaba el trasero de los monos.
Con una cuchara.

   Fuego de siempre dormía en los pedernales
y los escarabajos borrachos de anís
olvidaban el musgo de las aldeas.

   Aquel viejo cubierto de setas
iba al sitio donde lloraban los negros

mientras crujía la cuchara del rey
y llegaban los tanques de agua podrida.

    Las rosas huían por los filos
de las últimas curvas del aire,
y en los montones de azafrán
los niños machacaban pequeñas ardillas
con un rubor de frenesí manchado.

    Es preciso cruzar los puentes
y llegar al rubor negro
para que el perfume de pulmón
nos golpee las sienes con su vestido
de caliente piña.

    Es preciso matar al rubio vendedor de aguardiente,
a todos los amigos de la manzana y de la arena,
y es necesario dar con los puños cerrados
a las pequeñas judías que tiemblan llenas de burbujas,
para que los cocodrilos duerman en largas filas
bajo el amianto de la luna,
y para que nadie dude de la infinita belleza
de los plumeros, los ralladores, los cobres y las cacerolas de las cocinas.

    ¡Ay Harlem! ¡Ay Harlem! ¡Ay Harlem!
¡No hay angustia comparable a tus rojos oprimidos,
a tu sangre estremecida dentro del eclipse oscuro,
a tu violencia granate sordomuda en la penumbra,
a tu gran rey prisionero con un traje de conserje! (OC, I, pp. 459–60)

[With a spoon, he gouged out crocodiles' eyes and spanked monkeys' behinds. With a spoon. An age-old fire slept in the flints and beetles drunk on anisette forgot about the moss of the villages. That old man covered in mushrooms was going to the place where the blacks wept as the king's spoon crunched and the tanks of putrid water arrived. The roses fled along the blades of the last curves of the air and on the piles of saffron children battered small squirrels with a blush stained with frenzy. It's necessary to cross the bridges and reach the black murmur so that the perfume of lungs can hit our temples with its dress of hot pineapple. It's necessary to kill the blond vendor of moonshine, and all the friends of apple and sand; it's necessary to raise clenched fists to small Jewish women who tremble, filled with bubbles, so that the king of Harlem can sing with his crowd, so that the crocodiles can sleep in long rows beneath the asbestos of the moon, and so that no one can doubt the infinite beauty of feather dusters, graters, copper pans and casseroles of the kitchens. Oh, Harlem! Oh, Harlem! Oh, Harlem! No anguish compares to your oppressed reds, to your blood shuddering inside the dark eclipse, to your maroon violence, deaf and dumb in the half-light, to your great prisoner king, in his doorman's uniform!]

The king of Harlem is presented as a parody of an African king in order to emphasize how diminished he and, by association, all blacks are in New York. Thus, in the first stanza, he is given a spoon instead of a mace and is reduced to gouging out crocodile eyes and spanking monkeys' behinds in a reflex that is absurd, humiliating and an offence to nature. In the third stanza, his crunching spoon provides the soundtrack to pitiful scenes of an old man covered in mushrooms, men weeping, and tanks filled with putrid water. In the seventh stanza the king's humiliation is sealed with the image of him in a doorman's uniform, emblematic of Africans' fall into white servitude. This representation of the king carries over into the second section, where the poem's initial image is reprised amidst more weeping black figures as well as mulattoes whose desire to be white – 'llegar al torso blanco' ['attain a white torso'] (OC, I, p. 461) – is evidence, in Lorca's mind, of the white man's corrupting influence and the submission of some members of the black community to the erroneous white ideal.

Yet alongside these abject images, rebellion and violence are brewing, stirred up by the poet-speaker's exhortations. We sense this first, in the second stanza, in the fire sleeping in flints that are yet to spark, and in the fleeing roses and violent behaviour of children, in the fourth. Then there is the unequivocal declaration, in the sixth stanza, about the necessity 'to kill the blond vendor of moonshine' ('Es preciso matar al rubio vendedor de aguardiente' [OC, I, p. 460]) and, as shockingly, 'to raise clenched fists to small Jewish women' ('dar con los puños cerrados | a las pequeñas judías' [OC, I, p. 460]). All this so that finally the king of Harlem 'can sing with his crowd' ('para que el rey de Harlem cante con su muchedumbre' [OC, I, p. 460]) and herald the arrival of another order where 'crocodiles can sleep in long rows beneath the asbestos of the moon' ('para que los cocodrilos duerman en largas filas | bajo el amianto de la luna' [OC, I, p. 460]) and where the 'infinite beauty' ('infinita belleza' [OC, I, p. 460]) of African Americans can emerge from amidst the symbols of servitude – 'feather dusters, graters, copper pans and casseroles of the kitchens' ('los plumeros, los ralladores, los cobres y las cacerolas de las cocinas' [OC, I, p. 460]) – that have until now defined them, in the same way as the doorman's uniform has defined – and imprisoned – the king.

In the second section, a nightmarish night-time scene gives way to talk of blood, as tensions mount with the prospect of violence:

>Tenía la noche una hendidura y quietas salamandras de marfil.
>Las muchachas americanas
>llevaban niños y monedas en el vientre
>y los muchachos se desmayaban en la cruz del desperezo.
>
>Ellos son.
>Ellos son los que beben el whisky de plata junto a los volcanes
>y tragan pedacitos de corazón por las heladas montañas del oso.
>
>Aquella noche el rey de Harlem,
>con una durísima cuchara,
>arrancaba los ojos a los cocodrilos
>y golpeaba el trasero de los monos.
>Con una cuchara.
>Los negros lloraban confundidos
>entre paraguas y soles de oro,
>los mulatos estiraban gomas, ansiosos de llegar al torso blanco,
>y el viento empañaba espejos
>y quebraba las venas de los bailarines.
>
>Negros, Negros, Negros, Negros.
>
>La sangre no tiene puertas en vuestra noche boca arriba.
>No hay rubor. Sangre furiosa por debajo de las pieles,
>viva en la espina de puñal y en el pecho de los paisajes,
>bajo las pinzas y las retamas de la celeste luna de cáncer.
>
>Sangre que busca por mil caminos muertes enharinadas y ceniza de nardo,
>cielos yertos en declive, donde las colonias de planetas
>rueden por las playas con los objetos abandonados.
>
>Sangre que mira lenta con el rabo del ojo,
>hecha de espartos exprimidos, néctares de subterráneos.
>Sangre que oxida al alisio descuidado en una huella
>y disuelve a las mariposas en los cristales de la ventana.
>
>Es la sangre que viene, que vendrá
>por los tejados y azoteas, por todas partes,
>para quemar la clorofila de las mujeres rubias,
>para gemir al pie de las camas ante el insomnio de los lavabos
>y estrellarse en una aurora de tabaco y bajo amarillo.

>   Hay que huir,
> huir por las esquinas y encerrarse en los últimos pisos,
> porque el tuétano del bosque penetrará por las rendijas
> para dejar en vuestra carne una leve huella de eclipse
> y una falsa tristeza de guante desteñido y rosa química. (OC, I, pp. 460–61)

[There was a crack in the night and still ivory salamanders. American girls carried babies and coins in their bellies and the boys fainted, stretched out on their cross. They're the ones. The ones who drink silver whisky beside volcanoes and swallow pieces of heart on the frozen mountains of the bear. That night the king of Harlem, with a very hard spoon, dug out the crocodiles' eyes and slapped the monkeys' behinds. With a spoon. The blacks cried in confusion among umbrellas and golden suns, the mulattoes stretched rubber, eager to attain a white torso, and the wind clouded over mirrors and shattered the veins of the dancers. Blacks, Blacks, Blacks, Blacks. Blood has no doors in your night lying face-up. There's no blushing. Blood furious beneath the skin, alive in the thorn of the dagger and in the breast of landscapes, beneath the pincers and broom of the heavenly moon of cancer. Blood that searches a thousand roads for deaths dusted with flour and the ash of spikenards, for rigid, descending skies in which colonies of planets roll around the beaches with abandoned objects. Blood that looks slowly from the corner of an eye, made from pressed esparto grasses, nectars of subways. Blood that oxidizes careless trade wind in a footprint and dissolves butterflies on windowpanes. It's the blood that's coming, that will come over tiled and flat rooves, everywhere, to burn the chlorophyll of blond women, to groan at the foot of beds before the insomnia of washbasins and burst into an aurora of tobacco and low yellow. It's time to run away! To run away along street corners and hide locked away on the top floors. Because the marrow of the forests will penetrate the cracks to leave in your flesh the faint trace of an eclipse and the false sorrow of a stained glove and chemical rose.]

The women who are pregnant with coins, the boys who are stretched out on crosses, the whisky drinkers and the devourers of hearts: these are all representatives of a compassionless world that will suffer the vengeance of the city's black population. The rhythmic 'Negros, Negros, Negros, Negros' [OC, I, pp. 461 and 462], here and in the fourth section, conveys a mounting sense of foreboding, a premonition of the bloodletting that will overwhelm the city. Hence, the blood that 'has no doors' ('no tiene puertas' [OC, I, p. 461]), that runs 'furious beneath the skin' ('furiosa por debajo de las pieles' [OC, I, p. 461]), that 'searches a thousand roads for deaths' ('que busca por mil caminos muertes' [OC, I, p. 461]), that 'looks slowly' ('que mira lenta' [OC, I, p. 461]), that 'oxidizes' ('que oxida') (OC,

I. p. 461), and that 'will come over tiled and flat rooves, everywhere' ('que vendrá | por los tejados y azoteas, por todas partes' [OC, I, p. 461]). New York's white citizens have no option but to flee ('Hay que huir' [It's time to run away'] [OC, I, p. 461]), and even then, they may not escape 'the marrow of the forests' ('el tuétano del bosque' [OC, I, p. 461]) that, as an agent of this cataclysm, reinforces the binary logic identifying African Americans with nature in stark opposition to modernity.

This logic is recast in the third section as a battle between North and South. Here, the blacks who are in the employ of whites seek out the king as the south wind blows menacingly and as shapes in the clouds augur the devastation to come:

> Es por el silencio sapientísimo
> cuando los camareros y los cocineros y los que limpian con la lengua
> las heridas de los millonarios
> buscan al rey por las calles o en los ángulos del salitre.
>
> Un viento sur de madera, oblicuo en el negro fango,
> escupe a las barcas rotas y se clava puntillas en los hombros.
> Un viento sur que lleva
> colmillos, girasoles, alfabetos
> y una pila de Volta con avispas ahogadas.
>
> El olvido estaba expresado por tres gotas de tinta sobre el monóculo.
> El amor, por un solo rostro invisible a flor de piedra.
> Médulas y corolas componían sobre las nubes
> un desierto de tallos, sin una sola rosa. (OC, I, p. 462)

[It's in the all-knowing silence that waiters and cooks and those who clean the wounds of millionaires with their tongues look for the king along the streets and the corners of saltpetre. A wooden south wind, slanting in the black mud, spits at the broken boats and drives tacks into the shoulders. A south wind bearing fangs, sunflowers, alphabets, and a battery with drowned wasps. Oblivion was expressed by three drops of ink on the monocle. Love, by a single invisible face at stone level. Bone marrow and corollas composed on the clouds a desert of stems, without a single rose.]

In the fourth and final section, the poet foresees a new order where an African sun will shine:

> A la izquierda, a la derecha, por el Sur y por el Norte,
> se levanta el muro imposible

Lorca, the Modern 115

para el topo y la aguja del agua.
No busquéis, negros, su grieta
para hallar la máscara infinita.
Buscad el gran sol del centro
hechos una piña zumbadora.
El sol que se desliza por los bosques
seguro de no encontrar una ninfa,
el sol que destruye números y no ha cruzado nunca un sueño,
el tatuado sol que baja por el río
y muge seguido de caimanes.

 Negros, Negros, Negros, Negros.

 Jamás sierpe, ni cebra, ni mula
palidecieron al morir.
El leñador no sabe cuándo expiran
los clamorosos árboles que corta.
Aguadad bajo la sombra vegetal de vuestro rey
a que cicuta y cardos y ortigas turben postreras azoteas.

 Entonces, negros, entonces, entonces,
podréis besar con frenesí las ruedas de las bicicletas,
poner parejas de microscopios en las cuevas de las ardillas
y danzar al fin, sin duda, mientras las flores erizadas
asesinan a nuestro Moisés casi en los juncos del cielo.

 ¡Ay, Harlem disfrazada!
¡Ay, Harlem, amenazada por un gentío de trajes sin cabeza!
Me llega tu rumor,
me llega tu rumor atravesando troncos y ascensores,
a través de láminas grises,
donde flotan tus automóviles cubiertos de dientes,
a través de los caballos muertos y los crímenes diminutos,
a través de tu gran rey desesperado,
cuyas barbas llegan al mar. (OC, I, pp. 462–63)

[To the left, to the right, to the South and to the North, the wall rises unperturbed by the mole and the needle of water. Don't look, blacks, for a crack in which to find the infinite mask. Look for the great sun at the centre once you have turned into a buzzing pineapple. The sun slips through the woods certain it will find no nymph there. The sun that destroys numbers and has never crossed a dream, the tattooed sun that descends the river and bellows followed by caimans. Blacks, Blacks, Blacks, Blacks. Never did a serpent or zebra or mule turn pale on their death. The woodcutter does not know when the clamorous trees he cuts expire. Wait beneath the vegetal shadow of your king for the hemlock and thistles and nettles to disturb the highest rooftops. Then, blacks, then, then, you'll be able to wildly kiss the wheels of bicycles, place pairs of microscopes in the dens of squirrels and dance at last without hesitation, as bristling flowers murder our Moses almost in the bulrushes of heaven. Oh, Harlem in disguise! Oh, Harlem, threatened by a headless crowd of suits! Your murmur reaches me, your murmur reaches me crossing through tree trunks and elevators, through grey metal sheets, where float your automobiles covered in teeth, through dead horses and diminutive crimes, through your great, despairing king, whose beard reaches the sea.]

'Look for the great sun' ('Buscad el gran sol' [OC, I, p. 462]), exhorts the poet; the sun which 'destroys numbers' ('destruye números' [OC, I, p. 462]); the sun that, in a possible reference to tribal markings, bears tattoos ('tatuado sol' [OC, I, p. 462]); the sun that 'descends the river and bellows followed by caimans' ('baja por el río | y muge seguido de caimanes' [OC, I, p. 462]), reptiles that, though native to the Americas, evoke, all the same, the crocodile species associated with Africa. The shadow the king casts is vegetal because of his association with nature, and the revolution the king will bring will see nature overcome the city, with 'hemlock and thistles and nettles' ('cicutas y cardos y ortigas' [OC, I, p. 463]) reaching even 'the highest rooftops' ('postreras azoteas' [OC, I, p. 463]). That Moses should be murdered by 'bristling flowers' ('flores erizadas' [OC, I, p. 463]) and therefore excluded from the new order can be explained by this biblical figure's status as law giver, 'rendered obsolete in the future space where law and order are replaced by a naturalized and effortless necessity'.[13] Moreover, as Llera (p. 75) argues, Moses, as representative of the Judeo-Christian tradition, is equally, in Lorca's mind, a representative of the white man's world. In the final stanza, the poet's insistence that he can hear their murmur, reinforces his ideological identification with New York's African Americans and, consequently, his ideological disidentification, as Nandorfy (p. 137) puts it, with his own community. Yet, although he calls the prophet 'our Moses' ('nuestro Moisés' [OC, I, p. 463]) in recognition of the world to which he himself belonged, Lorca's position in respect of modernity means that he does not belong to the 'headless crowd of suits' ('gentío de trajes sin cabeza' [OC, I, p. 463]),

---

13 Martha Nandorfy, *The Poetics of Apocalypse: García Lorca's 'Poet in New York'* (Lewisburg, PA: Bucknell University Press / London: Associated University Presses, 2003), p. 137.

just as 'Harlem in disguise' ('Harlem disfrazada' [OC, I, p. 463]) does not belong to it either. Essentially, Lorca's 'El rey de Harlem' is an exhortation to Harlem's blacks to throw off their disguises and reinstall their king and nature's dominion in a world oppressed by modernity.

In a letter he wrote to his family in early November 1929, Lorca described the distress and confusion he had witnessed in New York's financial district during the Wall Street Crash of late October. He wrote of how, amidst the general hysteria and desperation, he had met a friend who had lost her entire fortune; and how he had seen a banker, who had jumped from the sixteenth floor of a hotel, lifted dead from the pavement (EC, p. 662). Lorca's account, though, betrays a mixture of horror and fascination. He watched the spectacle of catastrophe for more than seven hours, unable to drag himself away (EC, p. 661). His final reflections on what he saw are telling. 'Este espectáculo', he wrote, 'me dio una visión nueva de esta civilización, y lo encontré muy natural. No quiero decir que me gustara, pero sí que lo observé con gran sangre fría y que me alegré mucho de haberlo presenciado' ['This spectacle offered me a new vision of this civilization, and I found it very natural. I don't mean to say that I liked it, but rather that I observed it cold-bloodedly and was happy to have witnessed it'] (EC, p. 662). Despite his supposed detachment, Lorca admitted that he was drawn to the spectacle like a bystander watching a shipwreck. He said he felt pity for its victims who had been 'expuestos a terribles presiones y al refinamiento frío de los cálculos de dos o tres banqueros dueños del mundo' ['exposed to the terrible pressures and the cold refinement of calculations by two or three bankers']; but he also made a point of characterizing them as 'gente con el espíritu cerrado a todas las cosas' ['people with spirits closed to all things'] (EC, p. 622). Although the Wall Street Crash clearly provided Lorca with ample justification for his views on the ruthless world of capital, his pity for its victims was nonetheless tempered by his disdain for those citizens whose financial downfall had been preceded by spiritual loss.

It is as much against the background of the spiritual vacuum reigning in Wall Street as the brutal impact of the crash itself that Africa makes an appearance in the poem 'Danza de la muerte' ['Dance of Death'] (OC, I, pp. 469–72), this time via the figure of the mask. Throughout, variations on an initial exclamatory refrain alert us to the presence of the masked figure: 'El mascarón. ¡Mirad el mascarón! | ¡Cómo viene del África a New York!' ['The mask. Look at the mask! How it comes from Africa to New York!'] (OC, I, p. 469); 'El mascarón. ¡Mirad el mascarón! | ¡Arena, caimán y miedo sobre Nueva York!' ['The mask. Look at the mask! Sand, crocodile and fear over New York!'] (OC, I, p. 469); 'El mascarón. ¡Mirad el mascarón! | ¡Qué ola de fango y luciérnaga sobre Nueva York!' ['The mask. Look at the mask! Such a wave of mud and fireflies over New York!'] (OC, I, p. 470); 'El mascarón. ¡Mirad el mascarón! | ¡Cómo escupe veneno de bosque | por la angustia imperfecta de Nueva York!' ['The mask. Look at the mask! How it spits its venom of the forest over the imperfect anguish of New York!'] (OC, I, p. 472).

Taking its cue from 'El rey de Harlem', the poem's tone and images are, as the refrain demonstrates, violent and vindicatory, Africa once more aligned with a nature that is set to overrun the urban landscape. In its vindictive role, the masked figure is not out of place in New York's snow-covered streets (the poem is dated December 1929). It is there on a day of reckoning to defy the machine world and remind the worshippers of mammon that their fall was inevitable:

> Cuando el chino lloraba en el tejado
> sin encontrar el desnudo de su mujer
> y el director del banco observaba el manómetro
> que mide el cruel silencio de la moneda,
> el mascarón llegaba a Wall Street.
>
> No es extraño para la danza
> este columbario que pone los ojos amarillos.
> De la esfinge a la caja de caudales hay un hilo tenso
> que atraviesa el corazón de todos los niños pobres.
> El ímpetu primitivo baila con el ímpetu mecánico,
> ignorantes en su frenesí de la luz original.
> Porque si la rueda olvida su fórmula,
> ya puede cantar desnuda con las manadas de caballos:
> y si una llama quema los helados proyectos,
> el cielo tendrá que huir ante el tumulto de las ventanas.
>
> No es extraño este sitio para la danza, yo lo digo.
> El mascarón bailará entre columnas de sangre y de números,
> entre huracanes de oro y gemidos de obreros parados
> que aullarán, noche oscura, por tu tiempo sin luces,
> ¡oh salvaje Norteamérica!, ¡oh impúdica!, ¡oh salvaje,
> tendida en la frontera de la nieve! (OC, I, p. 470)

[When the Chinese man wept on the roof unable to find the nude of his wife, and the director of the bank observed the manometer that measures the cruel silence of money, the mask arrived on Wall Street. These cemetery niches that turn eyes yellow are not a strange place for the dance. Between the sphinx and the bank vault there's a taut wire that pierces the hearts of all poor children. The primitive impetus dances with the mechanical impetus, ignorant, in their frenzy, of the original light. For if the wheel forgets its formula, it can sing nude with herds of horses; and if a flame burns the frozen plans, the sky will have to flee before the tumult of windows. This isn't a strange place for the dance, I say. The mask will dance between columns of blood and numbers, between hurricanes of gold and the groans of unemployed workers who will howl, dark night, for your unlit time. O savage, shameless, savage North America! Stretched out on the frontier of the snow!]

Money, poor children, the mechanical, the wheel, the 'columns of blood and numbers' ('columnas de sangre y de números'), the 'hurricanes of gold' ('huracanes de oro'), the 'groans of unemployed workers' ('gemidos de obreros parados'): the mask has come from Africa to dance amidst them all and thus remind wintry America of its savagery and shamelessness.

In the final stanzas, it is made clear that only the mask has the moral right to dance as it heralds Wall Street's return to nature amid the sound of hissing cobras:

¡Que no baile el Papa!
¡No, que no baile el Papa!
Ni el Rey,
ni el millonario de dientes azules,
ni las bailarinas secas de las catedrales,
ni constructores, ni esmeraldas, ni locos, ni sodomitas.
Sólo este mascarón,
este mascarón de vieja escarlatina,
¡sólo este mascarón!

Que ya las cobras silbarán por los últimos pisos,
que ya las ortigas estremecerán patios y terrazas,
que ya la Bolsa será una pirámide de musgo,
que ya vendrán lianas después de los fusiles
y muy pronto, muy pronto, muy pronto.
¡Ay, Wall Street! (OC, I, p. 471)

[Don't let the Pope dance! No, don't let the Pope dance! Nor the King, nor the millionaire with blue teeth, nor the dry ballerinas of the cathedrals, nor the builders, nor the emeralds, nor the insane, nor the sodomites. Only this mask, this mask of old crimson. Only this mask! Cobras will hiss on the top floors, nettles will shake patios and terraces, the Stock Exchange will be a pyramid of moss, the jungle vines will arrive after the rifles and all so soon, so very soon, so very soon. Oh, Wall Street!]

Among those identified as unworthy to dance in 'Danza de la muerte' is the Pope, who is also the object of criticism in the ode 'Grito hacia Roma' (Desde la torre del Chrysler Building)' ['Cry to Rome (From the Tower of the Chrysler Building)'] (OC, I, pp. 525–27). Although the ode does not mention him by name, the Pope is self-evidently the man dressed in white who is characterized in terms that negate his Christian role:

> Manzanas levemente heridas
> por finos espadines de plata,
> nubes rasgadas por una mano de coral
> que lleva en el dorso una almendra de fuego,
> peces de arsénico como tiburones,
> tiburones como gotas de llanto para cegar una multitud,
> rosas que hieren
> y agujas instaladas en los caños de la sangre,
> mundos enemigos y amores cubiertos de gusanos
> caerán sobre ti. Caerán sobre la gran cúpula
> que unta de aceite las lenguas militares,
> donde un hombre se orina en una deslumbrante paloma
> y escupe carbón machacado
> rodeado de miles de campanillas.
>
> Porque ya no hay quien reparta el pan y el vino,
> ni quien cultive hierbas en la boca del muerto,
> ni quien abra los linos del reposo,
> ni quien llore por las heridas de los elefantes.
> No hay más que un millón de herreros
> forjando cadenas para los niños que han de venir.
> No hay más que un millón de carpinteros
> que hacen ataúdes sin cruz
> No hay más que un gentío de lamentos
> que se abren las ropas en espera de la bala.
> El hombre que desprecia la paloma debía hablar,
> debía gritar desnudo entre las columnas
> y ponerse una inyección para adquirir la lepra
> y llorar un llanto tan terrible
> que disolviera sus anillos y sus teléfonos de diamante.
> Pero el hombre vestido de blanco
> ignora el misterio de la espiga,
> ignora el gemido de la parturienta,
> ignora que Cristo puede dar agua todavía,
> ignora que la moneda quema el beso de prodigio
> y de la sangre del cordero al pico idiota del faisán. (OC, I, pp. 525–26)

[Apples lightly grazed by fine silver swords, clouds torn by a coral hand that carries on its back an almond of fire, arsenic fish like sharks, sharks like teardrops to blind the masses, roses that wound and needles embedded in the blood's tubes, enemy worlds and love covered in worms will fall upon you. They will fall upon the great dome that smears military tongues with oil, where a man urinates on a dazzling dove and spits crushed coal surrounded by thousands of little bells. Because there is no one to share out bread and wine, or to grow herbs in the mouths of the dead, or unfold the linen of repose, or weep for the wounds of elephants. There are only a million blacksmiths forging chains for children yet to come. Only a million carpenters making coffins with no crosses. Only a crowd of laments that undo their clothing, awaiting a bullet. The man who despises the dove ought to have spoken, ought to have shouted naked between the columns and injected himself with leprosy and let forth a cry terrible enough to dissolve his rings and diamond telephones. But the man dressed in white knows nothing of the mystery of the ear of wheat, knows nothing of the moans of a woman in labour, knows not that Christ can still give water, knows not that a coin burns the kiss of wonder and gives the blood of the lamb to the pheasant's idiotic beak.]

The ode is commonly understood to be an expression of Lorca's outrage at the Lateran Treaty, agreed in February 1929 and ratified by Italy's parliament in June the same year. The Treaty saw the Vatican recognized as an independent state in return for its tacit support of then prime minister, Benito Mussolini. When he 'ought to have spoken' ('debía hablar' [OC, I, p. 525]), when he 'ought to have shouted naked between the columns' ('debía gritar desnudo entre las columnas' [OC, I, p. 525]) – presumably of St. Peter's Basilica – when he ought even to have 'injected himself with leprosy and let forth a cry terrible enough to dissolve his rings and diamond telephones' ('ponerse una inyección para adquirir la lepra | y llorar un llanto tan terrible | que disolviera sus anillos y sus teléfonos de diamante' [OC, I, p. 526]), when, in short, the Pope ought to have railed against Fascism, the man in white ('el hombre vestido de blanco' [OC, I, p. 526]), characterized as the man 'who despises the dove' ('que desprecia la paloma' [OC, I, p. 525]), said nothing.

'Grito hacia Roma', in some respects, represents a shift in focus for *Poeta en Nueva York*, although its overall message – that the peoples of the world have been abandoned even by their spiritual leaders – can also be applied to the specific circumstances of New York's residents living in a spiritual void. There are other poems in the collection where Lorca looks away momentarily from the horrors of the urban landscape to consider other issues, such as personal identity, loss and belonging. These include, for example, the introspective '1910 (Intermedio)' ['1910 (Intermezzo)']

Figure 10 Self-portrait in New York, 1929

(OC, I, p. 448), 'Fábula y rueda de los tres amigos' ['Fable and Circle of Three Friends'] (OC, I, pp. 449–51) and 'Tu infancia en Menton' ['Your childhood in Menton'] (OC, I, pp. 452–53). There are also the poems the poet wrote during his visit to Vermont where, in August 1929, he stayed with his friend, Philip Cummings, whom he had met at the Residencia de Estudiantes the previous year. 'Era mi voz antigua | ignorante de los densos jugos amargos' ['My former voice was ignorant of the dense and bitter juices'], he laments in 'Poema doble del Lago Eden' ['Double Poem of Lake Eden'] (OC, I, pp. 489–90); while, in 'Cielo vivo' ['Living Sky'] (OC, I, pp. 491–92), he is more assertive when he writes that 'Yo no podré quejarme | si no encontré lo que buscaba' ['I cannot complain if I never found what I was looking for'] (OC, I, pp. 491 and 492).

While not as intimate as these, 'Oda a Walt Whitman' ['Ode to Walt Whitman'] (OC, I, pp. 528–32) is, in a different way, among the most personal poems of the New York collection inasmuch as it represents Lorca's most explicit treatment of homosexuality to that point. The ode, as Roberts (p. 139) notes, 'offers a complex and revealing self-portrait of Lorca as a gay man', revealing 'what it was that Lorca felt he owed to Whitman not just as a writer but, more importantly, as an iconic homosexual figure' (Roberts p. 139). In his ode, Lorca mythologizes the American poet 'into a fertility god', rendering him 'the American counterpart to the divine kings, Attis, Osiris, and Adonis'[14]:

> Ni un solo momento, viejo hermoso Walt Whitman,
> ha dejado de ver tu barba llena de mariposas,
> ni tus hombros de pana gastados por la luna,
> ni tus muslos de Apolo virginal,
> ni tu voz como una columna de ceniza;
> anciano hermoso como la niebla
> que gemías igual que un pájaro
> con el sexo atravesado por una aguja,
> enemigo del sátiro,
> enemigo de la vid
> y amante de los cuerpos bajo la burda tela. (OC, I, p. 529)

[Not for one moment, handsome old man, Walt Whitman, have I lost sight of your beard full of butterflies, or your corduroy shoulders worn out by the moon, or your virginal thighs like those of Apollo, or your voice like a column of ash; old man, as handsome as the mist, you who

---

14 Richard Saez, 'The Ritual Sacrifice in Lorca's Poeta en Nueva York', in *Lorca: A Collection of Critical Essays*, ed. by Manuel Duran (Prentice Hall: Englewood Cliffs, N. J., 1962), pp. 108–29 (p. 126).

moaned like a bird with its sex pierced by a needle, enemy of the satyr, enemy of the vine, and lover of bodies beneath rough cloth.]

Lorca extols Walt Whitman's Apollonian virtue in contrast to the bacchanalian impulses alluded to by the satyr and the vine of which Whitman is cast as an enemy. The bird's mutilated sex recalls, as Saez (p. 125) observes, 'the eunuch priests of Attis', the figurative castration with which Whitman is associated serving as an emblem of his purity, self-sacrifice and restraint.[15] Championing Whitman's virile yet discreet homosexuality – the reserve of a man who conceals his amorous activity beneath 'la burda tela' ['rough cloth'] – Lorca uses his ode to pass judgment on those homosexuals (whom he refers to by the derogatory term *maricas*) whose effeminacy and perceived lack of modesty, in contrast to Whitman's discretion, offend him. In the following stanzas, Lorca's sympathy for the closeted, who suffer their desires in silence, is in stark contrast to the outrage he feels towards those who flaunt their sexuality and seek women's attention:

> Puede el hombre, si quiere, conducir su deseo,
> por vena de coral o celeste desnudo.
> Mañana los amores serán rocas y el Tiempo
> una brisa que viene dormida por las ramas.
>
> Por eso no levanto mi voz, viejo Walt Whitman,
> contra el niño que escribe
> nombre de niña en su almohada,
> ni contra el muchacho que se viste de novia
> en la oscuridad del ropero,
> ni contra los solitarios de los casinos
> que beben con asco el agua de la prostitución,
> ni contra los hombres de mirada verde
> que aman al hombre y queman los labios en silencio.
> Pero sí contra vosotros, maricas de las ciudades
> de carne tumefacta y pensamiento inmundo,
> madres de lodo, arpías, enemigos sin sueño
> del Amor que reparte coronas de alegría.
>
> Contra vosotros siempre, que dais a los muchachos
> gotas de sucia muerte con amargo veneno.

---

[15] According to James George Frazer, *The Golden Bough. A Study in Magic and Religion*, Abridged Edition (London: Papermac, 1987), p. 347, the priests of Attis 'regularly castrated themselves on entering the service of the goddess [Cybele]'.

Contra vosotros siempre,
Faeries de Norteamérica,
Pájaros de la Habana,
Jotos de Méjico,
Sarasas de Cádiz,
Apios de Sevilla,
Cancos de Madrid,
Floras de Alicante,
Adelaidas de Portugal.

¡Maricas de todo el mundo, asesinos de palomas!
Esclavos de la mujer, perras de sus tocadores,
abiertos en las plazas con fiebre de abanico
o emboscados en yertos paisajes de cicuta. (OC, I, p. 531)

[Man is able, if he wishes, to guide his desire through a vein of coral or celestial nude. Tomorrow loves will be rocks and Time, a breeze asleep amid branches. That's why I don't raise my voice, old Walt Whitman, against the little boy who writes a girl's name on his pillow, nor against the young lad who dresses as a bride in the darkness of the closet, nor against the solitary men in casinos who drink with disgust the water of prostitution, nor against the men with green stares who love other men and burn their lips in silence. But I do against you, *maricas* of the cities, with your swollen flesh and dirty thoughts, mothers of mire, harpies, sleepless enemies of the Love that bestows garlands of joy. Always against you, who give boys drops of foul death with bitter poison. *Fairies* of North America, *Pájaros* of Havana, *Jotos* of Mexico, *Sarasas* of Cadiz, *Apios* of Seville, *Cancos* of Madrid, *Floras* of Alicante, *Adelaidas* of Portugal. *Maricas* the world over, murderers of doves! Slaves to woman. Their dressing table bitches. Opening in public squares with all the fever of fans or lying in wait in the rigid landscapes of hemlock.]

As Roberts (p. 140) points out, these lines are 'disturbingly homophobic and misogynistic'. Yet, in some respects, their insensitive and bigoted depiction of the '*maricas* of the cities' is consistent with Lorca's broader representation in *Poeta en Nueva York* of what he sees as the corrupting influence of modern city life on people and things; a corrupting influence to which, in his view, the *maricas* have also fallen victim. Overall, in 'Oda a Walt Whitman', Lorca still has his sights firmly on the ills of America's machine society as he, in a familiar paradigm, aligns the American poet with nature and against the industrial world:

Y tú, bello Walt Whitman, duerme a orillas del Hudson
con la barba hacia el polo y las manos abiertas.

> Arcilla blanda o nieve, tu lengua está llamando
> camaradas que velen tu gacela sin cuerpo.
> Duerme, no queda nada.
> Una danza de muros agita las praderas
> y América se anega de máquinas y llanto.
> Quiero que el aire fuerte de la noche más honda
> quite flores y letras del arco donde duermes
> y un niño negro anuncie a los blancos del oro
> la llegada del reino de la espiga. (OC, I, p. 532)

[And you, beautiful Walt Whitman, sleep on the banks of the Hudson, with your beard towards the pole and hands open. Soft clay or snow, your tongue is calling comrades to watch over your bodiless gazelle. Sleep, there's nothing left. A dance of walls stirs the prairies and America drowns in machines and tears. I want the strong air of the deepest night to blow away flowers and letters from the arch where you sleep and a black child to announce to the whites of gold the coming of the kingdom of the ear of wheat.]

Whitman serves as a role model for the poet as he bears witness to the excesses and injustices of the city. He declares that he has not lost sight of Whitman's beard, not even for a moment ('Ni un solo momento' [OC, I, p. 529]), thus acknowledging that the American poet has been a constant reference point: an idealized figure by which he has measured himself. And if, as in 'rey de Harlem', he can prophesize the coming of a new order – the kingdom of the ear of corn – it is because he has been able, Whitman-like, to withstand the city's onslaught.

Lorca spent the Spring of 1930 in Cuba, where he would give a series of lectures and recitals. The island seemed to him to be a home from home, Havana being 'una mezcla', as he put it to his family, 'de Málaga y Cádiz, pero mucho más animada y relajada por el trópico' ['a mixture of Malaga and Cadiz, but much more spirited and relaxed, being tropical'] (EC, p. 681). 'El ritmo de la ciudad', he added, 'es acariciador, suave, sensualísimo, y lleno de un encanto que es absolutamente español, mejor dicho, andaluz. Habana es fundamentalmente española, pero de lo más característico y más profundo de nuestra civilización' ['The city's rhythm is a caress, soft, very sensual, and filled with a charm that's absolutely Spanish, or better said, Andalusian. Havana is fundamentally Spanish, but in the sense of that which is most characteristic and profound of our civilization'] (EC, p. 681). 'Esta isla', he wrote in another letter to his family, 'es un paraíso. Cuba. Si yo me pierdo, que me busquen en Andalucía o en Cuba' ['This island is a paradise. Cuba. If ever I'm lost, people should look for me in Andalusia or Cuba'] (*EC*, p. 686). He considered his lectures a success, and he expressed his affinity with the easy-going Cuban people, including its black community, who all received him well. 'No olvidéis vosotros', he wrote, 'que en América ser poeta es algo más que ser príncipe en Europa' ['Don't forget that in the Americas being a poet is more than being a prince in Europe'] (*EC*, p. 686).[16] Little wonder, then, that his poem, 'Son de negros en Cuba' ['*Son cubano* of the Blacks in Cuba'] (*OC*, I, pp. 541–42), should represent a release from the anguished tones of his New York poems:

> Iré a Santiago.
> Brisa y alcohol en las ruedas.
> Iré a Santiago.
> Mi coral en la tiniebla.
> Iré a Santiago.
> El mar ahogado en la arena.
> Iré a Santiago.
> Calor blanco, fruta muerta.
> Iré a Santiago.
> ¡Oh bovino frescor de cañavera!
> ¡Oh Cuba! ¡Oh curva de suspiro y barro!
> Iré a Santiago. (*OC*, I, pp. 541–42)

[I'm off to Santiago. Breeze and alcohol on the wheels. I'm off to Santiago. My coral in the dark. I'm off to Santiago. The sea drowned in the sand. I'm off to Santiago. White heat, dead fruit. I'm off to Santiago. O bovine freshness of the cane fields! O Cuba! O curve of sigh and clay! I'm off to Santiago.]

The positivity Lorca expressed in his letters from Cuba is matched by the equally positive rhythms of 'Son de negros en Cuba', the poem's title referring to a musical genre – *son cubano* – that was born in Cuba and has its origins in both Africa and Spain. But if 'Son de negros en Cuba' is an accurate reflection of the tone of his Cuban letters, there is, conversely, a huge disparity between the tone of the letters Lorca wrote from New York and that of the poems he wrote there. The broad context for this disparity, as we have seen, is his focus on the dehumanizing consequences of machine society, capitalism and urban life. This focus places Lorca among those writers and artists whose engagement with modernity was,

---

16 For an account of Lorca's time in Cuba, see Gibson 1989, pp. 282–302, and Stainton, pp. 251–59.

at its core, sceptical, suspicious and deeply critical. But in order to make full sense of the disparity, we need also to consider the values of Lorca the poet as well as those of Lorca the man. In his preamble to his 1932 recital of his New York poems in Madrid, Lorca suggested that the title of the event ought to have been 'Nueva York en un poeta' ['New York in a Poet'] rather than 'Un poeta en Nueva York' (OC, III, p. 347). In this way, he drew attention to the importance of the city's impact on him as a poet as opposed simply to his experience of the city as a man who happened to be a poet as well. This is fitting because what many of his New York poems reveal is that, for Lorca the poet, poetry was itself a victim of the cult of modernity.

Before Lorca's departure for New York, Dalí had judged his *Romancero gitano* to be old-fashioned and commonplace. Buñuel had put in his tuppence worth too, in a letter to their mutual friend from the Residencia, Pepín Bello: 'It's a poetry', wrote Buñuel, 'that has the finesse and apparent modernity which any poetry needs nowadays in order to please the [critics]. But between this and having anything to do with the genuine and great poets of today there is a deep gulf' (see Gibson 1989, p. 220). Lorca also saw in Buñuel's and Dalí's Surrealist film, *Un Chien Andalou* [*An Andalusian Dog*], which premiered in Paris in 1929, a personal dig at himself. 'Andalusian dog' was, as it so happens, the nickname given jokingly to the more traditional southern poets in the Residencia de Estudiantes.[17] Lorca, it seems, was convinced that he alone was the model for the film's male protagonist and complained of the fact to friend and philologist, Angel del Río: 'Buñuel has made a tiny piece of shit called *An Andalusian Dog* – and I'm the dog' (Gibson 1989, p. 229). Lorca, then, had good personal reasons to dislike Surrealism. Yet it is clear also that his professional view of Surrealism had, in any case, always been ambivalent. In *Poeta en Nueva York*, however, he appears finally to have made up his mind. For despite its surrealistic veneer, the collection seems to be a deliberate attempt to denounce the incoherence and chaos of Surrealist production. This is the implication of Lorca's conscious association of surrealistic devices with his indictment of the negative consequences of modern living. It was no coincidence

---

17 See Jenaro Talens, *The Branded Eye: Buñuel's 'Un Chien andalou'*, trans. by Giulia Colaizzi (Minneapolis and London: University of Minnesota Press, 1993), p. 39; Phillip Drummond, 'Surrealism and Un Chien Andalou', *Un Chien Andalou: Luis Buñuel and Salvador Dalí* (London: Faber and Faber, 1994), pp. v–xxiii (p. ix); and Ian Gibson 1997, p. 195.

Figure 11 Lorca in Havana with a newspaper boy in 1930

that, in the wake of the criticism that his ballads were not sufficiently modern, he should travel to the most modern city in the world only then to produce a damning critique of modernity. That he should do so with reference to the aesthetics of Surrealism was a sign that he had decided that Surrealism was only fit to communicate an experience of modernity that was ugly, discordant and dissonant.

Chapter Three

Lorca, the Feminist

FEMINIST CONTEMPORARIES OF Lorca such as Margarita Nelken, María Martínez Sierra or Carmen de Burgos, and indeed women before and after them, rarely figure on either secondary school curricula or, for that matter, university syllabi, at least not in the United Kingdom. By contrast, Lorca's theatre, primarily his women-centred trilogy of rural tragedies – *Bodas de Sangre* [*Blood wedding*], *Yerma* [*Yerma*] and *La casa de Bernarda Alba* [*The House of Bernarda Alba*] – has been a permanent feature of school reading lists for many years, cementing Lorca's place in the popular imagination as Spain's most prominent defender of women.

While Lorca never did declare himself to be a feminist, his theatre is notable, as Roberta Johnson remarks, for its 'acute awareness of women's status within Spanish society, especially regarding class, education, work, and marriage' and, according to Roberta Ann Quance, for 'its sympathetic treatment of the repression of women's bodies and their desire'.[1] His rural tragedies, written between 1932 and 1935, are a case in point, and it is surely no coincidence that their exploration of the experience of women should have taken place during Spain's Second Republic, at a time when women's issues had moved to the forefront

---

1   Roberta Johnson, in 'Federico García Lorca's Theater and Spanish Feminism', *Anales de la literatura española contemporánea*, 33.2, El Teatro de Federico García Lorca en la Construccíon de la Identidad Colectiva Española (2008), 251–81 (p. 252) and Roberta Ann Quance, 'Federico García Lorca. Mediating Tradition and Modernity for a World Audience', in *A Companion to World Literature*, ed. by Ken Seigneurie (John Wiley & Sons, 2019), pp. 1–11 (p. 8) <https://doi.org/10.1002/9781118635193.ctwl0264>.

of Spanish politics.[2] Founded in 1931, Spain's Second Republic sought to improve the condition of women in the country and challenge the structural inequalities that had denied them the same access to education as men, the same rights at work, and had made 'married women legally subordinate to their husbands', including in the acquisition and disposal of property.[3] These inequalities had been legitimized by the ideology of the Catholic Church which proclaimed the importance of the family above all else and insisted that women's sole vocation was to marry and become mothers (see Lannon, p. 275). Now 'the new Constitution of the Second Republic described Spain as a democratic Republic of workers and introduced universal suffrage. It separated Church and State, secularized education, and instituted civil marriage and divorce'

2 Several other of Lorca's plays also seem to reveal feminist sensibilities. *La zapatera prodigiosa* [*The Shoemaker's Prodigious Wife*], for example, written in 1924 and first performed in 1930, is a comic treatment of the challenges facing a young girl in her marriage with an old man. The eponymous protagonist of *Mariana Pineda* [*Mariana Pineda*], which Lorca began writing in 1923 but only premièred in 1927, is based on a real historical figure from Granada considered to be a martyr for the liberal cause in early nineteenth-century Spain. Despite the view that its plot, rather than having a political focus, 'is really about the impossibility of attaining – or maintaining – a true love that is reciprocated', as Andrew A. Anderson argues (in 'Federico García Lorca', in *Twentieth-Century Spain and the Civil War*, ed. by David T. Gies, Cambridge Histories Online [Cambridge University Press, 2008], 595–608 [p. 602] <https://doi.org/10.1017/CHOL9780521806183.047>), the play lends itself to readings that foreground Lorca's interest in the role of women in the public domain. See, for example, Daniela Dimitrova Slivkova, *Federico García Lorca's 'Mariana Pineda': Erasing the Dividing Line Between the Lyrical-Feminine and the Heroic-Masculine* (Northern Illinois University, 2013). Another of Lorca's plays, *Doña Rosita la soltera o El lenguaje de las flores* [*Doña Rosita the Spinster or The Language of Flowers*], with its distinctly provincial middle-class setting, was first staged in 1935. As Wright (p. 56) points out, the play 'is often viewed as a comment on the limited options available to women in early twentieth-century Spain', although the plight of the spinster of the title might equally reveal a condition that is altogether more personal: a 'Tragic stasis or immobility against the passing of time, trading on unfulfilled desires' (Wright, p. 56).
3 Frances Lannon, 'Gender and Change: Identity and Reform in the Second Republic', in *A Companion to Spanish Women's Studies*, ed. by Xon de Ros and Geraldine Hazbun (Woodbridge: Tamesis, 2011), pp. 273–85 (p. 275).

(Lannon, p. 274). Most importantly, it granted men and women equal civil and political rights (see Lannon, p. 274).

Even before the advent of the Second Republic, feminist arguments in favour of granting women equal rights had already taken root in Spain. Although the Granada Lorca grew up in was, by all accounts, a city 'completely divided along gender lines' (Johnson, p. 251), the Madrid he first experienced as a student in 1919 would have been starkly different. There, 'feminist manifestations (if not a movement) [had been] increasing [...] from the 1890s onwards', receiving 'significant impetus during the First World War (1914–18), when many women entered the workforce' (Johnson, p. 251). Although, as Johnson rightly notes, scholarship has tended to focus on Lorca's male friends in Madrid, not least because the prestigious Residencia de Estudiantes, where he was lodging, only admitted male residents, he also counted many women among his friends and acquaintances – feminists and artists 'who moved in artistic circles associated with the Residencia' (Johnson, p. 253) and who most certainly had a deep and lasting influence on his thinking.[4] Amongst other things, they would have impressed on him the importance of education for women, an issue that would also have been current at the Residencia as a result of the Krausist ideas circulating there, women's education considered by Krausism to be 'a cornerstone for the progress of the Spanish nation' (Johnson, p.256).[5]

---

4   Johnson offers an important corrective to the almost exclusive attention that biographical scholarship has given to Lorca's male friends. Johnson (p. 253) points out that there was a parallel Residencia de Señoritas where Lorca's sister, Concha, resided in the mid-1930s and that counted 'several notable "liberated women"' among its residents. Johnson (pp. 254–66) discusses Lorca's acquaintances and friendships among this group, including feminist writer Carmen Burgos, stating that 'The themes and ominous tone of Lorca's rural tragedies have much in common with some of Carmen de Burgos's feminist novelettes (she wrote her own Andalusian rural tragedy titled *Los inadaptados* [1901])' (Johnson, p. 255). Johnson (pp. 255–66) also notes that Lorca attended *tertulias* (literary gatherings) organized by Margarita Nelken, one of Spain's 'new women'.
5   For a brief introduction to Krausism and its influence on republicanism, see Enrique Montero, 'Reform Idealized: The Intellectual and Ideological Origins of the Second republic', in *Spanish Cultural Studies: An Introduction: The Struggle for Modernity*, ed. by Helen Graham and Jo Labanyi (Oxford: OUP, 1995), pp. 124–33.

The issue of education was fundamental because traditionally women's formal education in Spain had 'focused on the domestic arts and hand work – sewing and embroidery – in addition to [only] rudimentary reading and writing' (Johnson, p. 256). Such limited education inevitably tied women to the domestic setting, offering them little prospect of obtaining meaningful work outside the home; work that might allow them 'independence from men and the necessity of marriage, often a marriage for purely economic reasons' (Johnson, p. 257), irrespective of the suitability of the match at a personal or affective level. 'Marriage and work are intertwined in Spanish feminist theory [...] of the 1920s and 1930s' (Johnson, p. 257), and its influence can be seen in Lorca's rural trilogy in the way he focuses 'on female protagonists from various levels of the landed classes who would not have meaningful work to occupy their time' (Johnson, p. 257); women who either find themselves in unhappy marriages or who are desperately seeking a love that will abstract them from the monotony of domestic life.

Love, as Chris Perriam notes, is a primary concern, along with death, of Lorca's work generally.[6] Importantly, in the rural trilogy, as well as in other plays, it is explored primarily via women's experience of the social constraints that prevent them from loving as they want. Thus, Lorca offers 'accounts of disempowerment and power from an equality-interested perspective, or a perspective that links sexuality and gender roles to social control' (Perriam, p. 160). His are 'socially grounded representations of femininity' (Perriam, p. 160), the dramatic situations he creates for his women being dependent on their 'experiencing the limitations of both their gender and their class' (Johnson, p. 257).

Clearly, Lorca's work can be read in the context of first-wave feminism, namely feminism of the late nineteenth century and early twentieth century.[7] Significantly, his depiction of women's experience in the plays of his rural trilogy, all written during the first years of the Second Republic, coincided with the mood for change encouraged by Republicanism after

---

6 Chris Perriam, 'Gender and Sexuality', in *A Companion to Federico García Lorca*, ed. by Federico Bonaddio (Woodbridge: Tamesis, 2007), pp. 149–69 (p. 152).

7 Perriam (p. 161) notes how *Yerma*, as well as other works, can be read in accordance with the interrogation by second-wave feminism – feminism of the 1960s onwards – of (and here he quotes Claire Colebrook's *Gender*) the 'direct relation between bodies and genders' and its rejection of 'the ways in which female bodies had been interpreted or gendered'.

years of feminist debate. The trilogy's rural focus is also significant given the particular hardships experienced by rural communities and given their relatively scant exposure to the progressive ideologies of large towns and cities. Considering that feminism was 'primarily an urban phenomenon' (Johnson, pp. 251–52, citing A. A. Anderson), as was the new, independent woman who 'manifested her modern status in her dress and hair styles' and 'was beginning to make an impression in the Spanish public sphere' (Johnson, p. 252), the rural setting, by contrast – steeped in tradition – offered Lorca the perfect stage on which to convey most intensely the limitations experienced by women. Yet, as was the case with his *Romancero gitano*, these real-life concerns – his very real interest in real lives – did not compel Lorca to abandon or compromise his artistic priorities. For his undoubtable concern for the condition of women and for the human condition more broadly was not incompatible with a sustained interest in the poetic qualities of his texts. In fact, as we shall see, his choice of the tragic mode for his plays meant not only that they would be governed by a poetic logic but also that their exploration of the real lives of women in Spain could have resonance, beyond the Spanish context, for all women and, indeed, for humanity generally.

The first of the trilogy, *Bodas de sangre*, was written in 1932 and premiered a year later. It is divided into three acts: the first is divided, in turn, into three scenes; the second and third, into two each. The play centres on a betrothal, wedding and the bride's subsequent flight with her lover; and there is evidence to suggest that it was inspired by a real-life crime committed in the summer of 1928 in Níjar, an Andalusian village in the province of Almería.[8] It is, though, not with the bride that the play opens but instead with the bridegroom's mother. This is significant because in Madre [Mother], as she is referred to, Lorca has fashioned a spokesperson for traditional customs and values and an exemplar of moral rectitude and social obedience. She is also, arguably, the play's most tragic figure, both because Lorca ascribes customs and values to her that others will inevitably fail to uphold and because he makes her the perennial victim of a cycle of violence that began with the murder of her husband and eldest son in a feud with the Félix family and will continue with the loss of her

---

8   For details of the play's source, see H. Ramsden, 'Introduction', in Federico García Lorca, *Bodas de sangre*, Hispanic Texts (Manchester and New York: Manchester University Press, 1980), pp. ix–xlix; and also C. B. Morris, *García Lorca: Bodas de sangre*, Critical Guides to Spanish Texts (London: Grant & Cutler / Tamesis, 1980), pp. 16–19.

younger son, on his wedding day, at the hands of his wife's lover, who is a member of the Félix clan also.

Unlike the bride, Madre is not torn between, on the one hand, the expectations that society heaps on women and, on the other, the pull of personal desires. She knows her duty and her place, and her resolve to adhere to society's codes will not be shaken even by the terrible loss of her loved ones. Moreover, her generic name gives her universal significance in the same way as Novia [Bride] and Novio [Bridegroom] and the generic names of other characters (Mother-in-Law, Father, Wife, Neighbour, Young Girl etc.) also have universal implications. Thus, her tragedy is able to extend beyond her personal circumstances to stand for the predicament of all women who hold fast to the rules that society dictates to them. It is no accident that the only character to whom Lorca gives a proper name is Novia's lover, Leonardo. In this way, Lorca foregrounds Leonardo's role as outsider and transgressor of societal norms, signalling that the desire he embodies (illicit given the circumstances) is the very thing that gives human beings their individuality.

Scene 1 of the play opens with the word *madre*, uttered by Novio as he enters a yellow painted room where Madre awaits. He asks Madre for the knife (not *a* knife, but *the* knife), which he needs to cut grapes from the vines in the family's vineyards. His request prompts Madre to reflect with anger and sorrow on the lives taken by knives and other weapons, including the lives of her husband and first son. She condemns these instruments of irreparable violence and wonders how her son even dare carry a knife or how she herself can allow such a thing in the house in the first place: 'No sé [...] cómo dejo a la serpiente dentro del arcón' ['I don't know how I'm able to allow the snake to be kept in the chest'].[9] Madre's lament presages the inescapable violence of a tragedy in which the aforementioned knife will claim the lives of two more men and deprive her of an heir in the process. Lorca, as we will see, gives property and inheritance an especial importance in this tragedy. Yet, although they are, in great part, what drive events to their inevitable conclusion, Lorca does not allow these material matters to obscure the deeply felt personal toll of Madre's grief.

The conversation between Novio and Madre soon turns to the bride-to-be, and it is here that we begin to discern Madre's strong attachment to a traditional view of women and of their social role and function. Asked

---

9 Federico García Lorca, *Obras completas*, II, ed. Arturo del Hoyo, 22nd ed. (Madrid: Aguilar, 1986), p. 703.

what she thinks about the bride-to-be, Madre acknowledges that the girl seems hardworking and discreet, though her suspicion that she may already have had a sweetheart reveals the doubts she harbours about Novia's moral character. These doubts are latent in her declaration that she herself only ever had eyes for her husband, the implication being that Novia, by contrast, might be less self-disciplined. Indeed, even after her husband's death, all Madre looked at was 'la pared de enfrente' ['the wall opposite'] (OC, II, p. 706). Madre is also sorry she never had the opportunity to find out what the girl's own mother was like, no doubt because this would have offered her other clues as to the character of her son's future wife. For a moment, though, her negative thoughts give way to the happy prospect of grandchildren. Madre wants at least six grandchildren or as many as her son desires, given that, unlike his father, he has plenty of space at home. And granddaughters amongst them too, since women face few of the perils that, as Madre knows from personal experience, men generally do. In a later scene, Madre explains that '¡Los varones son del viento!' ['Men come and go on the wind'] and 'Tienen por fuerza que manejar armas' ['are obliged to handle weapons'] (OC, II, p. 756). Girls, on the other hand, 'no salen jamás a la calle' ['never set foot in the street'] (OC, II, p. 756). After all, in Madre's mind a woman's vocation is simply to be a mother and housemaker, which is why she assumes that her granddaughters will be as content as she is to pass their time indoors sewing and embroidering: 'Que yo quiero bordar y hacer encaje y estar tranquila' ['Because I want to embroider and make lace and be in peace'] (OC, II, p. 707). The reference to embroidery is as telling here as it is elsewhere in Lorca's work. For, as Johnson (p. 256) points out, 'in Lorca's plays, traditional, domestically-oriented women are often associated with embroidery, an important synecdoche for the divide between the "new woman" and the "tradition-bound woman".'

Before Novio exits, Madre reassures her son that she will indeed love his future wife. Yet the optimism she offers him despite herself is short-lived. At the end of the scene, a neighbour confirms not only that Novia has previously had a sweetheart but, to Madre's horror, that the man in question is a Félix. Mother promises to say nothing about this to her son; after all, Leonardo was only eight years old at the time of the feud between their families. And yet her earlier admission to her son that the mere mention of Novia throws her off balance – despite the girl's evident homemaking abilities – becomes, in retrospect, deeply foreboding: 'Amasa su pan y cose sus faldas, y siento sin embargo, cuando la nombro, como si me dieran una pedrada en la frente' ['She kneads bread and sews skirts, yet when I mention her, I feel as if someone had hit me in the face with a stone'] (OC, II, p. 705). Madre's unease can no longer be shrugged off with the excuse that what irks her is merely the prospect of her son leaving home.

The betrothal of Novia to Novio is sealed in Act 1, Scene 3, when Madre and the bride's father, Padre, meet to discuss the engagement. Much of their discussion revolves around property. Each family owns land and, as Leonardo's mother-in-law suggests in Scene 2, with the marriage of Novia to Novio 'se van a juntar dos buenos capitales' ['two fine fortunes will be united'] (OC, II, p. 720). Leonardo's relatively modest income and meagre prospects were, it seems, at the root of the failure of his relationship with Novia whose betrothal to Novio is, in contrast, deemed suitable not because of any mutual affection but because it makes financial sense. In the context of their union, even the prospect of grandchildren has an economic value. In Act 2, Scene 2, after the wedding, Padre expresses his hope that the couple will have children quickly and that they be sons at that – because the land requires unpaid labour or, as he puts it, 'brazos que no sean pagados' ['arms that are not paid'] (OC, II, p. 756). And he continues: 'Hay que sostener una batalla con las malas hierbas, con los cardos, con los pedruscos que salen no se sabe dónde. Y estos brazos tienen que ser de los dueños, que castiguen y que dominen, que hagan brotar las simientes. Se necesitan muchos hijos' ['You need to do battle with weeds, thistles, stones that pop up from who knows where. And these arms must belong to the owners, to punish and tame, to sow the seed. You need many sons'] (OC, II, p.756).

As well as land and property, Madre and Padre also discuss their children's personal virtues, and here Lorca ensures that the very strict limits placed on women come to the fore. Padre's exultation of his daughter's skills situates her responsibilities firmly in the domestic and private sphere: 'Hace las migas a las tres, cuando el lucero. No habla nunca; suave como la lana, borda toda clase de bordados y puede cortar una maroma con los dientes' ['She makes breakfast at three, with the morning star. She never speaks; she's as soft and gentle as wool, makes all sorts of embroidery and can cut a rope with her teeth'] (OC, II, p. 727). And while Madre clearly values her son's self-restraint when she declares 'Mi hijo es hermoso. No ha conocido mujer. La honra más limpia que una sábana puesta al sol' ['My son is handsome. He has never known a woman. His honour is as pristine as a white sheet in the sun'] (OC, II, p. 727), the responsibility for maintaining the honour and integrity of the family falls squarely on Novia. Marriage for Novia must mean (in Madre's own words) 'Un hombre, unos hijos y una pared de dos varas de ancha para todos los demás' ['One man, children and a wall three foot thick against everyone else'] (OC, II, p. 729). Novia knows the obligations of a wife and assures Madre that she will meet them. Later, in a desperate rush to get to church before her feelings for Leonardo get the better of her, it is clear from her declaration to Novio that she is fully aware of the solitary existence awaiting her: 'Estoy deseando ser tu mujer y quedarme sola contigo, y no oír más voz que la tuya' ['I can't wait to become your wife and to be alone with you, and not hear any other voice but yours'] (OC, II, p. 750). But her apparent acceptance of her future as a wife contrasts starkly with the passionate declarations Lorca has her make to Leonardo as they flee the wedding reception together. Here she roundly rejects the security marriage can provide, unable to resist a love more powerful than the conventions that normally bind married couples:

> No quiero
> contigo cama ni cena,
> y no hay minuto del día
> que estar contigo no quiera,
> porque me arrastras y voy,
> y me dices que me vuelva
> y te sigo por el aire
> como una brizna de hierba. (OC, II, p. 785)

[I want neither bed nor board from you, and there's not a minute of the day that I don't want to be with you, because you pull me towards you and I go, and you tell me to return and I follow you through the air like a wisp of grass.]

After the wedding, Madre spells out to her son a husband's role in ensuring that a wife is obedient, making light of domestic violence in the process: 'Con tu mujer procura estar cariñoso, y si la notas infatuada o arisca, hazle una caricia que le produzca un poco de daño, un abrazo fuerte, un mordisco y luego un beso suave. Que ella no pueda disgustarse, pero que sienta que tú eres el macho, el amo, el que mandas' ['Try to be affectionate with your wife, and if ever she turns conceited or offish, give her a caress that hurts her a little, a strong embrace, a bite and then a gentle kiss. Not to upset her, but she needs to know you're a man, her master, the one who gives the orders'] (OC, II, p. 769). It is clear from her advice that Madre not only willingly submits to the patriarchal code but has taken it upon herself to be its guardian also: 'Así aprendí de tu padre. Y como no lo tienes, tengo que ser yo la que te enseñe estas fortalezas' ['I learnt this from your father. And as he's no longer here for you, I need to be the one to show you how to be firm with your wife'] (OC, II, p. 769).

Ultimately, though, the very conventions intended to maintain order prove to be patriarchy's tragic flaw as human desire confounds the strictures imposed on men and especially women.[10] Imprisoned by convention, Lorca's characters become its victims, turning on one another in a desperate attempt to avenge dishonour, but condemned all the same to live a life of shame. Their hopeless plight is epitomized by Novia who continues to be tormented by the notion of her honour even as she flees with Leonardo:

> Con los dientes,
> con las manos, como puedas,
> quita de mi cuello honrado
> el metal de esta cadena,
> dejándome arrinconada
> allá en mi casa de tierra. (OC, II, p. 783)

[With your teeth, with your hands, however you can, cut from my honest neck the metal of this chain, and leave me forgotten in my house of earth.]

Honour weighs so heavily upon Novia that she insists that she is pure even after the damage has been done and desire and vengeance have led to the deaths of her husband and lover. As Madre lashes out at her, Novia is willing to take the punishment, imploring a neighbour who tries to separate the two women to let Mother be: 'Que quiero que sepa que soy limpia, que estaré loca, pero que me pueden enterrar sin que ningún hombre se haya mirado en la blancura de mis pechos' ['It's that I want her to know that I'm pure, it may be that I'm mad, but they can bury me and no man will have gazed on the whiteness of my breasts'] (OC, II, p. 795). As for Madre, however much she might want to blame Novia for what has happened, Lorca shows her role as guardian of the code to be as futile as Novia's attempt to ignore desire and live the life others have designed for her and all women.

Yerma, which Lorca began writing in 1933 and premiered in 1934, centres on a farming community and the relationship between its eponymous

---

10 For a development of this idea, see Federico Bonaddio, 'Federico García Lorca's *Blood Wedding*: Patriarchy's Tragic Flaws', in *Patriarchal Moments*, ed. by Cesare Cuttica and Gaby Mahlberg (London: Bloomsbury, 2016), pp. 163–69.

protagonist and her husband, Juan, a shepherd. The play is divided into three acts, each with two scenes. The couple's means are more modest than those of Novia and Novio in *Bodas de sangre*; yet, despite the different social status Lorca attributes to them, Yerma and Juan are no less beset by preoccupations with reputation and family honour. Desire continues to be the destabilizing force that it was in *Bodas de sangre*, although now Lorca makes its focus not a lover but rather Yerma's desperate need to have a child. Desire's machinations thus remain within the boundaries of marriage, although these boundaries are tested as Yerma's frustrations cause her increasingly to question the obligations of a dutiful wife and the suitability of her marriage itself.[11] The play culminates in Yerma strangling Juan: an unpremeditated act of desperation and anger which, perversely, represents Yerma's only possible escape from her childless marriage given that she is unable and unwilling to break her marriage vows.

Whereas, in *Bodas de sangre*, Lorca gives Novia a binary choice, torn as she is between the man she ought to marry and the man she loves, the dilemma he gives Yerma is altogether more complex. She is trapped in a relationship with a man she will neither leave nor cheat on; a man with whom she has been unable to have a child even though her only reason for marrying was so that she could have children. Juan, for his part, seems unconcerned by the prospect of not having children. Yerma conflates her husband's lack of concern with the scant affection he offers her and with the lack of passion in the bedroom, seeing in it the cause of their childlessness. In Act 2, Scene 2, Yerma tells her friend, María, that her marriage does little more than cater for her basic needs: 'Mi marido me da pan y casa' ['My husband gives me bread and a roof over my head'] (OC, II, p. 849). And when, in Act 3, Scene 1, she is visiting Dolores, a conjuror whose prayers, she hopes, will bring her the child she so desires, she is even more forthright about the problems in her relationship: 'Él va con sus ovejas por sus caminos y cuenta el dinero por las niches. Cuando me cubre cumple con su deber, pero yo le noto la cintura fría, como si tuviera el cuerpo muerto, y yo, que siempre he tenido asco de las mujeres calientes, quisiera ser en aquel instante como una montaña de fuego' ['He

---

11 As Johnson (p. 268) notes, 'Unsuitable marriage [...] is a prominent secondary theme that competes with and complicates Yerma's pain over frustrated maternity.' See Delgado (pp. 88–89) on the controversy that greeted the play on its opening. This controversy 'marked the play as a potent statement on oppression and social discontent' (Delgado, p. 88), dividing opinions on Lorca's depiction of an unhappy marriage along political lines of left and right.

accompanies his sheep along their paths and counts his money at night. When he lies with me, he does his duty, but I notice he's cold around the waist, as if his body were dead, and I, who've always been disgusted by randy women, yearn at that moment to be like a mountain of fire'] (OC, II, p. 859). Yerma concludes that Juan does not want children, and 'como no lo ansía, no me los da' ['as he doesn't want them, he won't give them to me'] (OC, II, p. 859).

In Yerma's mind, therefore, her marriage is loveless as well as childless, and yet she is still made to suffer the constraints which, in her community, come with the role of being a wife; particularly the obligation to stay at home, out of public view, which limits her opportunities for contact with other men and, consequently, helps to avoid any suspicion of infidelity or provide reason for others to gossip. Madre's view, in *Bodas de sangre*, on the meaning of marriage for women springs to mind: 'una pared de dos varas de ancha para todos los demás' ['a wall three foot thick against everyone else'] (OC, II, p. 729). Contrary to Yerma's impressions, we could read Juan's accommodation with the childless state of his marriage and his insistence that he wants to look after his wife as signs that he cares deeply for her, notwithstanding the lack of passion in their relationship. After all, on more than one occasion, Lorca has other characters refer to him as being a good man. And yet, despite this, it is difficult not to arrive at a negative appraisal of Juan and judge him on the basis of his severely chauvinistic ideas about a woman's place and his conventional obsession with reputation and honour, all of which intensify Yerma's feelings of entrapment, suffocation, and neglect.

Between Acts 1 and 2 some three years have passed and Yerma and Juan have been married five years. In the intervening years, Yerma's increasing melancholy and her unwillingness to remain indoors have prompted Juan to ask his two sisters to live with them so that they can help his wife with the housework and, presumably, keep an eye on her. There were already signs of Juan's disapproval of Yerma being out of doors as early as Act 1, Scene 2, when he catches her talking to Víctor, a shepherd and friend since childhood. 'Debías estar en casa' ['You should have been home'] (OC, II, p. 829), Juan tells her, adding 'No comprendo en qué te has entretenido' ['I don't understand what kept you'] (OC, II, p. 829) and 'Así darás que hablar a las gentes' ['This way you'll start people talking'] (OC, II, p. 829). When Yerma questions whether he trusts her – 'Juan, ¿qué piensas?' [Juan, what are you thinking?'] (OC, II, p. 829) – he insists that he is not worried about her but only about what people might say: 'No lo digo por ti, lo digo por las gentes' ['I'm not saying it because of you, I'm saying it because of other people'] (OC, II, p. 829).

Whether Juan trusts Yerma or not, in Act 2 the issue has still not been put to rest. In Act 2, Scene 1, we learn from the conversation between five washerwomen that Yerma and her husband are already the subject of gossip. None of the washerwomen has seen Yerma with another man, but rumour has it that other people have. Thus, it comes as no surprise when, in Scene 2, on finding that Yerma is not at home, Juan should become angry that neither of his sisters accompanied her when she left the house. As family members, his sisters are also implicated in the matter of his honour: 'Mi vida está en el campo, pero mi honra está aquí. Y mi honra es también la vuestra' ['My life is in the fields, but my honour is here (at home). And my honour is also yours'] (OC, II, p. 841). When, moments later, Yerma does return (she has been out to fetch fresh water), the conversation quickly turns to her absences from home. Yerma's behaviour makes it impossible for Juan to have peace of mind; he makes clear his views on the matter in terms that, as much as anything, reveal the limitations of his own experience and thinking: 'Es que no conoces mi modo de ser? Las ovejas en el redil y las mujeres en su casa. Tú sales demasiado' ['Don't you know the way I am? Sheep in their pens and women in their homes. You go out too much'] (OC, II, p. 842). Juan's way of thinking is narrow and crude, and he remains insensitive to the crisis of identity Yerma is experiencing as a result of not having been able to become a mother. 'Yo no sé quién soy' ['I don't know who I am'] (OC, II, p. 845), she confesses, pleading with Juan to trust her and allow her the space to deal with her issues: 'Déjame andar y desahogarme. En nada te he faltado' ['Let me wander out so I can breathe more easily. I've never failed you'] (OC, II, p. 845). Yet it is like talking to a brick wall, so entrenched is Juan in his ways: 'No me gusta que la gente me señale. Por eso quiero ver cerrada esta puerta y cada persona en su casa' ['I don't like people pointing at me. That's why I want to see our door closed and each person in their home'] (OC, II, p. 845). And when Yerma argues that talking to people is not a sin ('Hablar con la gente no es pecado' [OC, II, p. 845]), Juan's retort is that it can appear to be one ('Pero puede parecerlo' [OC, II p. 845]). As David Gilmore explains, 'Masculine hono[u]r depends upon feminine shame, or modesty, and a man therefore depends upon the good behaviour of his womenfolk as guarantee of his public esteem.'[12]

---

12 David Gilmore, *Aggression and Community: Paradoxes of Andalusian Culture* (New Haven and London: Yale University Press, 1987), p. 127.

In Act 3, Scene 1, matters come to a head when Juan and his sisters find Yerma at the house of Dolores, the conjuror. For Juan, Yerma's nightly outings are a cause of dishonour, but his resentment of his wife, it seems, runs deeper still. When Dolores defends Yerma by saying she has done nothing wrong, Juan vents frustrations that have built up since the start of their marriage: 'Lo está haciendo desde el mismo día de la boda. Mirándome con dos agujas, pasando las noches en vela con los ojos abiertos al lado mío y llenando de malos suspiros mis almohadas' ['She's been wrong since the day we got married. Looking daggers at me, awake all night with her eyes wide open by my side and filling my pillows with unhappy sighs'] (OC, II, p. 862). His protestations, of course, however revelatory of his personal suffering, unwittingly reveal his lack of understanding of Yerma's predicament and his general insensitivity to what is, deep down, her grief at her childlessness. In Act 2, Scene 2, Juan responded just as insensitively to his wife's distress. 'Quiero beber agua', she explained, 'y no hay vaso de agua, quiero subir al monte y no tengo pies, quiero bordar mis enaguas y no encuentro los hilos' ['I want to drink water but there's no glass or water, I want to climb the hill, but I have no feet, I want to embroider my petticoats, but I can't find my thread'] (OC, II, p. 845). But Juan's response only rubbed salt in the wound and shifted the focus back to his own anxieties about his reputation: 'Lo que pasa es que no eres una mujer verdadera y buscas la ruina de un hombre sin voluntad' ['The truth is you are not a real woman and you're trying to ruin a helpless man'] (OC, II, p. 845).

In Act 3, Scene 1, the question of honour returns to confound Juan's expressions of helplessness and personal hurt which, otherwise, might have drawn our sympathy. 'Yo no puedo más' ['I can't stand it anymore'] (OC, II, p. 862)', he exclaims. 'Porque se necesita ser de bronce para ver a tu lado una mujer que te quiere meter los dedos dentro del corazón y que se sale de noche fuera de su casa, ¿en busca de qué? ¡Dime!, buscando qué? Las calles están llenas de machos. En las calles no hay flores que cortar' ['You'd have to be made of bronze to put up with a woman who wants to jab her fingers into your heart and who goes out at night, looking for what? Tell me! Looking for what? The streets are full of men. There aren't any flowers to pick in the streets'] (OC, II, p. 862). Such is Juan's obsession with what people might say, that it renders him blind to the connections Yerma is seeking with him in her heart-felt explanations. 'Te busco a ti. Te busco a ti, es a ti a quien busco día y noche, sin encontrar sombra donde respirar. Es tu sangre y tu amparo lo que deseo' ['It's you I'm looking for. I'm looking for you, it's you I look for night and day, without finding any shade where to draw breath. It's your blood, your help I want'] (OC, II, p. 863).

Lorca has Yerma defend her honour here and throughout the play: 'Si pudiera dar voces también las daría yo para que se levantaran hasta los muertos y vieran esta limpieza que me cubre' ['If I could shout I would to rouse even the dead so that they could see the purity in which I'm covered'] (OC, II, p. 862); 'Haz conmigo lo que quieras, que soy tu mujer, pero guárdate de poner nombre de varón en mis pechos' ['Do with me what you will, I'm your wife, but take care not to pin another man's name on my breasts'] (OC, II, p. 863). Despite Juan's bewilderment and suspicions, Yerma will not betray him. As she tells María, in Act 2, Scene 2, even if Juan and his sisters are right to think that she likes another man, 'lo primero de mi casta es la honradez' ['in my family, honour comes first'] (OC, II, p. 849). In a first encounter with Vieja 1ª (First Old Woman), in Act 1, Scene 2, Yerma admits to this passer-by that she has never felt aroused by Juan. She did, however, feel something of the sort when, on one occasion, Víctor lifted her in his arms to cross a ditch when she was just fourteen. Later, in Act 2, Scene 2, when Víctor announces that he is leaving the community to join his brothers at his father's behest, Yerma reminds him of this intimate moment in their youth: 'Siendo zagalón me llevaste una vez en brazos, ¿no recuerdas?' ['When you were a strapping young lad, you once carried me in your arms, don't you remember?'] (OC, II, p. 853). And yet, despite the love interest that Víctor represents, at no point does Lorca allow Yerma to be tempted to lie with him and betray her husband, even though doing so might bring her the child she so desires. 'No soy una casada indecente' ['I'm not an inmoral wife'] (OC, II, p. 859), she tells Dolores and Vieja 1ª; 'pero yo sé que los hijos nacen del hombre y de la mujer. ¡Ay, si los pudiera tener yo sola!' ['but I know that children are born of a man and a woman. Oh, if only I could have them all by myself!'] (OC, II, p. 859).

Yerma's conformity with the values of her community is self-evident, in her attachment to fidelity and, of course, to the vocation of motherhood itself. Although society's expectation that women will marry and have children cannot fully explain the intensity of frustrated desire with which Lorca has endowed Yerma, it is a factor, nonetheless. After five years of marriage, Juan may have forgotten all about having children, but not so Yerma: 'Los hombres tienen otra vida: los ganados, los árboles, las conversaciones, y las mujeres no tenemos más que esta de la cría y el cuido de la cría' ['Men have another life: their flocks, trees, conversations, we women have only children and caring for children'] (OC, II, p.

844). Yerma's words are a reminder of women's exclusion from the public sphere, even though she says them here not so much to challenge the restriction of women to the private and domestic domain as to emphasize how important it is to her and all women to have children. Indeed, we see early on in the play that Yerma, despite her childlessness, cannot help but act and think like a mother. Surrounded by characters who are, or who are due to become, mothers – all of which foregrounds her own lack – Lorca ensures there is plenty of opportunity for Yerma to make known her views on motherhood as well as lament her childless condition. When, in Act 1, Scene 1, her friend, María, who is expecting a child, notes how people say 'que con los hijos se sufre mucho' ['you suffer a lot with children'] (OC, II, p. 813), Yerma's indignation is telling: 'Mentira. Eso lo dicen las madres débiles, las quejumbrosas. ¿Para qué los tienen?' ['That's a lie. That's what weak and whiny mothers say. Why do they have them?'] (OC, II, p. 813). In Yerma's view, a mother's suffering is healthy, beautiful and an integral part of her role: 'Tener un hijo no es tener un ramo de rosas. Hemos de sufrir para verlos crecer. Yo pienso que se nos va la mitad de nuestra sangre. Pero esto es bueno, sano, hermoso. Cada mujer tiene sangre para cuatro o cinco hijos, y cuando no los tienen se les vuelve veneno, como me va a pasar a mí' ['Having children isn't like getting a bunch of roses. We have to suffer to see them grow. I think we lose half our blood in the process. But that's good, healthy, beautiful. Each woman has enough blood for four or five children, and when they don't have any it turns to poison, as is going to be the case with me'] (OC, II, p. 813).

Similarly, in Act 1, Scene 2, Lorca has Yerma chide Muchacha 1ª [First Girl] for leaving her child asleep at home all alone. Yerma lectures her on just how vulnerable small children are: 'es que no os dais cuenta lo que es un niño pequeño. La causa que nos parece más inofensiva puede acabar con él. Una agujita, un sorbo de agua' ['it's just that you don't realize what a small child is. What might seem to us the most harmless thing could do away with him. A tiny needle, a sip of water'] (OC, II, p. 822). Muchacha 2ª [Second Girl] challenges Yerma and emphasizes instead the burden for women of having children: 'Si tuvieras cuatro o cinco, no hablarías así' ['If you had four or five, you wouldn't talk this way'] (OC, II, p. 823). Like Yerma, this young woman has no children; unlike Yerma, she sees her childlessness as a blessing: 'De todos modos, tú y yo, con no tenerlos, vivimos más tranquilas' ['In any case, you and I, as we don't have any, can live a more tranquil life'] (OC, II, p. 823). Yerma's indignation at the girl's attitude confirms the traditional view she has of the integral connection between marriage and motherhood: '¿Por qué te has casado?' ['Why did you get married?'] (OC, II, p. 823). The girl's reply, by contrast, reveals a less than traditional attitude on her part. The fact is that, like every other young woman, including Yerma, she was simply married off. 'Si seguimos así', Muchacha 2ª adds wryly, 'no va a haber solteras más que las niñas' ['If things continue like this, the only single women will be little girls'] (OC, II, p. 823). And as for the institution of marriage itself, she sees no point in it. All it really means is that she now finds herself, at nineteen years of age, having to do the cooking and washing, both of which she hates. She complains: 'pues todo el día he de estar haciendo lo que no me gusta. ¿Y para qué? ¿Qué necesidad tiene mi marido de ser marido? Porque lo mismo hacíamos de novios que ahora. Tonterías de los viejos' ['so all day long I have to do things I don't like. And what for? Why does my husband have to be my husband? Before we were married, we used to do the same things as we do now. It's just old people's nonsense'] (OC, II, pp. 823–24). Muchacha 2ª suggests that Yerma might think her mad, but what she has learnt from life is that 'toda la gente está metida dentro de sus casas haciendo lo que no le gusta. Cuánto mejor se está en medio de la calle' ['everyone's stuck indoors doing things they don't want to do. It's so much better to be outside'] (OC, II, p. 824). Yerma, still indignant, tells her not to say such things and dismisses her as being a little girl. But, in effect, this 'little girl' has voiced complaints that represent major issues for women; not only the extreme pressure women feel to bear children, but the limitations that marriage places on their personal choices and freedoms, banishing them to the home and a life of domestic servitude. That Yerma should ignore most of what Muchacha 2ª says is a consequence of her fixation with motherhood. She is far more interested in finding out about the herbal remedies and prayers that the girl's mother has recourse to in the hope that her daughter will one day fall pregnant. In any case, Yerma, despite her suffering, is resigned to her marriage. As she later puts it to Juan, 'Vivo sumisa a ti, y lo que sufro lo guardo pegado a mis carnes' ['I'm always submissive to you and I keep my suffering to myself'] (OC, II, p. 843).

Lorca uses Muchacha 2ª as a foil to highlight Yerma's obsession with motherhood along with the conformity that defines her. Yet it is not long before Yerma's frustrations bring her to a position that is closer to the young girl's. Life indoors quickly becomes unbearable for Yerma as she begins to feel the limitations of her marriage more acutely, not only in terms of her childlessness but also the little affection and understanding she receives from her husband. While it is never clear whether Yerma or Juan (or indeed both of them) suffer from infertility, in the final scene of the play (Act 3, Scene 2), set on the site of a shrine where a pilgrimage quickly turns into a fertility rite, Yerma meets an old pagan woman who points the finger of blame squarely at Juan:

> Ni su padre, ni su abuelo, ni su bisabuelo se portaron como hombres de casta. Para tener un hijo ha sido necesario que se junte el cielo con la tierra. Están hechos con saliva. En cambio, tu gente no. Tienes hermanos y primos a cien leguas a la redonda. Mira qué maldición ha venido a caer sobre tu hermosura (OC, II, p. 874).

> [Neither his father, nor his grandfather, nor his great-grandfather conducted themselves like men of good stock. Heaven and earth had to come together for them to have a child. They're made of saliva. On the other hand, for your people it was different. You have brothers and cousins for a hundred leagues around. Look what curse has come to fall on your beauty.]

The possible causes of Yerma's and Juan's childlessness are, however, less important than the impact of childlessness on their relationship. For, whatever its origins, it provokes a crisis of identity in Yerma and, most painfully of all, undermines her sense of womanhood. Her traditional view that a woman's vocation is to become a mother makes this inevitable, just as it is inevitable that the idea that marriage is the only proper setting to have children will shake the foundations of her childless marriage with Juan.

At the end of Act 1, when Lorca has Juan chide Yerma for using foul language because he considers it to be unbecoming of a woman, his words elicit a response from Yerma that comes from a place of deep hurt and confusion: 'Ojalá fuera yo una mujer' ['If only I were a woman'] (OC, II, p. 830). Then, in Act 2, Scene 2, when Juan angrily voices his disapproval of Yerma's absences from the home, Lorca has her retaliate by claiming that the obligation to stay at home which Juan might normally expect of a wife is no longer applicable given that theirs is not a normal marriage:

> Justo. Las mujeres dentro de sus casas. Cuando las casas no son tumbas. Cuando las sillas se rompen y las sábanas de hilo se gastan con el uso. Pero aquí, no. Cada noche, cuando me acuesto, encuentro mi cama más nueva, más reluciente, como si estuviera recién traída de la ciudad (OC, II, pp. 842–43).

> [You're right. A woman in her home. But that's when her home isn't a tomb. When chairs break and sheets wear out with use. But not here,

no. Each night, when I go to bed, the bed seems newer, shinier, as if it had just been brought from town.]

When Juan finally tires of her challenges and tells her not to engage in conversation with anyone but remember she is a married woman, Yerma's exasperation is summed up in one ironic exclamation: '¡Casada!' ['Married!'] (OC, II, p. 845).

As in *Bodas de sangre*, the very conventions intended to maintain order fail the characters. Despite seeing the limitations of her marriage, Yerma cannot entertain the thought of leaving Juan or of having a child by any other man. 'No lo quiero, no lo quiero' ['I don't love him, I don't love him'] (OC, II, p. 859), she tells Dolores, 'y, sin embargo, es mi única salvación. Por honra y por casta. Mi única salvación' ['and yet he is my only salvation. For honour and for family. My only salvation'] (OC, II, p. 859). When, in the play's final scene, the old pagan woman invites Yerma to leave Juan for her son, Yerma's refusal is unequivocal:

¡Calla, calla, si no es eso! Nunca lo haría. Yo no puedo ir a buscar. ¿Te figuras que puedo conocer otro hombre? ¿Dónde pones mi honra? El agua no se puede volver atrás ni la luna llena sale a mediodía. Vete. Por el camino que voy seguiré. ¿Has pensado en serio que yo me pueda doblar a otro hombre? ¿Qué yo vaya a pedirle lo que es mío como una esclava? Conóceme, para que nunca me hables más. Yo no busco. (OC, II, p. 875)

[Be quiet, be quiet, it's not that! I would never do that. I can't go looking. Do you think I could have another man? What about my honour? Water can't flow back from where it's come nor can the moon come out at midday. Go away. I'll continue on the path I'm on. Did you really think that I could yield to another man? That I could ask him for what is mine like some slave? Know who I am, so that you never speak to me again. I'm not looking.]

Once again, Yerma refers to her honour, but the words Lorca gives her also have feminist echoes with their insistence that she will not, for anything, submit herself to the will of another man. In essence, Yerma, unable to leave Juan, will, at the very least, be the owner of her own sorrow. She will not barter it away even in the hope of being given a child. Her insistence in this respect becomes desperately clear at the play's tragic end. Juan, displaying more affection than Lorca has allowed him to do at any time, insists that it is Yerma whom he wants and that together they can be happy without children. This is not what Yerma wants to hear. Resigned to her condition which, echoing the old pagan woman, she now refers to as being *marchita* or barren (also the literal meaning in Spanish of her name, Yerma), Lorca has her strangle Juan and thus put an end to any hope that she will one day become a mother.

Lorca began writing *La casa de Bernarda Alba*, the third play of his trilogy, in 1935. He completed it in 1936, although it would not be performed until 1945, in Buenos Aires. Divided into three acts, it centres on the authoritarian rule of a mother, Bernarda Alba, over her five daughters: Angustias, Magdalena, Amelia, Martirio and Adela. After her husband's funeral, Bernarda imposes eight years of mourning on her daughters during which time all but the eldest, Angustias (Bernarda's daughter from a previous marriage), are forbidden to marry. Bernarda's fanatical notions of modesty and decency mean that her daughters are also forbidden to leave the house or have any sort of contact with men. The notion of honour that compelled Juan to restrict his wife's movements in *Yerma* now finds its most extreme expression in Lorca's creation of Bernarda and her draconian rules.

With *La casa de Bernarda Alba*, 'Lorca's concentration on women reaches its climax'.[13] There are no men on stage, and there are only third-person references to the play's principal male figure, Pepe el Romano. The figure of Pepe el Romano is, nonetheless, crucial. At once engaged to Angustias, the object of Martirio's infatuation, and the lover of Bernarda's youngest daughter Adela, he is the catalyst for the conflict that takes place in the house. Despite his physical absence from the stage, Pepe's figure looms large as the play explores Bernarda's daughters' emotional torment and their competition with one another to be with him. Absent in body, his persona and, with it, the desires he represents are aggrandized. As Bernarda's eighty-year-old mother, María Josefa, exclaims during one of her delirious yet revelatory turns, 'Pepe el Romano es un gigante. Todas lo queréis. Pero él os va a devorar porque vosotras sois granos de trigo. No granos de trigo. ¡Ranas sin lengua!' ['Pepe el Romano is a giant. You all want him. But he will devour you all because you are but grains of wheat. Not grains of wheat. Frogs without tongues!'] (OC, II, p. 1058). And devour them he does, the rising passions and tensions in the house culminating in Adela taking her own life in the belief that her mother has shot and killed her lover. Yet in the midst of it all, Bernarda is more responsible than Pepe el Romano or any other character – in this or, indeed, in the other plays in the trilogy – for

---

[13] Felicity Rosslyn, 'Lorca and Greek Tragedy', *The Cambridge Quarterly*, 29.3 (2000), 215–36 (p. 228).

propelling events towards their tragic conclusion. The characterization of Bernarda is all-important, with the play's focus of blame on a single, despotic figure distinguishing it from *Bodas de sangre* and *Yerma* where the source of tragedy is more diffuse.

Despite the fact that Lorca subtitled his play *Drama de mujeres en los pueblos de España* [*Drama of Women in the Villages of Spain*] and included an advisory note to indicate that its three acts are intended as 'un documental fotográfico' ['a photographic documentary'] (OC, II, p. 973), it is not clear that the extreme circumstances portrayed in *La casa de Bernarda* are a wholly accurate depiction of women's reality in Spain. For a start, Lorca took as his inspiration for Bernarda the very specific case of one Frasquita Alba Sierra who lived with her family in the village of Asquerosa where Lorca had spent part of his childhood.[14] Frasquita, moreover, was just a starting point for Bernarda who, as Gibson (1989, p. 437) notes, is 'a grotesque magnification' of the former resident of Asquerosa. Against the background of the Second Republic's concern with women's rights, Lorca's employment of a large dose of dramatic licence helped to drive home his point about the limitations women traditionally faced. But the magnification of Frasquita's 'domineering temperament' (Gibson 1989, p. 436) in Bernarda, along with the concentration of blame for the play's tragic outcome in this single, despotic figure, suggest that *La casa de Bernarda* was also informed by other contemporary concerns. 'It cannot have been by chance', writes Gibson (1989, p. 437), 'that Lorca wrote a play on the theme of despotism at a time when everyone with any sense knew there was a very real possibility of a right-wing *coup* in Spain.'

Traditional views of women were, of course, bound up with the ideology of Spain's ultra-conservative right. So, the play's focus on women is not inconsistent with the broader political implications of its pronouncement in favour of individual liberty at a time when tensions in the country were running high and political views were becoming increasingly polarized.

---

14 Frasquita and her family lived next door to Lorca's cousins and across the street from where Lorca's father had bought his first house in the village. Like Bernarda, Frasquita was a widow who remarried. She had three children by her first marriage and another four by her second. Yet, although Frasquita may have been 'a woman of domineering temperament' (Gibson 1989, p. 436), she and her family served only as a starting point for Lorca, as did the other real-life figures who inspired characters in the play (see Gibson 1989, pp. 436–37). Moreover, Frasquita died a year before her second husband and therefore 'could at no time have ruled as a widow over the children of both marriages' (Gibson 1989, p. 436), as Bernarda does.

At this critical moment in Spain's history, 'Lorca's theatre', as David Johnston puts it, 'becomes a site of cultural resistance to simplistic politics, with its accompanying social weapon of crude opprobrium'.[15]

At one level, Bernarda is, like Madre in *Bodas de sangre*, an example of a woman who reproduces patriarchal law, morality and prejudice. Bernarda's views on women, particularly when it comes to their relations with the opposite sex, are not unfamiliar, reprising the ultra-conservative attitudes we see in both *Bodas de sangre* and *Yerma*. 'Las mujeres en la iglesia no deben de mirar más hombre que al oficiante' ['Women in church ought to look at no man other than the priest'] (OC, II, p. 981), she opines on learning that Pepe el Romano has been spotted at her husband's funeral; 'y ese porque tiene faldas. Volver la cabeza es buscar el calor de la pana' ['and only then because he is dressed in skirts. To turn one's head is to seek the heat in corduroy trousers'] (OC, II, p. 981). And when Bernarda reaffirms her authority in face of her daughter Magdalena's early irritation at the thought of being shut away for eight years with little else to do than embroider her trousseau, she does so in terms that defer to the traditional division between the sexes: 'Aquí se hace lo que yo mando. Ya no puedes ir con el cuento a tu padre. Hilo y aguja para las hembras. Látigo y mula para el varón' ['Here you do what I say. You can't go telling tales to your father now. Needle and thread for the girls. The whip and mule for the boys'] (OC, II, p. 986). Bernarda is also beset by the same seemingly petty concerns about appearances that we saw in Yerma's husband and that ultimately serve to silence women. Whatever troubles there might be at home, what is important to Bernarda is that they should remain within the walls of her house. Ultimately, she seems less concerned about her daughters' feelings than about keeping up appearances, convinced that the residents of her village would like nothing more than to see her family fall into moral decline. When, in Act 3, Angustias is reluctant to make peace with Martirio after her sister stole her photograph of Pepe el Romano from beneath her pillow, Bernarda's primary concern is that her family maintain a façade of unity and respectability: 'Cada uno sabe lo que piensa por dentro. Yo no me meto en los corazones, pero quiero buena fachada y armonía familiar' ['Each person knows what they think inside. I don't pry into people's hearts, but I want a united front and family harmony'] (OC, II, p. 1046). Honour and shame are what matter most,

---

15 David Johnston, 'The Cultural Engagement of Stage Translation: García Lorca in Performance', in *Voices in Translation: Bridging Cultural Divides*, ed. by Gunilla Anderman (Clevedon: Multilingual Matters, 2007) pp. 78–93 (p. 80).

and Bernarda believes that any error of judgment, once made public, is irreparable. Thus, towards the play's conclusion, when Adela locks herself in her bedroom before taking her own life, Bernarda reminds her that she now has nowhere to hide: 'Abre. No creas que los muros defienden de la vergüenza' ['Open the door. Don't think that the walls can hide your shame'] (OC, II, p. 1065).

Bernarda's concern with honour extends to other members of the household; for, however fanatical Bernarda may be, the convention is deeply rooted in the community and each member stands to suffer from another's tarnished reputation. Thus, it is also in the interest of La Poncia, the head maid, that Adela keep away from her eldest sister's fiancé. She reminds Adela in Act 2 that she has her eye on her: '¡Velo! Para que las gentes no escupan al pasar de pronto por esta puerta' ['I'm keeping watch! So that people won't end up spitting when they pass our door'] (OC, II, p. 1015). La Poncia may not have the authority that Bernarda has over her daughters, but she does, like her employer, have a reputation to protect: 'No os tengo ley a ninguna, pero quiero vivir en casa decente. ¡No quiero mancharme de vieja!' ['I don't have loyalty towards any of you, but I want to live in a decent house. I don't want to be tainted in my old age!'] (OC, II, p. 1015). Lorca shows that, as ever, the honour code affects women disproportionately, the bar of expectation being significantly lower for men. As La Poncia remarks to Criada [Maid] in Act 3, 'No es toda la culpa de Pepe el Romano. Es verdad que el año pasado anduvo detrás de Adela y estaba loca por él, pero ella debió estarse en su sitio y no provocarlo. Un hombre es un hombre' ['It's not all Pepe el Romano's fault. It's true that he went after Adela last year and that she was crazy for him, but she ought to have kept her place and not provoked him. After all, a man is a man'] (OC, II, p. 1054). For La Poncia, men's 'natural' weakness makes it all the more important that a woman demonstrate moral fortitude. Hence her advice to Adela, in Act 2, to leave her sister, Angustias, in peace, adding that 'si Pepe el Romano te gusta, te aguantas' ['if you like Pepe el Romano, keep it to yourself'] (OC, II, p. 1014).

There are other moments in the play where Lorca brings to the fore the injustices women face. For example, there is the early exchange, in Act 1, between Amelia and Martirio, on the subject of their friend Adelaida. The reason Adelaida was not at their father's funeral, it transpires, is that her fiancé would not let her out of the house. Adelaida's story is, by now, all too familiar: 'Antes era alegre; ahora ni polvos echa en la cara' ['She used to be happy; now she doesn't even powder her face'] (OC, II, p. 992). She is, moreover, a victim of hearsay – 'De todo tiene la culpa esta crítica que no nos deja vivir' ['It's all the fault of this gossip that doesn't let us live'] (OC, II, p. 993) – even though, if the gossip is to be believed, it is her father who should bear all the shame rather than she or anyone else. For, according to Bernarda, he murdered the husband of his first wife in order to marry her, and if he is not in prison for this crime, it is because, as Martirio argues, 'los hombres se tapan unos a otros las cosas de esta índole y nadie es capaz de delatar' ['men cover up these sorts of things for one another and no one is ever prepared to speak up'] (OC, II, p. 993). Adelaida's father was, moreover, a philanderer. After abandoning his first wife for another woman, he remarried and had an affair with his second wife's daughter – none other than Adelaida's mother, whom he married when his second wife, driven to madness, died. Both her grandmother and mother were, therefore, at some point, Adelaida's father's spouse. A sordid tale, perhaps; but one in which Adelaida herself is blameless. And yet it is still she who is forbidden to go out because of her fiancé's fears that, if she did venture from the home, history would somehow repeat itself.

Little wonder, then, that Lorca should have Martirio conclude that she is better off without a man. Enrique Humanes, the one man rumoured to have been her suitor, went off with a woman whom Amelia thinks 'fea como un demonio' ['ugly as sin'] (OC, II, p. 994). At this comment, Martirio's damning view of men surfaces again and with it her bitter acknowledgment of the limited prospects awaiting most women: '¡Qué les importa a ellos la fealdad! A ellos les importa la tierra, las yuntas, y una perra sumisa que les dé de comer' ['They don't care about ugliness! All they care about is land, oxen, and a submissive bitch who'll give them their food'] (OC, II, p. 994). 'Nacer mujer es el mayor castigo' ['To be born a woman is the greatest punishment'] (OC, II, p. 1020), laments Amelia later, in Act 2, as she speaks out against the double standards that make it perfectly acceptable for La Poncia to pay for her son to have sex because 'Los hombres necesitan estas cosas' ['Men need this sort of thing'] (OC, II, p. 1020), while, as Magdalena points out, women are not even allowed to look at the opposite sex: 'ni nuestros ojos siquiera nos pertenecen' ['not even our eyes are our own'] (OC, II, p. 1020). 'Se les perdona todo' ['They are forgiven everything'] (OC, II, p. 1020), complains Adela; and, by implication, women are forgiven nothing at all. How significant, therefore, that the principal example of female sexuality, other than Adela's passionate desire for Pepe el Romano, should be the wanton behaviour of one Paca la Roseta who, La Poncia alleges in Act 1, wilfully had sex with a group of men who carried her off to the olive groves at night after tying her husband to a tree. Lorca shows us how, in the popular imaginary, female desire, when not censored altogether, is exiled to the realms of the forbidden or downright indecent, making it always – to reprise Adela's words – unforgivable. He reminds us, in other words, that there is no middle ground, no healthy acceptance, no possibility of its normalization or recognition, and no chance, ultimately, of forgiveness. Unsurprisingly, the account of Paca la Roseta that Lorca puts into the mouth of La Poncia is both lurid and judgmental. 'Dicen que llevaba los pechos fuera' ['They say she had her breasts out'] (OC, II, p. 989), La Poncia tells Bernarda, 'y Maximiliano la llevaba cogida como si tocara la guitarra. ¡Un horror!' ['and Maximiliano held her in his arms as if he were playing a guitar. Dreadful!'] (OC, II, p. 989). Then, when they returned the next morning, 'Paca la Roseta traía el pelo suelto y una corona de flores en la cabeza' ['Paca la Roseta wore her hair loose and a crown of flowers on her head'] (OC, II, p. 989). Bernarda can only conclude that Paca la Roseta is the one bad woman in the village, the woman's anomalous status confirmed when La Poncia reminds Bernarda that she is not originally from the village anyway. Paca la Roseta, therefore, is an exception; so too, her behaviour, which transgresses all the codes of modesty and decency.

As unforgivable, if not more so, than Paca la Roseta's behaviour is the crime committed by La Librada's daughter, an unmarried woman who kills her baby and buries it under rocks in order to hide her shame, not knowing who its father is. When her crime is discovered after dogs dig up the infant corpse, Lorca has the whole village, bar Adela, bay for her blood. Without question, the young woman has committed a crime, but she is also a victim of the codes that drive women to such desperate acts. La Librada might not inspire sympathy in anyone other than Adela, but the savage reaction that Lorca attributes to the unforgiving villagers, including Martirio – 'Que pague lo que debe' ['May she pay what she owes'] (OC, II, p. 1039) – and Bernarda – 'y que pague la que pisotea su decencia' ['and may she who tramples on her modesty pay the price'] (OC, II, p. 1039); '¡Matadla! ¡Matadla!' ['Kill her! Kill her!'] (OC, II, p. 1039) – makes clear that she does deserve our sympathy after all.

Just as we are compelled to feel sympathy for the plight faced by La Librada's daughter, so too are we moved by the dilemmas of so many of the characters of Lorca's trilogy who are similarly victims of the codes they are bound to follow and profess. We can even forgive the petulant tantrums of Bernarda's daughters who are set against one another by their mother's wholly unreasonable rules. But when it comes to Bernarda, her case is altogether different. For while she may have something in common with Madre in *Bodas de sangre* who, like her, internalizes and reproduces patriarchal law, Bernarda, unlike Madre, is cast unequivocally as a tyrant and, as such, is inseparable from the oppressive instinct and bigotry she displays. We can, for example, at least try to understand Martirio's condemnation of La Librada's daughter; after all, Martirio is a young, impressionable woman whose judgment is possibly no more than a displacement of her own deep-set frustrations. Yet, by contrast, the venom Lorca injects into Bernarda's verbal assault is shocking and betrays an intolerance and insensitivity on her part that make it near impossible to make allowances for her. 'Sí' ['Yes'], she cries, 'que vengan todos con varas de olivo y mangos de azadones, que vengan todos para matarla' ['let them all come with olive branches and hoes, let them all come to kill her'] (OC, II, p. 1038). In a play in which, incidentally, black and white are the colours that dominate – the whitewashed walls of the house and the black clothes of the women in mourning – there is no ambiguous grey area but, instead, wrong and right, set in diametric opposition. Bernarda, symbol of denial and oppression, occupies the former position, while Adela, symbol of desire and freedom, occupies the latter.[16] And importantly, in her position at the opposite pole to Bernarda, Adela suffers none of the internal conflict that afflicts either Novia or Yerma who struggled to break free from the conventions of honour and decency. Adela is a naïve and pure expression of liberty and desire, the counterpoint to the despotism embodied by the figure of Bernarda and a foil to her insensitivity and intransigence.

Lorca establishes Bernarda's entirely despotic credentials early on in the play. Our first glimpse of her is in the opening interaction between La Poncia and Criada as they clean and prepare the house to receive the mourners from her husband's funeral. The maids, naturally focused on domestic matters, characterize Bernarda as penny-pinching, domineering and demanding. '¡Quisiera que ahora, que no come ella, que todos nos muriéramos de hambre! ¡Mandona!' ['As she doesn't eat, she'd have us all die of hunger. The bossy boots!'] (OC, II, p. 974), La Poncia complains, tempted to eat the bread and chorizo reserved for the guests. And she exhorts Criada to make sure the place is spotless, acutely aware of Bernarda's impossible standards: 'Si Bernarda no ve relucientes las cosas

---

[16] 'Visually too the play's palette of black and white may serve to evoke the colour scheme of a black and white photograph' (Delgado, p. 106). Delgado (p. 106) also sees in the 'painterly manner' of Lorca's use of colour in *La casa de Bernarda Alba* a debt to Strindberg's *Miss Julie* and Wedekind's *Spring Awakening*.

me arrancará los pocos pelos que me quedan' ['If Bernarda doesn't find everything sparkling clean, she'll tear the last hairs from my head'] (OC, II, p. 975). 'Tirana de todos los que la rodean' ['Tyrannical over all that's around her'] (OC, II, p. 975), she adds. 'Es capaz de sentarse encima de tu corazón y ver cómo te mueres durante un año sin que se le cierre esa sonrisa fría que lleva en su maldita cara' ['She's capable of plonking herself on your heart and watching you die the whole year long without ever wiping that cold smile from her damned face'] (OC, II, p. 975). Thus, when Bernarda finally appears, it comes as no surprise that Lorca should have her immediately criticize her maids' preparations. 'Menos gritos y más obras' ['Less shouting and more work'] (OC, II, p. 979), Bernarda says, chastising Criada. 'Debías haber procurado que todo esto estuviera más limpio para recibir al duelo' ['You ought to have ensured the place was cleaner for the mourners'] (OC, II, p. 979).

The next comments uttered by Bernarda reveal her dreadful class snobbery. Still expressing her dissatisfaction with Criada's work, Bernarda explains her maid's shortcomings in terms that betray a brutal and bigoted view of the world: 'Los pobres son como los animales. Parece como si estuvieran hechos de otras sustancias' ['The poor are like animals. It seems they are made of other stuff'] (OC, II, p. 979). When one of the guests suggests that the poor also experience feelings of sorrow, Bernarda's retort is equally blunt: 'Pero las olvidan delante un plato de garbanzos' ['But they forget them as soon as they're tucking into a chickpea stew'] (OC, II, p. 979).

In light of the polarization of political opinion in Spain and the Left's defence of the rights of workers and landless labourers in a country where the vast majority of households were made up of working-class or peasant families, that the theme of class should appear in *La casa de Bernarda Alba* is highly significant. Class, of course, impacts on all of the plays of the trilogy, since the dilemmas in which especially the female characters find themselves cannot be dissociated from the circumstances of the rural classes to which they belong and which would have been starkly different from those experienced, for example, by the urban middle class during the Second Republic. It is an issue that is foregrounded in *Bodas de sangre*, where it is precisely Leonardo's landless condition that makes him an unsuitable husband for Novia. But in *La casa de Bernarda Alba*, the issue of class is altogether more pronounced, compounding the negative characterization of a tyrannical woman who believes herself and her family to be better than everyone else. It is Bernarda's snobbery, we learn, that circumvented the possibility of marriage between Martirio and Enrique

Humanes. As Bernarda tells La Poncia in Act 2, '¡Mi sangre no se junta con la de Humanes mientras yo viva! Su padre fue gañán' ['My blood will not mix with that of the Humanes family for as long as I live! His father was a labourer'] (OC, II, p. 1032). No one in the neighbourhood is good enough for her daughters. 'No hay en cien leguas a la redonda quien se pueda acercar a ellas' ['There's no one for one hundred leagues around who can come close to them'] (OC, II, p. 991), Bernarda tells La Poncia in Act 1, adding that 'Los hombres de aquí no son de su clase. ¿Es que quieres que las entregue a cualquier gañan?' ['The men around here are not of their class. Would you have me give them to any old labourer?'] (OC, II, p. 991). And when La Poncia suggests, impertinently, that in other parts her daughters might seem relatively poor, Bernarda reacts angrily, reminding La Poncia of her place and that what they have together is not friendship but a contractual relationship: 'Me sirves y te pago. ¡Nada más!' ['You serve me, and I pay you. Nothing more!'] (OC, II, p. 991).

Intolerant, intransigent, and a snob to boot, Bernarda is incapable of understanding the simplest of truths which, ironically, only La Poncia, her class inferior, seems able to articulate: 'Tus hijas están y viven como metidas en alacenas. Pero ni tú ni nadie puede vigilar por el interior de los pechos' ['Your daughters are and live as if they were shut away in a closet. But neither you nor anyone else can guard over what's inside their hearts'] (OC, II, p. 1051); 'Son mujeres sin hombre, nada más. En estas cuestiones se olvida hasta la sangre' ['They are women without men, nothing more. In such matters not even blood counts'] (OC, II, p. 1055). Bernarda, though, thinks she can seal her daughters off from the world and from worldly desire. She is incapable of understanding the irrepressible character of her daughters' emotions or ever countenancing the force of resistance that her draconian rules will meet.

Adela, for her part, demonstrates all the courage that her sister, Martirio, does not have. Martirio's reflex is to fall back on the codes in which she has been instructed: 'No es ese el sitio de una mujer honrada' ['This is not the place for a respectable woman to be'] (OC, II, p. 1059), she tells Adela when she spots her out in the yard. Adela, by contrast, will not give in: 'He visto la muerte debajo de estos techos', she tells her sister, 'y he salido a buscar lo que era mío, lo que me pertenecía' ['I've seen death beneath these roofs and I've gone out to look for what is mine, for what belongs to me'] (OC, II, p. 1060). Pepe el Romano may have been attracted by Angustias's wealth, but Adela knows that he loves her and no one else: 'Vino por el dinero, pero sus ojos los puso siempre en mí' ['He came for the money, but he only ever had eyes for me'] (OC, II, p. 1060).

Adela's desire for Pepe el Romano is reminiscent of the irrepressible force that sweeps Novia away in *Bodas de sange*, and it is cast in equally natural terms: 'Aquí no hay ningún remedio. La que tenga que ahogarse que se ahogue. Pepe el Romano es mío. Él me lleva a los juncos de la orilla' ['There's no other way. Whoever must drown will drown. Pepe el Romano is mine. He takes me to the reeds on the shore'] (OC, II, p. 1061). Unlike her mother, Adela is not afraid of what people might think or say. Moved by her indomitable passion, she is determined to be with Pepe el Romano even if he marries someone else. She will, moreover, display her love for him publicly, in defiance of the codes of modesty and decency:

> Ya no aguanto el horror de estos techos después de haber probado el sabor de su boca. Seré lo que el quiera que sea. Todo el pueblo contra mí, quemándome con sus dedos de lumbre, perseguida por los que dicen que son decentes, y me pondré la corona de espinas que tienen las que son queridas de algún hombre casado. (OC, II, p. 1062)
>
> [I can't stand the horror of living beneath this roof after tasting his mouth. I will be whatever he wants me to be. The whole village against me, burning me with their pointed fingers aflame, persecuted by those who call themselves decent, and I will wear the crown of thorns worn by the sweethearts of married men.]

Adela is speaking for herself here, but her pronouncement also speaks for women like Paca la Roseta and La Librada's daughter who either wilfully or out of desperation defy society's rules just as Adela defies Bernarda's. Her voice has even broader resonance when she counters her mother's insults after Martirio accuses her of sleeping with Pepe el Romano: '¡Aquí se acabaron las voces de presidio!' ['Enough of these jailer's words!'] (OC, II, p. 1063), she cries, before taking her mother's staff, breaking it in two and exclaiming 'Esto hago yo con la vara de la dominadora' ['This is how I treat the tyrant's rod'] (OC, II, p. 1063). Thus, Adela's actions are cast, in exemplary terms, as a defence against not just her mother's but, indeed, all tyranny.

In the very last moments of the play, the negative qualities Lorca attaches to Bernarda – her intolerance, intransigence and snobbery – combine to ensure that she makes a tragic miscalculation. After learning that Adela has been meeting Pepe el Romano in secret, she rushes to fetch her shotgun and shoots at him as he waits outside the house. Worst still, she insinuates that she has killed him when, in fact, she knows that he made his escape on horseback. It is, in the end, this lie that seals her youngest daughter's fate. Adela's final act of defiance is to take her own life rather than live without Pepe el Romano whom she now believes dead. This tragic moment is also the moment of Bernarda's ultimate failure as a mother, and yet her character is so flawed that she is unable, even at this point, to recognize her own culpability or to realize that the control she seeks is illusory. Instead, she falls back on the codes she unquestioningly lives by, insisting that Adela died a virgin and challenging those around her to say any different. Bernarda is so proud, observes Criada, 'que ella misma se pone una venda en los ojos' ['that she herself covers her eyes in a blindfold'] (OC, II, p. 1053). As was the case with Novia in *Bodas de sangre* and the eponymous protagonist of *Yerma*, the question of purity remains a priority even in the face of death. Yet, unlike Novia, Madre or Yerma, Bernarda does not draw our sympathy. The events of the play take place in the shadow of her tyranny; so, when her final command – '¡Silencio!' ['Silence!'] (OC, II, p. 1066) – brings the play to a close, it is not a victim of society's codes we hear, but rather a despot resorting, obstinately, to censorship.

The finale of *La casa de Bernarda Alba* clearly resonates with the political moment in Spain and seems to be premonitory of the silence that would later be imposed by the Francoist regime. 'Once again in this play', writes Felicity Rosslyn (p. 229), 'we see the fearful cost of control which refuses to compromise life itself.' And Rosslyn (p. 229) adds: 'Beyond the drama of Bernarda's family we see foreshadowed the fate of the whole of Spain, embarking in this same year on a civil war that will terminate in ferocious Fascist control, and require the silencing of all its major artists.'

All three plays in Lorca's rural trilogy deal, then, as we have seen, with real-life concerns. They 'synchronize with the feminist discourse of [the] day' and 'reflect the problems real Spanish women confronted in a highly misogynist milieu' (Johnson, pp. 252–53). Additionally, *La casa de Bernarda Alba* had particular resonance for the grave political moment in which Spain found itself in the mid-1930s. Even so, Lorca's concern in these plays for real-life issues did not preclude, as we have noted also with regard to his poetry, a continued interest in art in and of itself. The way he chose to approach the subject of his plays, or for that matter his poetry, was driven as much by aesthetic considerations as it was by his interest in real life affairs. Which may explain why Lorca's public pronouncements on the role of politics in art tend to be inconclusive, marking him neither as a pure aesthete nor as a committed political writer. It has even been reported, Nigel Dennis reminds us, that Lorca had 'doubts about the ability of any politically committed writer to write anything of serious literary value'.[17] Lorca insisted that he himself could never be a political writer. 'Yo nunca seré político' ['I'll never be political'], he exclaimed, according to the poet Dámaso Alonso, at a reading he gave to friends of his then newest play, *La casa de Bernarda Alba*. And he added: 'Yo soy revolucionario, porque no hay un verdadero poeta que no sea revolucionario. ¿No lo crees tú así? [...] Pero político no lo seré nunca, ¡nunca!' ['I'm a revolutionary because all true poets are revolutionary. Don't you agree? But political, that I'll never be, never!'] (cited by Dennis, p. 189). As Lorca himself appears to be suggesting here, being a revolutionary poet is not the same as being a revolutionary in the political sense. And yet, against the background of intense political polarization, his public pronouncements increasingly sounded politically partisan, even though, on closer inspection, they clearly stop short of being party-political.

Rather than the product of party politics or 'a specific political allegiance', Lorca's 'political' outlook is perhaps best characterized as emerging from 'an instinctive liberal humanitarianism, inspired by a sense of solidarity with all mankind' (Dennis, p. 188). Thus, when he criticizes nationalism in an interview he gave in 1936, he does so on the basis of this humanitarian spirit: 'Yo soy hermano de todos y execro al hombre que se sacrifica por una idea nacionalista abstracta por el solo hecho de que ama a su patria con una venda en sus ojos. [...] Desde luego no creo en la frontera política' ['I am everyone's brother and I loathe anyone who sacrifices themselves for an abstract nationalist idea simply because they love their country with a blindfold pulled over their eyes. [...] Naturally, I don't believe in political borders'] (*OC*, III, p. 683).

In the same interview, Lorca rejects art for art's sake and insists that, at this dramatic moment in time, 'el artista debe llorar y reír con su pueblo' ['artists must cry and laugh with their people'] (*OC*, III, p. 681). These might sound like the words of a committed socialist; after all, Lorca is quoted as saying elsewhere that he would always be on the side of the poor (see Gibson 1989, p. 396). But if Lorca's solidarity with the Romani people in *Romancero gitano* and with African Americans in *Poet en Nueva York* tells us anything, it is that his ability to 'cry and laugh' with the people did not in any way diminish his interest in matters artistic.

In 1934, Lorca gave an interview on the subject of his involvement with the state-sponsored student theatre group, La Barraca. In it, he shrugs off any worry that a change of government under the Republic might threaten the troupe's subvention. And, tellingly, he does so by placing his

---

17 Nigel Dennis, 'Politics', in Bonaddio (2007), pp. 170–89 (p. 188).

Figure 12 Lorca with the Barraca troupe in front of a tour bus in 1933

trust in a universal and self-evidently apolitical concept of the value of art – in this case, of Spanish classical theatre specifically: '¿qué Gobierno, cualquiera que sea su orientación política, va a desconocer la grandeza augusta del clásico teatro español, de nuestro mayor timbre de gloria, y no va a comprender que es el más seguro vehículo de la elevación cultural de todos los pueblos y habitantes de España?' ['what Government, whatever its political orientation, is not going to be aware of the august majesty of our Spanish classical theatre, of our most glorious mark of distinction, and not understand that it is the surest vehicle for the cultural elevation of every village and inhabitant of Spain?'] (OC, III, p. 596). La Barraca was a 'showpiece' of the Republic's 'enlightened cultural policies', and so its activities 'inevitably became charged with political meaning' (Dennis, p. 184). Yet, for Lorca, the work of the troupe, which allowed him to indulge his passion for the theatre, clearly had a significance that extended well beyond politics.

The same can be said of the plays of his rural trilogy which, for all their concern with real-life issues, retain a deeply poetic quality. 'El teatro que ha perdurado', declared Lorca in an interview for the theatre publication *Escena* in 1935, 'siempre es el de los poetas. Siempre ha estado el teatro en manos de los poetas. Y ha sido mejor el teatro en tanto más grande el poeta' ['The theatre that has lasted is always that of the poets. Theatre has always been in the hands of poets. And the greater the poet, the better the theatre'] (OC, III, p. 628). Lorca was referring here to dramatic and not lyric poets, and yet, in his own plays, it is, more often than not, the voice of the lyric poet we hear breaking through the dialogue. As Renée M. Silverman explains, 'Lorca turns the lyric into his preferred instrument for the sounding and silencing of desire's song, since lyric most directly plays the chords of passion, fantasy, and longing.'[18] Take, for example, Novia's emotional outpouring to Madre at the end of *Bodas de Sangre*, where ecphonesis, repetition and symbolism combine to heighten Novia's sense of helplessness in face of her indomitable desire:

> Yo era una mujer quemada, llena de llagas por dentro y por fuera, y tu hijo era un poquito de agua de la que yo esperaba hijos, tierra, salud; pero el otro era un río oscuro lleno de ramas, que acercaba a mí el rumor de sus juncos y su cantar entre dientes. Y yo corría con tu hijo que era como un niñito de agua, frío, y el otro me mandaba cientos de pájaros

---

18 Renée M. Silverman, 'The Lyric Performance of Tragedy in Federico García Lorca's *Blood Wedding*', *South Atlantic Review*, 74.3 (Summer 2009), 45–63 (p. 49).

que me impedían el andar y que dejaban escarcha sobre mis heridas de pobre mujer marchita, de muchacha acariciada por el fuego. Yo no quería, ¡óyelo bien!, yo no quería, ¡óyelo bien! Yo no quería. ¡Tu hijo era mi fin y yo no le he engañado, pero el brazo del otro me arrastró como un golpe de mar, como la cabezada de un mulo, y me hubiera arrastrado siempre, siempre, siempre, siempre, aunque hubiera sido vieja y todos los hijos de tu hijo me hubiesen agarrado de los cabellos! (OC, II, p. 796)

[I was a burnt woman, covered in wounds inside and out, and your son was a drop of water that I hoped would give me children, land, health; but the other man was a dark river filled with branches, who brought to me the sound of his reeds and murmuring song. And I ran with your son who was like a small child of the water, cold, and the other man sent hundreds of birds my way that prevented me from walking and left frost on the wounds of this poor withered woman, this girl caressed by fire that I am. I didn't want to, believe me! I didn't want to, believe me! I didn't want to. Your son was my purpose and I didn't deceive him, but the other man's arm threw me off course like the crash of the sea, like the headbutt of a mule, and he would have done so forever, ever, ever, ever, even in my old age and even if the sons of your son had pulled me back by the hair.]

In *Yerma*, there are echoes of the nature symbolism we find here in Novia's speech; for example, in Yerma's pithy yet indignant response, in Act 3, Scene 2, to the old pagan woman's offer to her of her son as a solution for her childlessness: 'Yo soy como un campo seco donde caben arando mil pares de bueyes y lo que tú me das es un pequeño vaso de agua de pozo. Lo mío es dolor que ya no está en las carnes' ['I am like a dry field large enough for a thousand oxen to plough and what you are giving me is a small glass of well water. Mine is a pain that exceeds the flesh'] (OC, II, p. 875). For Yerma, despite her personal anguish, the old woman's son is no more a solution than is Madre's son – that 'drop of water' – for Novia.

The lyrical quality of Yerma's lines renders them sufficiently enigmatic for them to be open to interpretation. Paul McDermid, for example, sees in Yerma's admission that hers is 'a pain that exceeds the flesh' evidence of Lorca's concern with 'an impossible, transcendent Love, and as such, universal.'[19] In McDermid's view, 'Yerma cannot physically have a child because it is not a child of flesh and blood she seeks. Rather, Yerma is

---

19 Paul McDermid, *Love, Desire and Identity in the Theatre of Federico García Lorca* (Woodbridge: Tamesis, 2007), p. 146.

motivated by the desire to transcend her material being and "reproduce" her Self on the symbolic plane of the soul' (McDermid, p. 146). In other words, frustrated in the material world, Yerma 'strives for union with an ideal' (McDermid, p. 149) – and McDermid cites numerous instances in Lorca's work where physical frustrations are similarly redirected onto a non-physical plane (for example, the Gitano nun and Preciosa in their corresponding poems in *Romancero gitano*). Thus, in Yerma's declaration to Maria, in Act 2, Scene 2, that 'Acabaré creyendo que yo misma soy mi hijo' ['I'll end up believing I'm my own child'] (OC, II, p. 848), the 'child', in McDermid's reading, becomes the very embodiment of Yerma's integrity, selfhood and becoming.

There are, of course, less arcane interpretations to be had. Yerma follows her declaration to María with an account of the chores she undertakes that are normally reserved for men: 'Muchas veces bajo yo a echar comida a los bueyes, que antes no lo hacía, porque ninguna mujer lo hace, y cuando paso por lo oscuro del cobertizo mis pasos me suenan a pasos de hombre' ['I often go down to feed the oxen, something I didn't do before, because no woman does, and as I make my way through the darkness of the shed my footsteps seem to me to be a man's'] (OC, II, p. 848). Here we see that Yerma is not only her own child but also takes on a man's role. If anything, what she seems to be communicating is her loneliness and her experience of a life led outside of the paradigm of the family unit (parents and child) that she considers normal. Perhaps, then, what we ought to understand by her shifting identities is that, from the perspective of her solitude, she can, at best, only imagine the family trinity she so desperately craves and [that she] herself plays the parts that a yet-to-be-born child and an uncaring husband (as Yerma sees Juan) cannot or will not.

Here and elsewhere, the possibility of coming to different interpretations is facilitated by the lyrical vein running through the play which, significantly, Lorca subtitled not a 'tragedy' (as he did *Bodas de sangre*) or even a 'drama' (as he did *La casa de Bernarda Alba*), but rather a 'tragic poem'. Beyond the particularities of Yerma's and Juan's relationship, the lyricism in *Yerma* also has resonances for the broader theme of sterility (often creative sterility) that extends across Lorca's poetic oeuvre. *Yerma*, like many of Lorca's poems, is an elegy to fecundity, lamenting its loss irrespective of who or what is the cause. This lament is reprised in a range of lyrical utterances in the play, in the form of songs, prayers, soliloquies and dialogue. For example, *Yerma* opens with a lullaby that, out of Yerma's mouth, becomes a passionate elegy to a child that is yet to be born. The desire to have children expressed here inevitably foregrounds Yerma's barrenness:

> Te diré, niño mío, que sí,
> tronchada y rota soy para ti.
> ¡Cómo me duele esta cintura
> donde tendrás tu primera cuna!
> ¿Cuándo, mi niño, vas a venir?
>
> ¡Cuando tu carne huela a jazmín! (OC, II, p. 808)

[I will say yes, my child, cut and broken I am for you. How painful my waist where you will have your first cradle! When, my child, will you come? When your flesh smells of jasmine!)

Appending an initial rendition of this stanza are lines that, in their use of fertility-symbols, epitomize this cradle song's poetic character: '¡Que se agiten las ramas al sol | y salten las fuentes alrededor!' ['Let the branches shake in the sun | and fountains spring forth all around!'] (OC, II, p. 808). Act 2 similarly opens with a song replete with symbolism. Sung by six washerwomen and interspersed by their gossiping on the subject of Yerma's sisters-in-law and whether or not she has been looking at another man, it contains allusions to the cycle of sexual union, fertility and birth: 'Dime si tu marido | guarda semilla | para que el agua cante | por tu camisa' ['Tell me if your husband has seed so that water may sing through your nightdress'] (OC, II, p. 837); 'Por el aire ya viene | mi marido a dormir, | Yo, alhelíes rojos | y él, rojo alhelí' ['With the breeze comes my husband to sleep, I, red wallflowers, and red wallflower he'] (OC, II, pp. 837–38); 'Hay que juntar flor con flor | cuando el verano seca la sangre del segador' ['Flower with flower must be joined when summer the reaper's blood has dried'] (OC, II, p. 838); 'Y abrir el vientre a pájaros sin sueño | cuando a la puerta llama temblando el invierno' ['And a belly open to sleepless birds when at the door winter calls all ashiver'] (OC, II, p. 838); 'Para que un niño funda | yertos vidrios del alba' ['So that a child may melt the stiff glass of the dawn'] (OC, II, p. 838).

The washerwomen's eulogy to fecundity, however, which also serves to reaffirm 'the basic assumptions and definitions of the community' (Silverman, p. 49), is soured by a brief lament – a couplet, once-repeated, reminding us of Yerma's despair: '¡Ay de la casada seca! | ¡Ay de la que tiene los pechos de arena!' ['Alas the barren wife! Alas she who has breasts of sand!'] (OC, II, pp. 837 and 839). This lament for fecundity echoes in Yerma's admission to the old pagan woman that she is a 'campo seco' ['dry field'] (OC, II, p. 875); in the old woman's riposte – 'Pues sigue así. Por tu gusto es. Como los cardos del secano, pinchosa, marchita' ['Then continue as you are. It's the way you like it. Like the thistles of the dry lands, you're prickly and withered'] (OC, II, p. 875); in the women's prayer, at the shrine – 'Sobre su carne marchita | florezca la rosa amarilla' ['On her withered flesh may the yellow rose blossom'] (OC, II, p. 868) – and in Yerma's own prayer – 'Señor, abre tu rosal | sobre mi carne marchita' ['Lord, may your rose bush open on my withered flesh'] (OC, II, p. 869), 'Sobre mi carne marchita | la rosa de maravilla' ['On my withered flesh the rose of wonder'] (OC, II, p. 869); and also in the male dancers' chants during the fertility rite at the shrine – '¡Ay, con el vientre seco | y la color quebrada!' [Oh, she with a dry belly and a brittle colour!'] (OC, II, p. 871). The lament resonates more deeply still in Yerma's soliloquy, in Act 2, Scene 2, delivered as if in a dream:

¡Ay, qué prado de pena!
¡Ay, qué puerta cerrada a la hermosura!,
que pido un hijo que sufrir, y el aire
me ofrece dalias de dormida luna.
Estos dos manantiales que yo tengo
de leche tibia, son en la espesura
de mi carne dos pulsos de caballo
que hacen latir la rama de mi angustia.
¡Ay, pechos ciegos bajo mi vestido!
¡Ay, palomas sin ojos ni blancura!
¡Ay, qué dolor de sangre prisionera
me está clavando avispas en la nuca!
Pero tú has de venir, amor, mi niño,
porque el agua da sal, la tierra fruta,
y nuestro vientre guarda tiernos hijos,
como la nube lleva dulce lluvia. (OC, II, pp. 846–47)

[Alas, what field of sorrow! Alas, what door closed to beauty! I ask for a child to suffer, and the breeze offers me dahlias of a sleeping moon. These two springs I have of lukewarm milk are, in the thicket of my flesh, the two heartbeats of horses that make the branch of my anguish rebound. Alas, blind breasts beneath my dress! Alas, doves without eyes or white plumage! Oh what pain of captive blood nails wasps into my nape! But you have to come, love, my child, because water gives salt, the land, fruit, and our belly bears tender children as a cloud bears sweet rain.]

And, finally, we hear the lament in Yerma's last words after killing Juan and, with him, her only hope of becoming a mother: 'Con el cuerpo seco para siempre. ¿Qué queréis saber? ¡No os acerquéis, porque he matado a mi hijo, yo misma he matado a mi hijo!' ['With my body forever dry. What do you want to know? Stay away, because I've killed my son, I myself have killed my son!'] (OC, II, p. 880).

It goes without saying that the lyrical agility Yerma and other characters demonstrate in constructing their metaphors must be credited to the poet who has conceived them. And although, as Quance (p. 9) suggests, we should be careful not to treat the source of their lyrical outpourings as being 'in the author's psyche', it is nonetheless true that they have connections with ideas that appear elsewhere in Lorca's work, in particular his poetry. The lyrical treatment of fertility in *Yerma* is a case in point, for it has its precedents in numerous poems.[20]

'Chopo muerto' ['Dead Poplar'] (OC, I, pp. 108–09), dated 1920, from Lorca's first collection of poems, *Libro de poemas*, is an elegy to a dead poplar that in turn represents the poet's own figurative demise. It alludes, as I have suggested elsewhere, to the death of lyricism rooted in turn-of-the-century symbolism in anticipation of poetic renewal.[21] But most relevant to our discussion here are the images of sterility that emerge from the poem's nature symbolism: 'Fue tu espíritu fuerte | el que llamó a la muerte, | al hallarte sin nidos, olvidado | de los chopos infantes del prado' ['It was your strong spirit that called death to you, on finding yourself without nests, forgotten by the infant poplars of the field'] (OC, I, p. 108); '¡Qué amargura tan honda | para el paisaje | el héroe de la fronda | sin ramaje!' ['How deeply bitter it is for the landscape to see the hero of foliage without a leaf'] (OC, I, p. 109); 'Ya no serás la cuna | de la luna, | ni la mágica risa | de la brisa, | ni el bastón de un lucero | caballero. | No tornará la primavera | de tu vida, | ni verás la sementera | florecida. | Serás nidal de ranas | y de hormigas' ['No longer will you be the moon's cradle, nor the breeze's magical laughter, nor the gentleman-star's cane. The spring of your life will not return, nor will you see sown fields bloom. You will be a nest for frogs and ants'] OC, I, p. 109).

There is a similar lament, though this time voiced by the tree directly, in 'Canción del naranjo seco' ['Song of the Dry Orange Tree'] (OC,

---

20 Stainton, p. 288, notes that Lorca often 'summons the motif of the unborn child'. She suggests that the origin of this conceit was Lorca's own childlessness (see Stainton, pp. 332–33).
21 See Bonaddio, 2010, pp. 41–43.

I, p. 389), from *Canciones*. Here the orange tree cannot bear to see its barren condition in the shadow it casts: 'Leñador. | Córtame la sombra. | Líbrame del suplicio | de verme sin toronjas' ['Woodcutter. Cut down my shadow. Release me from the torture of seeing myself without fruit']. The orange tree's anguish can also be read as a metaphor for the poet's anxieties in face of the prospect of creative sterility. This prospect looms ever larger in *Poeta en Nueva* York which, as we have already seen, is replete with images of sterility as the disorientated and out-of-place poet struggles with the creative challenges posed by the inhuman, alienating city. Hence, the image of thwarted creativity in the opening poem, 'Vuelta de paseo' – 'mariposa ahogada en el tintero' ['butterfly drowned in an inkwell'] (OC, I, p. 447) – or the ripped sails of boats on the Hudson, in 'Navidad en el Hudson', along with the river's 'grey sponge', that is also the poet's own ('¡Oh esponja mía gris!' [OC, I, p. 479]), and the poet with his 'throat just cut' ('¡Oh cuello mío recién degollado!' [OC, I, p. 479]).

La casa de Bernarda is, on the surface, more prosaic in style than *Yerma* and *Bodas de sangre*.[22] And yet Lorca's qualification of the play as a 'photographic documentary', while seeming to suggest a realist focus, reflects, as much as anything, a symbolic approach evidenced by its colour scheme: the mourning black of Bernarda's and her daughters' clothing and the white of the house's lime walls, both alluding, in turn, to the diametrically opposed 'black and white' positions of oppressive control, on the one hand, and the struggle for personal freedom, on the other. From both Bernarda's and Adela's perspectives there is no grey area, just the truth of their own positions in respect of obedience and desire. Moreover, the play's dialogue, for all its prosaism, is peppered with moments of symbolism that also betray a poetic approach. When, in Act 1, Amelia chides her mother for speaking ill of the funeral guests, Bernarda, giving no quarter, associates what she sees as the moral shortcomings of her fellow villagers with the stagnant water of wells: 'Es así como se tiene que hablar de este maldito pueblo sin río, pueblo de pozos, donde siempre se bebe agua con el miedo de que esté envenenada' ['This is how one must speak of this damned village with no river, village of wells, where one drinks water fearing that it is poisoned'] (OC, II, p. 984). And, against the background of a storm that is brewing both literally and figuratively, the play's water-symbolism extends to the inevitable, impending downpour,

---

22 Delgado (p. 104) suggests that it is perhaps Lorca's most performed play 'because of its ostensibly realist idiom that poses few interpretative challenges of the lyricism of [for example] *Doña Rosita* or *Blood Wedding*'.

La Poncia telling Criada in Act 3 that there is 'una tormenta en cada cuarto. El día que estallen nos barrerán a todas' ['a storm in each room. The day they explode they'll sweep us all away'] (OC, II, p. 1054), and Bernarda, as early as Act 2, herself admitting that 'Yo veía la tormenta venir, pero no creía que estallara tan pronto' ['I saw the storm coming, but I didn't think it would break so soon'] (OC, II, p. 1029). This pattern of symbolism encourages us to read Adela's inability to sleep, in Act 3, in equally symbolic terms. 'Voy a beber agua' ['I'm going for a drink of water'] (OC, II, p. 1055), she tells La Poncia, adding 'Me desperto la sed' ['I was woken up by thirst'] (OC, II, p. 1055). As the storm is reaching its peak, we can only infer that what Adela is really seeking to quench is not her thirst for water but her desire for Pepe el Romano.

Yet perhaps what is most deeply poetic about *La casa de Bernarda*, in common with the other plays in the trilogy, is its tragic character. Lorca's choice of the tragic mode for his plays implies an active, poetic vision of the world rather than the realism we would expect of mere observation and a documentary approach. In effect, the inevitability of the tragic ending of all three plays detaches them from the real world where futures are, by contrast, open-ended and thus unpredictable. Although they each have something – and something very important – to say about the real world, the plays are, much like poems, self-contained universes in of themselves, governed by tragedy's poetic logic – not poetic justice, but rather the patterns of inevitability which the tragic poet has crafted.

Lorca's ability to treat real-life issues without compromising his interest in the art of poetry may have something to do with the deeply poetic manner in which, in any case, he saw the world. 'La poesía', he explained in an interview published in the Madrid newspaper *La Voz* in 1936, 'es algo que anda por las calles. Que se mueve, que pasa a nuestro lado' ['Poetry is something that walks the streets. It moves, it passes by our side'] (OC, III, p. 671). And he added: 'Todas las cosas tienen su misterio, y la poesía es el misterio que tienen todas las cosas. Se pasa junto a un hombre, se mira a una mujer, se adivina la marcha oblicua de un perro, y en cada uno de estos objetos humanos está la poesía' ['All things have their mystery, and poetry is the mystery that all things have. One passes close to a man, one watches a woman, one discerns a dog's oblique steps, and in each of these human things there is poetry'] (OC, III, p. 671). In effect, there is no reason why Lorca's inclination to see poetry in all things would preclude him from having a social vision. What it did do, though, was colour that vision; so much so that he expressed social realities via the poetic mystery that he, as a poet, delighted in.

In Lorca's trilogy, tragedy's poetic logic plays out in symbolism. Unlike most of the examples we have considered thus far, it is a symbolism of which the characters are incognizant, even when it is contained in their very own utterances. While tragedy is, at one level, the product of the social codes – recognizable in real life – that coerce the plays' protagonists, it is also the product of something other-worldly, tying the characters, in spite of themselves, to a fate some of them have already unknowingly uttered. Take, for example, Bernarda's command in Act 3 that her stud horse be released into the courtyard and her fillies, locked away in the stables: 'El caballo garañón, que está encerrado y da coces contra el muro. [...] ¡Trabadlo y que salga al corral! [...] Debe tener calor' ['The stud horse that's locked up and kicking against the walls. Fasten him and let him out into the courtyard! He must be on heat!'] (OC, II, p. 1041); 'Pues encerrad las potras en la cuadra, pero dejadlo libre, no sea que nos eche abajo las paredes' ['Then lock the fillies up in the stable, but let him free, otherwise he might bring the walls down'] (OC, II, p. 1042). Here, desire finds its correlative in the figure of the horse, Bernarda's command – in metaphorical terms – casting Pepe el Romano as the stud horse and her daughters as the fillies. Even though Bernarda may want the sexes to be kept apart, the energy of desire, symbolized and embodied by the stud, is irrepressible; a fact that she is only able to acknowledge in respect of her horses but not, it seems, when it comes to human beings and the case of Pepe el Romano and her daughters. Bernarda is blind to the symbolic inferences in her utterances and to the inevitable fact that desire will bring down the walls of her house just as the stud horse would bring down the walls of its stable were it not first released into the yard. The inevitability of desire's resurgence is later represented by the stud horse again as it stands alone in the night, its white coat illuminating the courtyard for Adela, a subliminal reference to the desire that she is unable to contain within herself: 'El caballo garañón estaba en el centro del corral. ¡Blanco! Doble de grande, llenando todo lo oscuro' ['The stud was in the centre of the courtyard. White! Twice the size, filling all the darkness'] (OC, II, p. 1048).

Reinforcing the horse symbolism in *La casa de Bernarda Alba* is the fact that Pepe el Romano makes his visits to Bernarda's house on horseback. In this respect, he reminds us of Leonardo, in *Bodas de sangre*, whose horse-riding comes to symbolize his waywardness and sexual menace. The threat Leonardo poses eventually materializes in his and Novia's flight from the wedding reception – on horseback once again. Leonardo's riding is also the topic of conversation, in Act 1, Scene 2, in an early exchange that he has with his wife (Mujer) and mother-in-law (Suegra). Leonardo claims to have just returned from the blacksmith's, yet the frequency of his visits to the smithies to have his horse shoed and the fact that he runs his mount so terribly hard arouse the women's suspicions. 'Ayer', says Mujer, 'me dijeron las vecinas que te habían visto al límite de los llanos' ['Yesterday the neighbours told me they'd seen you at the edge of the plain'] (OC, II, p. 717). Bookending this exchange is a lullaby Mujer and Suegra sing to Leonardo's child, in which a horse figures once more, as in the following extracts:

> Nana, niño, nana
> del caballo grande
> que no quiso el agua.
> El agua era negra
> dentro de las ramas.
> [...]
> Duérmete, clavel,
> que el caballo no quiere beber.
> [...]
> Duérmete, rosal,
> que el caballo se pone a llorar.
> Las patas heridas,
> las crines heladas,
> dentro de los ojos
> un puñal de plata.
> Bajaban al río.
> ¡Ay, cómo bajaban!
> La sangre corría más fuerte que el agua.
> [...]
> No quiso tocar
> la orilla mojada,
> su belfo caliente
> con moscas de plata.
> A los montes duros
> solo relinchaba
> con el río muerto
> sobre la garganta.
> ¡Ay caballo grande
> que no quiso el agua!
> ¡Ay dolor de nieve,
> caballo del alba! (OC, II, pp. 713–14)

[Lullaby, child, lullaby of the big horse that did not want water. The water was black inside the branches. (...) Sleep, carnation, the horse does not want to drink. (...) Sleep, rose bush, the horse is crying. Its legs wounded, its mane frozen, inside its eyes a silver dagger. They went down to the river. Oh, how they went! The blood ran quicker than water. (...) It would not touch the damp shore, its lip hot with silver flies. At the harsh mountains it would only neigh with a dead river on its throat. Oh, big horse that did not want the water! Oh, pain of snow, horse of the dawn!]

Mujer's and Suegra's lullaby is a reworking of a cradle song from Granada that Lorca cited in a lecture he gave on the subject of Spanish lullabies in 1928. One important difference, though, is that, in his reworking, the horse is not prevented from drinking, as it is in the original, but does itself refuse to drink.[23] Thus, in becoming the subject – and a masculine subject at that – the horse acquires a symbolic connection with Leonardo, its refusal to drink becoming synonymous with Leonardo's attempts, early on in his story, to control his desire for Novia. By the same token, its crying, as Maria Cristina Assumma (p. 25) argues, symbolizes Leonardo's unhappiness in his self-imposed condition of repression and denial. Mujer's and Suegra's lullaby is clearly prescient, its ominous reference to blood and to a silver dagger in the horse's eyes foreshadowing the violence yet to come. But, importantly, Mujer and Suegra are not sybils. They are, rather, oblivious to the symbolism in their cradle song and to its contribution to the play's tragic narrative, just as Bernarda is oblivious to the symbolic implications of her pronouncements. The characters each make their contribution to the poetic construction of their tragic scenarios, their utterances being, albeit unbeknown to them, prescient of the events that will unfold and signs of the inevitable nature of the future that awaits them.

Undoubtedly, the most remarkable example of the poetry infusing Lorca's plays and their tragic vision comes in Act 3, Scene 1 of *Bodas de Sangre*, where the transition from something we might recognize as reality to an 'alternative world', as Bilha Blum puts it, 'is conveyed by a radical change of scenery and by an abrupt stylistic passage from prose to poetry'.[24] The scene opens with three woodcutters discussing Novia's and Leonardo's flight on horseback into the woods at night and the group that is pursuing them. Just like the washerwomen in *Yerma*, the woodcutters function much like a Greek chorus. Their reflections on the action are

---

23 See Maria Cristina Assumma, '"Estribillos de estribillos": la savia popular en el teatro lorquiano', *Anales de la literatura española contemporánea*, 34.2 (2009), 391–426 (p. 25).
24 Bilha Blum, '"¡Silencio, he dicho!": Space, Language, and Characterization as Agents of Social Protest in Lorca's Rural Tragedies', *Modern Drama*, 48.1 (Spring 2005), 71–86 (p. 76).

ominous – 'los buscan por todas partes' ['they're looking for them everywhere'] (OC, II, p. 772), 'Ya darán con ellos' ['They'll find them in the end'] (OC, II, p. 772), 'Cuando salga la luna los verán' ['They'll spot them when the moon comes out'] (OC, II, p. 773), 'los matarán' ['they'll kill them'] (OC, II, p. 773) – as they discuss not only the inevitability that the couple will be hunted down but also the wrongs and rights of their actions and the indomitable nature of their passion: 'Hay que seguir la inclinación; han hecho bien en huir' ['You have to follow your inclination; they did well to flee'] (OC, II, p. 773); 'Se estaban engañando uno a otro y al fin la sangre pudo más' ['They were deceiving one another and in the end the urge of blood won out'] (OC, II, p. 773); 'Ahora la estará queriendo' ['Now he'll be making love to her'] (OC, II, p. 774); 'El cuerpo de ella era para él y el cuerpo de él para ella' ['His body belonged to her and hers to him'] (OC, II, p. 774). And even though one woodcutter suggests that Novio will find them with or without the benefit of moonlight, it is the appearance of the moon that eventually seals the couple's fate. The moon, appearing in the form of a young, white-faced woodcutter, demands that the trees of the woods, which otherwise conceal Novia and Leonardo in the shadows they cast, make way for him. And he declares:

> No quiero sombras. Mis rayos
> han de entrar en todas partes,
> y haya en los troncos oscuros
> un rumor de claridades,
> para que esta noche tengan
> mis mejillas dulce sangre,
> y los juncos agrupados
> en los anchos pies del aire.
> ¿Quién se oculta? ¡Afuera digo!
> ¡No! ¡No podrán escaparse!
> Yo haré lucir al caballo
> una fiebre de diamante. (OC, II, p. 777)

[I don't want shadow. My rays must reach everywhere and on the dark tree-trunks there should be a murmur of light, so that on this night my cheeks may be smeared in sweet blood, and reeds clustered round the broad feet of the wind. Who is hiding? Out, I say! No! No, you cannot escape! I will make the horse gleam like a feverish diamond.]

The woodcutter-moon is then joined by the figure of death in the shape of an old beggar woman. Together they conspire to ensure that the couple is found and that Leonardo and Novio face each other in what will prove to be a mortal combat. 'Ilumina el chaleco y aparta los botones,' demands the old beggar woman, 'que después las navajas ya saben el camino' ['Light up their waistcoats and undo their buttons, after which the knives will know the way'] (OC, II, p. 778). 'Pero que tarden mucho en morir' ['But may they take long to die'], replies the blood-thirsty moon. 'Que la sangre me ponga entre los dedos su delicado silbo' ['May the blood put between my fingers its delicate hiss'] (OC, II, p. 778). 'No dejemos que pasen el arroyo', the old woman responds defiantly ['We must not let them cross the stream'] (OC, II, p. 779). Having taken human form, death is able to meet Novio in person and lead him through the woods to the couple for whom there is no escape.

The young woodcutter and the old beggar woman – each poetic figurations – are incarnations of the forces of destiny. Whereas, elsewhere in his plays, Lorca inscribes the tragic fate of his characters in the symbolism they unknowingly utter, here he gives it human form so it can walk, unrecognized, amongst them. His conception of theatre as 'la poesía que se levanta del libro y se hace humana' ['poetry that has stepped out of its book and become human'] (OC, III, p. 673) is nowhere more evident than in the figures of the young woodcutter and old beggar woman. Yet the idea that poetry provides the basis for theatre extends, beyond this very literal transposition of the moon and death, to encompass all of his characters, each of whom lacks the roundedness, the psychological depth, that we would expect of realism. As Gwynne Edwards explains, Lorca's characters 'are relatively flat and one dimensional'.[25] In other words, not being the contradictory beings that people are in real life, they 'are relevant only in so far as they contribute to the play's basic [tragic] structure and progression' (Ramsden 1980, p. xix), their function being tied, above all, to the poetic logic of the plays and to the delivery of the tragic plot.

Thus, for example, Madre, in *Bodas de sangre*, 'is driven almost entirely by grief, apprehension and vengeance', while 'the life of Yerma seems entirely circumscribed, firstly by her longing for a child and then, as she is progressively denied it, her despair in the face of that fact' (Edwards, p. 131). Similarly, Adela, in *La casa de Bernarda Alba*, is characterized almost entirely by her desire for Pepe el Romano.

This narrow focus for each of the characters means that their 'emotional lives [...] are enormously intensified' (Edwards, p. 131). Yet we could also argue that the lyricism in their utterances and the poetic logic governing the action and directing it towards a tragic conclusion risk

25 Gwynne Edwards, 'Federico García Lorca: "Para el teatro... dentro de muchos años"', *Anales de la literatura española contemporánea*, 17.1 (1992), 125–44 (p. 131).

distracting us from social concerns that might have been better served by a plainly realist approach. Poetry, at the level of speech or at the level of the tragic order crafted for the plays, is not essential to the consideration of society's problems. Poetry warrants, and gains, our appreciation on its own terms, as does the effect of tragedy itself, and while the emotional engagement that tragedy elicits is not incompatible with an understanding of social issues, it need not have any resonance beyond our cathartic experience of the plays' action. Much like the myths of the ballads of *Romancero gitano*, there is a sense in which the plays have their own independent, artistic life, their lyrical and symbolic craft, along with the pity and fear that tragedy inspires, becoming sources of pleasure in and of themselves, for all their connection with serious, real-life issues.[26]

Ultimately, the poetic character of his plays – their very literariness – demonstrates how Lorca retained his artistic priorities even when treating issues pertaining to the real world. Indeed, it seems likely that he did, after all, have doubts about the value of art that was solely politically motivated. Importantly, the plays' poetic character also gives them their universal dimension, even though it has been suggested, paradoxically, that particularity of location, including, for example, an Andalusian culture characterized by 'the paradoxical relations of passion and restraint' and an 'obsession with honour' (Rosslyn, p. 216), meant Lorca was well-placed to produce tragedy. There are clearly elements in the trilogy that are rooted in local values, behaviours and custom, such as 'arrangements for marriage, the importance of land, wives taking food to their husbands in the fields, the centrality of children to married life, and the crucial significance of offended honour' (Edwards, p. 129). There are also many references to the physical world of rural Spain: 'houses with thick walls', 'food and crops', 'flowers and plants', 'fields and mountains', 'dress and costume' (Edwards, p. 129). Yet the initial impression of the trilogy's rootedness eventually gives way to the universal implications of a poetry that emphasizes broad human concerns about love, loss, desire, freedom,

---

26 Aristotle, in his *Poetics*, notes the pleasure that poets produce from tragedy. See Aristotle, *Poetics*, trans. with intro. and notes by Malcolm Heath (London: Penguin Classics, 1996), New eEdition. On the one hand, he acknowledges that tragedy is cast in 'language made pleasurable', by which he means 'that which possesses rhythm and melody, i.e. song' (p. 9 of 49). On the other, he advises against relying on pleasures that are not distinctive of tragedy: 'one should not seek every pleasure from tragedy, but the one that is characteristic of it', namely 'the pleasure which comes from pity and fear' (p. 21 of 49).

death and fate. As Edwards (p. 130) suggests, what is important is not the 'Spanishness' of Lorca's theatre but rather 'the extent to which it is an embodiment of the human soul, to which its implications are universal'. It is this that, according to Edwards (p. 130), 'explains Lorca's rejection from the very beginning of his career as a dramatist of the particularized and localized preoccupations of naturalism'. And by way of illustration, Edwards (p. 130) cites Lorca's assessment of his 1930 play *La zapatera prodigiosa* [*The Shoemaker's Prodigious Wife*], an assessment which might equally apply to any one of the plays of his rural trilogy: 'La zapatera es [...] un ejemplo poético del alma humana y es ella sola la que tiene importancia en la obra' ['The shoemaker's wife is a poetic example of the human soul and it is only this that is important in the play'].

It was a notable achievement on Lorca's part to have given voice to so many memorable female characters in his rural trilogy as well as in other plays. 'When so many other contemporaneous male writers were creating silent or at best insipidly or shrilly tongued female characters', writes Johnson (p. 274), 'Lorca invested his finest poetic talent in writing leading parts for women in which their subjectivity is manifest in all its complexity'. And Johnson (p. 274) adds: 'In the socio-historical context in which Lorca was writing, that was feminism at its best.' In the terms in which it is framed here, there is no contradiction between Lorca's fixation with the art of poetry and his concern for the condition of women. As Johnson (p. 274) suggests, the 'eloquent poetic voice' Lorca gave to his female characters was, in and of itself, possibly his 'greatest gift to the enchained women of his time'. In effect, Lorca never lost sight of art even as he wrote about serious, real-life issues. We see this not only in his attention to the lyricism he bestowed on his subjects but also in his choice of the tragic mode. Importantly, while tragedy is, in one sense, an appropriate mode by which to evoke the inevitability of women's plight in communities stymied by tradition, its metaphysical implications – the diversion (however partial) of its source from social or personal flaws to some inescapable, metaphysical force – also engender readings that extend beyond the situation of women, whether in Spain or beyond, to acquire universal significance for the human condition. Lorca sought to transpose to the stage the poetry he perceived in real life – the poetry that is 'the mystery that all things have'. Real-life dramas – including 'the social tensions that vocal Spanish feminism was provoking' (Johnson, p. 258) – will have been important in their own right. Yet they also fed Lorca's interest in art and aesthetics, providing him with the very poetic substance for his plays.

Conclusion

CRITICS HAVE POINTED to the difficulty, even the senselessness, of looking for coherence across Lorca's work. 'My working hypothesis', writes Mayhew (2009, pp. 3–4), 'is that Lorca is an internally contradictory figure rather than a transparently cohesive one. It is extraordinarily difficult to arrive at a global sense of who he really was, of what his work, taken together, might signify.' As regards Lorca's life specifically, Stephen Roberts (p. 9), in his recent biography, reminds us of some of the contradictions and ambiguities, including the fact that he could be a friend both to Manuel Azaña, the Liberal-Socialist President of the Republic, and to José Antonio Primo de Rivera, eldest son of General Primo de Rivera, and founder of the Fascist Falange.

In some respects, our study of Lorca under the various motifs of the Gitano, the modern and the feminist acknowledges the possibility that there is no single Lorca to be had, whether in terms of the life he experienced or his thematic interests.[1] Even his reluctant and inconsistent engagement with the principles of the avant-garde reveals a Lorca who is often in two minds. And yet it would be disingenuous not to admit that we have, nonetheless, stubbornly sought to find some coherence across his most popular works, both in his reluctance to surrender to the principles of impersonality and irrationality in art and in the fact that he so often chose to tell stories about the real worlds of the marginalized and the oppressed.

---

1 Roberts (p. 9) argues that Lorca's life 'was not as smooth, rounded or limned as that of a symbol or an icon but rather as chaotic, unpredictable and open-ended as any other human life'.

Romancero gitano is an attempt to revitalize the traditional Spanish ballad. Lorca's decision to take on the ballad form and do so preserving the Gitano as its central motif was a bold one because of the hackneyed associations the form had acquired and the clichés about Gitanos it traditionally conveyed. Tackling the ballad necessarily meant tackling the clichés too. This he did by creating for his Gitanos mythical scenarios infused with lyricism and built upon complex metaphors. In this way, the poetic qualities of his ballads rescued them from the commonplaces often associated with the tradition. Which is why Lorca expressed surprise and dismay at Dalí's and Buñuel's criticism of his ballad book, made precisely on the grounds that his ballads had little new to offer. But novelty there was, and no little courage, in Lorca's very decision to write about Gitanos at a time when both the Spanish Romani people and the culture associated with them were habitually denigrated. Thus, his highly stylized treatment of his subject acquired significance beyond matters of artistic value, revealing not only an aesthetic but also a philanthropic appreciation of a people and culture that others, in their bigotry, reviled. For this reason, it is not surprising that amidst the pages of *Romancero gitano* we should find stories about the oppression Gitanos suffered. Lorca's ballads represent his own particular response to a climate of artistic innovation, but they are also evidence of his deep interest in the human subject.

Equally divided between artistic and human concerns is Lorca's *Poeta en Nueva York*. Whether by design or coincidence, Lorca found himself in the most modern of modern cities only a short while after his ballad book had been criticized by his friends for its lack of modernity. He seized the opportunity to return the favour and, with his New York poems, countered others' blind adulation of modernity by emphasizing the ugliness and disorder of Surrealism, modern art's flavour of the day. But his criticism went beyond the realm of art and aesthetics to include an attack on modern living also with poems that depicted the city as being oppressive, divisive, unnatural and dehumanizing. Thus, to those who regarded Andalusia's rural settings and folkloric traditions as material that was incompatible with a modern outlook Lorca retaliated by challenging the ideal of modernity itself.

In *Poeta en Nueva York*, Lorca also produced his most overt treatment of homosexuality up until that time, with his ode to the American poet, Walt Whitman. Critics have sought to map a symbology with specific reference to homosexuality (conceived of, more often than not, as a homosexuality silenced) across Lorca's entire oeuvre, particularly (though not exclusively) in respect of early collections of poems such as *Libro de poemas*, *Suites* and *Canciones*. Yet homosexuality, I would contend, is not the primary thematic concern of Lorca's most popular works, even though we might agree with the view offered by David Johnston in his biography 'that Lorca's sexuality, and above all the crisis of being homosexual in a society that gifted the word *macho* to the world, is a key to the very distinctive sense of life that informs his work'.[2] For such a view does not exclude the possibility that a play's or poem's thematic focus may extend beyond homosexuality or even lie elsewhere. Indeed, as Walters (p. 191) has pointed out in respect of the theme of love, Lorca's poetry, for example, 'contains a variety of perspectives', so we ought not to 'fall into the trap [...] which results from reading all of Lorca's utterances on amatory subjects as homosexually orientated, in defiance of the evidence'. And as Smith (p. 110) advises, it is important also to be wary of the simplistic view that somehow Lorca, as a homosexual, had, as I have put it elsewhere, 'a kind of insider's understanding of the sensibilities of women and the predicaments that they faced'.[3] Such advice applies especially to Lorca's plays, including his rural trilogy, where the lead protagonists are women. Nonetheless, what seems certain is that Lorca's New York experience, as well as his time in Cuba, when he found himself far from his habitual circles in Granada and Madrid, proved to be a catalyst for more overt and confident explorations of sexual identity. This is evident not only in 'Oda a Walt Whitman' but also his experimental play *El público*,

---

2   David Johnston, *Federico García Lorca* (Bath: Absolute Press, 1998), p. 22. For a treatment of homosexual symbolism in Lorca's work, see Sahuquillo's *Federico García Lorca and the Culture of Male Homosexuality* (Jefferson, N.C.: McFarland & Co., 2007) and Paul Binding's *Lorca: The Gay Imagination* (London: GMP, 1985).

3   Federico Bonaddio, 'Introduction. Biography and Interpretation', in *A Companion to Federico García Lorca*, ed. by Federico Bonaddio (Woodbridge: Tamesis, 2007), pp. 4–5. Smith (p. 110) refers to readings where 'critics might claim that the rebellious heroines of Lorca's drama are "really" men, disguised or displaced figures of the author's own sexual oppression' or where 'the (unexamined) "fact" of homosexuality serves to "explain" Lorca's supposed empathy with women and his understanding of the female predicament'.

which, like the ode, has become a key text in the study of the homosexual thematic of his work, contributing to his status as a gay icon.

In his rural trilogy of plays, Lorca once again succeeds in treating real-life subjects without compromising his artistic ideals. If anything, the lyricism in his characters' speeches, particularly those of his female leads, emphasizes their sense of desperation and estrangement in a world governed by patriarchal logic that leaves no room for the expression of individual personality or desire. While the themes of *Bodas de sangre*, *Yerma* and *La casa de Bernarda Alba* reflect contemporary debates about the condition of women in Spain, the characters' tragic condition has resonance for anyone whose individuality is negated by society's unyielding prescriptions. For while it is true that much of the plays' lyricism derives from local culture, such as popular song and children's lullabies, just as much of their poetic imagery is rooted in the reality of local custom and practice; the choice of the tragic mode, as well as the intensely lyrical character of the plays (albeit to a lesser degree in *La casa de Bernarda Alba*), allow them to have significance beyond the locality of southern Spain. Lorca was clearly familiar with contemporary real-life issues, but his was never going to be a documentarist approach. Instead, his continued interest in art and his own intensely poetic vision of the world ensured that the plays of his rural trilogy would be at once an exploration of the condition of women in Spain (and beyond) and of the human condition more generally, with particular focus on the question of personal freedoms.

As Spain drew ever closer to civil conflict, Lorca almost certainly felt pressure to shout ever louder his commitment to the defence of these freedoms. Hence the desperate cry we hear from Adela in *La casa de Bernarda* and its tragic extinction by the silence imposed by an unfeeling, ultra-conservative matriarch. Yet in an increasingly polarized Spain, even Lorca's depiction of infidelity in *Bodas de Sangre* or of a dysfunctional marriage in *Yerma* could offend conservative sensibilities. So too, retrospectively, his defence of the Gitanos and depiction of the Civil Guard in *Romancero gitano*, or the iconoclasm of a poem like 'Grito hacia Roma', in *Poeta en Nueva York*, with its explicit condemnation of the Pope. Indeed, as we look back at Lorca's work through the prism of Franco's dictatorship and, prior to that, the Spanish Civil War, it is the political significance of such depictions that stands, above all else, to monopolize our attention, and this despite his relative disinterest in party politics.

Ultimately, what we hope to have shown is that, for Lorca, there was no contradiction in tackling real-life topics while paying due attention to the artistic and aesthetic qualities of his texts. In this respect, for all his interest in real peoples' lives, his work managed to keep faith with the spirit of the avant-garde even if it did not follow its prescriptions for autonomous art to the letter. In effect, Lorca's ability to see poetry in the things of the world rendered the dichotomy of art versus life redundant and the need to assert the value of one over the other quite unnecessary. How significant that, in his famous lecture on the spirit of *duende*, which he delivered in Buenos Aires in 1933, he should choose to describe the impact of this mysterious, chthonic force in art in specifically bodily terms; this force that 'no está en la garganta' ['is not in the throat'], but 'sube por dentro desde la planta de los pies' ['rises up inside from the soles of the feet'] (OC, III, p. 307). 'Todas las artes', explained Lorca, 'son capaces de duende, pero dónde encuentran más campo, como es natural, es en la música, en la danza y en la poesía hablada, ya que estas necesitan un cuerpo vivo que interprete, porque son formas que nacen y mueren de modo perpetuo y alzan sus contornos sobre un presente exacto' ['All arts are capable of *duende*, but where it has most scope, as is natural, is in music, in dance and in poetry spoken out loud, since these require a live body to interpret them, because they are forms that are born and die in perpetuity and cast their silhouette over the exact present'] (OC, III, p. 311). Lorca, it appears, felt an irresistible pull, especially in art, towards the real experience of physical human beings. So it is no coincidence that his best loved works are those in which he was able to combine aesthetic endeavour with a deep and passionate concern for, to gloss the great Spanish thinker Miguel de Unamuno, men and women of 'flesh and bone'.[4] That is, for men and women 'who are born, suffer and die – above all die – who eat and drink and play and sleep and think and want, who can be seen and heard, brothers [and sisters], true brothers [and sisters]' (Unamuno, p. 25). Lorca may have been interested in art in and of itself, but this interest did not come at the expense of his ability – his responsibility even – as he himself put it, to 'cry and laugh' with the people. It is this ability that explains the intensely emotional character of so much of his work.

While some might frown, as did Dalí and Buñuel, at what they see as Lorca's folkloricism and his pandering to popular conceptions of Spain – to people's insatiable appetite for exotic tales of Gitanos or Spanish rural life – the truth of his success, I believe, lies elsewhere. If Lorca continues

[4] It is in these terms that the Spanish thinker and writer defined the subject of his inquiry in his philosophical treatise *Of the Tragic Sense of Life*. See Miguel de Unamuno, *Del sentimento trágico de la vida* (Madrid: Espasa Calpe, 1982), p. 25. Translations are my own.

to be read widely today it is because his depictions of marginalization and oppression are still relevant, not least because his poetic approach to his subjects endowed them with a timeless, universal quality. Moreover, against the background of his sustained interest in the aesthetic qualities of his art, Lorca's undoubted lyrical prowess means that his work can be read not only for what it tells us about the lives of real people, whether in Spain or beyond, but also, quite simply, for the pleasure that its poetic craft engenders.

Suggested Further Reading

ALTHOUGH I HAVE used Arturo del Hoyo's three-volume edition of Lorca's complete works (Madrid: Aguilar, 1986), increasingly the standard reference for scholars has become Miguel García-Posada's four-volume edition (Barcelona: Galaxia Gutenberg / Círculo de Lectores, 1997). The most comprehensive bilingual edition of Lorca's poetry is Christopher Maurer's revised edition of *Collected Poems* (New York: Farrar, Straus and Giroux, 2002). Christopher Maurer has also produced a bilingual edition of *Poeta en Nueva York* (New York: Farrar, Straus and Giroux, 1998), translations of uncollected poems and prose in *A Season in Granada* (London: Anvil Press, 1998), translations of Lorca's prose, in *Deep Song and other prose* (London: Marion Boyars, 1980), as well as Lorca's correspondence with Dalí, in *Sebastian's Arrows. Letters and Mementos of Salvador Dalí and Federico García Lorca* (Chicago: Swan Isle Press, 2004). Additionally, there is the collection, entitled *Selected poems with Parallel Spanish Text*, in the Oxford World Classics series (Oxford: OUP, 2007), translated by Martin Sorrell with an introduction and notes by D. Gareth Walters. This volume includes poems from both *Romancero gitano* and *Poeta en Nueva York*.

Reliable translations of Lorca's theatre include John Edmunds's *Federico García: Four Major Plays* (Oxford: OUP, 1999), which brings together all three plays of the rural trilogy, as well as *Doña Rosita la soltera o el lenguaje de las flores* [*Doña Rosita the Spinster or the Language of Flowers*], with an introduction by Nicholas Round and notes by Ann MacLaren; the bilingual edition of *Yerma*, from Ian R. McPherson, J. Minett and John E. Lyon (Warminster: Aris & Phillips, 1987); and Michael Dewell's and Carmen Zapata's translations, with an introduction by Christopher

Maurer, in the collection entitled *The House of Bernarda Alba and other plays* (London: Penguin, 1992). More recently, there is playwright Jo Clifford's translation of the rural trilogy (London: Nick Hern Books, 2017); J. S. Kline's easily accessible and very readable versions of the same, in *Four Final Plays*, published by Poetry in Translation on 14 March 2018 and available online at <https://www.poetryintranslation.com/PITBR/Spanish/LorcaPlayshome.php>; and Michael Kidd's *Four Key Plays* (Indianapolis / Cambridge: Hackett Publishing Company, 2019), which includes an introductory biographical sketch and critical guide.

Ian Gibson's *Federico García Lorca: A Life*, published in 1989 by Faber and Faber is still the most detailed of the biographies of Lorca available and remains an indispensable source of information on all aspects of Lorca's life, including his family, circle of friends and the places where he lived. Stephen Roberts's recent biography, *Deep Song: The Life and Work of Federico García Lorca* (London: Reaktion, 2020), though possibly less detailed, is an immensely readable study that includes a greater focus on the works themselves as it sets out to situate them in the context of Lorca's lived experience; so too Leslie Stainton's earlier study, *Lorca: A Dream of Life* (London: Bloomsbury, 1998), which succeeds in bringing to life both Lorca's personality and the literary and artistic circles in which he moved. As regards the circumstances of Lorca's death, Ian Gibson's authoritative *The Assassination of Federico García Lorca* (Harmondsworth: Penguin, 1983) remains unsurpassed. Gibson has also provided a guide to the Granada Lorca frequented, entitled *Lorca's Granada: a practical guide* (London: Faber and Faber, 1992).

When it comes to critical studies of Lorca's work, a good place to start is *A Companion to Federico García Lorca* (Woodbridge: Tamesis, 2007), which provides an overview of Lorca's polyvalent talent with chapters devoted to his poetry, theatre and drawing respectively, as well as to his interest in music and the cinema. There are also chapters that approach his work from the perspective of religion, gender and sexuality, and politics. A good book-length introduction to Lorca as a gay writer and to the codification of sexual identity in his work is Ángel Sahuquillo's *Federico García Lorca and the Culture of Male Homosexuality* (Jefferson, N.C.: McFarland & Co., 2007). More recently, Javier Herrero's *Lorca, Young and Gay: The Making of An Artist* (Newark, Delaware: Juan de la Cuesta, 2014) seeks to trace Lorca's early artistic growth and the development of his sexual identity as a young man. Indispensable to a study of the debt Lorca's work owes to Andalusia and its culture is C. Brian Morris's *Son of Andalusia: The Lyrical Landscapes of Federico García Lorca* (Liverpool:

Liverpool University Press, 1997). Cecelia J. Cavanaugh, on the other hand, examines the influence of science on Lorca's work in *New Lenses for Lorca: literature, art, and science in the Edad de plata* (Lewisburg: Bucknell University Press, 2013).

The decades-old series of critical guides to Spanish Texts, published by Grant & Cutler (London), still provides solid introductions to Lorca's key works. Thus we have, in the series, C. Brian Morris's guides to *Bodas de sangre* (1980) and to *La casa de Bernarda Alba* (1990); Andrew A. Anderson's guide to *Yerma* (2003); and Derek Harris's guide to *Poeta en Nueva York* (1978). Additionally, Herbert Ramsden's *Lorca's 'Romancero gitano': Eighteen commentaries* (Manchester: Manchester University Press, 1988) provides short but detailed studies of each of the ballads. For a focused study of the poetry, my own study, *Federico García Lorca: The Poetics of Self-Consciousness* (Woodbridge: Tamesis, 2010), is one of very few in English to span the entirety of Lorca's career. As regards his plays, Maria M. Delgado's, *Federico García Lorca* (London and New York: Routledge, 2008), in the Routledge Modern and Contemporary Dramatists series, offers a comprehensive study, including details of theatre productions and film adaptations. It begins with a very useful chapter on the mythology surrounding Lorca's life and personality.

Bibliography

Anderson, Andrew A., 'Federico García Lorca', in *Twentieth-Century Spain and the Civil War*, Cambridge Histories Online, ed. by David T. Gies (Cambridge University Press, 2008), 595–608 <https://doi.org/10.1017/CHOL9780521806183.047>

Aristotle, *Poetics*, trans. with intro. and notes by Malcolm Heath (London: Penguin Classics, 1996), New eEdition

Assumma, Maria Cristina, '"Estribillos de estribillos": la savia popular en el teatro lorquiano', *Anales de la literatura española contemporánea*, 34.2 (2009), 391–426

André Belamich, 'Presentación de las *Suites*', in Federico García Lorca, *Suites*, ed. by André Belamich (Barcelona: Ariel, 1983), pp. 9–26

Binding, Paul, *Lorca: The Gay Imagination* (London: GMP, 1985)

Blum, Bilha, '"¡Silencio, he dicho!": Space, Language, and Characterization as Agents of Social Protest in Lorca's Rural Tragedies', *Modern Drama*, 48.1 (Spring 2005), 71–86

Bonaddio, Federico, *Federico García Lorca: The Poetics of Self-Consciousness* (Woodbridge: Tamesis, 2010)

Bonaddio, Federico, 'Introduction: Biography and Interpretation', in *A Companion to Federico García Lorca*, ed. by Federico Bonaddio (Woodbridge: Tamesis, 2007), pp. 1–15.

Bonaddio, Federico, 'Federico García Lorca's *Blood Wedding*: Patriarchy's Tragic Flaws', in *Patriarchal Moments*, ed. by Cesare Cuttica and Gaby Mahlberg (London: Bloomsbury, 2016), pp. 163–69

Bradbury, Malcolm and James Walter McFarlane, eds, *Modernism 1890-1930* (London: Penguin Books, 1991)

Castro Lee, Cecilia, 'La "Oda a Salvador Dalí": significación y trascendencia en la vida y creación de Lorca y Dalí', *Anales de Literatura Española Contemporánea*, 11 (1986), 61–78

Cockburn, Jacqueline and Federico Bonaddio, 'Drawing', in *A Companion to Federico García Lorca* ed. by Federico Bonaddio (Woodbridge: Tamesis, 2007), pp. 84–100

Debicki, Andrew P., *Spanish Poetry of the Twentieth Century: Modernity and Beyond* (University Press of Kentucky, 1994)

Delgado, Maria M., *Federico García Lorca*, Routledge Modern and Contemporary Dramatists (London and New York: Routledge, 2008)

Delgado Morales, Manuel, 'Embroiderers of Freedom and Desire in Lorca's Poetry and Theater', in *Lorca, Buñuel, Dalí: Art and Theory*, ed. by Manuel Delgado Morales and Alice J. Poust (London and Toronto: Associated University Presses, 2001), pp. 37–51

Dennis, Nigel, 'Politics', in *A Companion to Federico García Lorca*, ed. by Bonaddio (Woodbridge: Tamesis, 2007), pp. 170–89

Drummond, Phillip 'Surrealism and Un Chien Andalou', *Un Chien Andalou: Luis Buñuel and Salvador Dalí* (London: Faber and Faber, 1994)

Edwards, Gwynne, 'Federico García Lorca: "Para el teatro... dentro de muchos años"', *Anales de la literatura española contemporánea*, 17.1 (1992), 125–44

Eliot, T. S., 'Tradition and the Individual Talent', *The Sacred Wood. Essays on Poetry and Criticism* (London and New York: Methuen, 1986), pp. 47–59

Frazer, James George, *The Golden Bough: A Study in Magic and Religion*, Abridged Edition (London: Papermac, 1987)

García Lorca, Federico, *Deep Song and other prose*, ed. and trans. by Christopher Maurer (London: Marion Boyars, 1980)

García Lorca, Federico, *Obras completas*, 3 vols, ed. by Arturo del Hoyo, 22nd edn (Madrid: Aguilar, 1986)

García Lorca, Federico, *Romancero gitano*, ed. by Derek Harris, Grant & Cutler Spanish Texts (London: Grant & Cutler, 1991)

García Lorca, Federico, *Epistolario completo*, ed. by Andrew A. Anderson and Christopher Maurer (Madrid: Cátedra, 1997)

García Lorca, Federico, *Obras completas*, ed. by Miguel García-Posada, 4 vols (Barcelona: Galaxia Gutenberg / Círculo de Lectores, 1997)

García Lorca, Federico, *Poemas en prosa*, ed. by Andrew A. Anderson (Comares / La Veleta, 2000)

García Lorca, Federico, *Collected Poems*, rev. bilingual edn, ed. by Christopher Maurer (New York: Farrar, Straus and Giroux, 2002)

García Lorca, Federico, *Four Final Plays*, trans. by J. S. Kline (Poetry in Translation, 2018), available at <https://www.poetryintranslation.com/PITBR/Spanish/LorcaPlayshome.php>

García Lorca, Federico, *Poet in New York* [Poet in New York], trans. by Pablo Medina and Mark Statman (New York: Grove Press, 2008)

Gibson, Ian, *Federico García Lorca: A Life* (London: Faber and Faber, 1989)

Gibson, Ian, *The Shameful Life of Salvador Dalí* (London: Faber and Faber, 1997)

Gilmore, David, *Aggression and Community: Paradoxes of Andalusian Culture* (New Haven and London: Yale University Press, 1987)
Graham, Helen and Jo Labanyi, eds, *Spanish Cultural Studies: An Introduction: The Struggle for Modernity* (Oxford: OUP, 1995)
Harris, Derek, *Federico García Lorca: 'Poeta en Nueva York'*, Critical Guides to Spanish Studies (London: Grant & Cutler / Tamesis, 1978)
Harris, Derek, 'Introduction', in Federico García Lorca, *Romancero gitano*, ed. by Derek Harris, Grant & Cutler Spanish Texts (London: Grant & Cutler, 1991), pp. 7–87
Harris, Derek, ed., *Metal Butterflies and Poisonous Lights: Language of Surrealism in Lorca, Alberti, Cernuda and Aleixandre* (Arncroach, Scotland: La Sirena, 1998)
Herrero, Javier, *Lorca, Young and Gay: The Making of An Artist* (Newark, Delaware: Juan de la Cuesta, 2014)
Huélamo Kosma, Julio, 'La influencia de Freud en Federico García Lorca', *Boletín de la Fundación Federico García Lorca*, 6 (1989), 59–83
Huidobro, Vicente, *Obras completas*, I (Santiago de Chile: Zig-Zag, 1964)
Johnson, Roberta, 'Federico García Lorca's Theater and Spanish Feminism', *Anales de la literatura española contemporánea*, 33.2, El Teatro de Federico García Lorca en la Construcción de la Identidad Colectiva Española (2008), 251–81
Johnston, David, *Federico García Lorca* (Bath: Absolute Press, 1998)
Johnston, David, 'The Cultural Engagement of Stage Translation: García Lorca in Performance', in *Voices in Translation: Bridging Cultural Divides*, ed. by Gunilla Anderman (Clevedon: Multilingual Matters, 2007) pp. 78–93
Lannon, Frances, 'Gender and Change: Identity and Reform in the Second Republic', in *A Companion to Spanish Women's Studies*, ed. by Xon de Ros and Geraldine Hazbun (Woodbridge: Tamesis, 2011), pp. 273–85
Llano, Samuel, 'Public Enemy or National Hero? The Spanish Gypsy and the Rise of Flamenquismo, 1898–1922', *Bulletin of Hispanic Studies*, 94.6 (2017), 977–1004
Llera, José Antonio, 'Federico García Lorca en Harlem', in *Cosas que el dinero puede comprar: Del eslogan al poema*, ed. by Luis Bagué Quílez (Madrid: Iberoamericana-Vervuert, 2018), pp. 51–79
Loughran, David, 'Myth, the Gypsy, and Two "Romances históricos"', *Modern Language Notes*, 87.2 (1972), 253–71
Maurer, Christopher, ed., *Sebastian's Arrows: Letters and Mementos of Salvador Dalí and Federico García Lorca* (Chicago: Swan Isle Press, 2004)
Maurer, Christopher, 'Poetry', in *A Companion to Federico García Lorca*, ed. by Federico Bonaddio (Woodbridge: Tamesis, 2007), pp. 16–38
Mayhew, Jonathan, *Apocryphal Lorca: Translation, Parody, Kitsch* (Chicago and London: The University of Chicago Press, 2009)

Mayhew, Jonathan, *Lorca's Legacy: Essays in Interpretation* (New York: Routledge, 2018), eBook

McDermid, Paul, *Love, Desire and Identity in the Theatre of Federico García Lorca* (Woodbridge: Tamesis, 2007)

Mérimée, Prosper, *'Carmen' and Other Stories*, trans. by Nicholas Jotcham, Oxford World's Classics (Oxford: Oxford University Press, 1998)

Mitchell, Timothy, *Flamenco Deep Song* (New Haven: Yale University Press, 1994)

Montero, Enrique, 'Reform Idealized: The Intellectual and Ideological Origins of the Second Republic', in *Spanish Cultural Studies: An Introduction: The Struggle for Modernity*, ed. by Helen Graham and Jo Labanyi (Oxford: OUP, 1995), pp. 124–33

Morris, C. Brian, *García Lorca: Bodas de sangre*, Critical Guides to Spanish Texts (London: Grant & Cutler / Tamesis, 1980)

Morris, C. Brian, *Son of Andalusia: The Lyrical Landscapes of Federico García Lorca* (Liverpool: Liverpool University Press, 1997)

Nandorfy, Martha, *The Poetics of Apocalypse: García Lorca's 'Poet in New York'* (Lewisburg, PA: Bucknell University Press / London: Associated University Presses, 2003)

Ortega y Gasset, José, 'Teoría de Andalucía', *Obras Completas*, VI (1941–1946), 5th edn (Madrid: Revista de Occidente, 1961), pp. 111–20. Originally published in *El Sol*, April 1927

Ortega y Gasset, José, 'La deshumanización del arte', *Obras completas*, III (1917–1928), 5th edn (Madrid: Revista de Occidente, 1962), pp. 353–86

Pabanó, F. M., *Historia y costumbres de los gitanos* (Barcelona: Montaner y Simón, 1915)

Perri, Dennis, 'Fulfillment and Loss: Lorca's View of Communication in the Twenties', *Hispania* 75.3 (September 1992), 484–91

Perriam, Chris, 'Gender and Sexuality', in *A Companion to Federico García Lorca*, ed. by Federico Bonaddio (Woodbridge: Tamesis, 2007), pp. 149–69

Quance, Roberta Ann, 'Federico García Lorca. Mediating Tradition and Modernity for a World Audience', in *A Companion to World Literature*, ed. by Ken Seigneurie (John Wiley & Sons, 2019), pp. 1–11 <https://doi.org/10.1002/9781118635193.ctwl0264>

Ramsden, Herbert, 'Introduction', in Federico García Lorca, *Bodas de sangre*, Hispanic Texts (Manchester and New York: Manchester University Press, 1980), pp. ix–xlix

Ramsden, Herbert, *Lorca's 'Romancero gitano': Eighteen commentaries* (Manchester: Manchester University Press, 1988)

Roberts, Stephen, *Deep Song: The Life and Work of Federico García Lorca* (London: Reaktion, 2020)

Rosslyn, Felicity, 'Lorca and Greek Tragedy', *The Cambridge Quarterly*, 29.3 (2000), 215–36

Saez, Richard, 'The Ritual Sacrifice in Lorca's Poeta en Nueva York', in *Lorca: A Collection of Critical Essays*, ed. by Manuel Duran (Prentice Hall: Englewood Cliffs, N. J., 1962), pp. 108–29

Sahuquillo, Ángel, *Federico García Lorca and the Culture of Male Homosexuality* (Jefferson, N.C.: McFarland & Co., 2007)

Silverman, Renée M., 'The Lyric Performance of Tragedy in Federico García Lorca's *Blood Wedding*', *South Atlantic Review*, 74.3 (Summer 2009), 45–63

Slivkova, Daniela Dimitrova, *Federico García Lorca's 'Mariana Pineda': Erasing the Dividing Line Between the Lyrical-Feminine and the Heroic-Masculine* (Northern Illinois University, 2013)

Smith, Paul Julian, *The Body Hispanic: Gender and Sexuality in Spanish and Spanish American Literature* (Oxford: Clarendon Press, 1989)

Sontag, Susan, 'Notes on "Camp"', in *Against Interpretation and other essays* (London: Penguin Classics, 2009), pp. 275–92

Stainton, Leslie, *Lorca: A Dream of Life* (London: Bloomsbury, 1998)

Talens, Jenaro, *The Branded Eye: Buñuel's 'Un Chien andalou'*, trans. by Giulia Colaizzi (Minneapolis and London: University of Minnesota Press, 1993)

Unamuno, Miguel de, *Del sentimento trágico de la vida* (Madrid: Espasa Calpe, 1982)

Walters, D. Gareth, *'Canciones' and the Early Poetry of Lorca* (Cardiff: University of Wales Press, 2002)

Washabaugh, William, *Flamenco: Passion, Politics and Popular Culture* (Oxford and Washington: Berg, 1996)

Whitworth, Michael H., ed., *Modernism* (Oxford: Blackwell, 2007)

Wright, Sarah, 'Theatre', in *A Companion to Federico García Lorca*, ed. by Federico Bonaddio (Woodbridge: Tamesis, 2007), pp. 39–62

Index

Aladrén, Emilio   14
Alberti, Rafael   14
Amor de Don Perlimplín con Belisa en su jardín [*The Love of Don Perlimplín for Belisa in Their Garden*]   3, 13
Así que pasen cinco años [*Once Five Years Pass*]   3
avant-garde
   Lorca's engagement with   2, 3, 4, 5, 12, 20, 32, 37, 71, 179, 183
Barraca, La   17, 161–63
Bello, José ('Pepín')   12, 128
Bodas de sangre [*Blood Wedding*]   3, 18, 131, 135–40, 141, 142, 149, 151, 152, 156, 157, 163–64, 165, 169, 171–76, 182
   class   157
   generic names   136
   honour   138–40, 156
   land and property   138, 157
   Leonardo   136, 138–40, 171–74
   lullabies   172–73
   lyricism   163–64, 175–76
   Madre [Mother]   135–38, 138–39, 140, 142, 152, 156, 160, 175
   Mujer [Leonardo's wife]   171–73
   Novia [Bride]   137–40, 141, 156, 157, 159, 160, 163–64, 171, 173, 174
   Novio [Bridegroom]   136–67, 138, 139, 141, 174, 175
   obligations of husband and wife   136–40
   old beggar woman   174–75
   Padre [Father]   138–39
   patriarchy   139–40
   symbolism   171, 173
   Suegra [Mother-in-Law]   171–73
   tragedy   151, 171–76
   Woodcutters   173–74
   Woodcutter-Moon   174–75
Buñuel, Luis   12, 69, 62 n.19, 104
   opinion of Lorca's work   14, 128, 180, 183
Burgos, Carmen de   131, 133 n.4
Canciones [*Songs*]   2, 2 n.5, 3, 13, 22, 71, 181
   'Canción del naranjo seco' ['Song of the Dry Orange Tree']   168–69
'Cante jondo. Primitivo canto andaluz' ['Deep Song. Primitive Andalusian Song']   27–28
Casa de Bernarda Alba, La [*The House of Bernarda Alba*]   3, 8, 18, 131, 150–61, 169–71, 175, 182
   Adela   150, 153, 154, 155, 156, 158–60, 169, 170, 171, 175, 182
   Adelaida   153–54
   Amelia   150, 153–54, 169
   Angustias   150, 153, 158
   Bernarda   150-3, 154, 155, 155–58, 159–60, 169–70, 171, 173
   inspiration for   151, 151 n.14
   despotism   151, 156, 160

195

Enrique Humanes 154, 157–58
honour 150, 152–53
La Librada's daughter 155–56, 159
Magdalena 150, 152, 154, 156
Martirio 150, 152, 153–54, 155, 156, 157, 158, 159
patriarchy 152, 156
Pepe el Romano 150, 152, 153, 154, 158–60, 170, 171, 175
Paca la Roseta 154–55, 159
sexuality 154–55
symbolism 156, 169–70, 171
tragedy 151, 159–60, 170
Cernuda, Luis 14
Chien andalou, Un [*An Andalusian Dog*] 128
Concurso del cante jondo [Competition of the Deep Song] 13, 27, 34 n.14
'Corazón bleu y Coeur azul' 13, 75–76, 93
Cubism 13, 72
Dalí, Salvador 62 n.19
  opinion of Lorca's work 21–22, 75–76, 128, 180, 183
  relationship with Lorca 12, 13, 18, 72
dehumanization 2, 4, 5, 20, 71
Diván del Tamarit [*Diwan of Tamarit*] 3
Eliot, T. S. 2
Expressionism 7, 82, 82 n. 7
Falla, Manuel de 13, 27
Fernández Almagro, Melchor 22
Fernández Montesinos, Manuel 18
flamenquismo [flamencoism] 26
Freud, Sigmund 57, 62 n.19
García Lorca, Federico
  Argentina trip 17
  Cuba trip 126–7, 181
  'Dalí epoch' 72
    See also 'Corazón bleu y Coeur azul', 'Oda a Salvador Dalí' ['Ode to Salvador Dalí']
  death 18
  drawings 13–14, 100
  education 10–12
  Gitano moniker 22–23
  interviews 4–5, 27, 31, 32, 33 n.13, 161, 161–63, 163, 170

  letters
    to family (from New York) 8, 77–79, 83, 86, 95–96, 96–97, 105, 117, 126–27
    to Francisco García Lorca (Lorca's brother) 38
    to Sebastià Gasch 14, 22, 74, 76
    to Jorge Guillén 22–23, 25, 40–41, 69
    to Melchor Fernández Almagro 22
  New York residence 3, 15, 71, 77–79, 95, 181
    Christmas 96–97
    Coney Island 83, 85–86
    Harlem 7, 105, 109, 117
      Harlem Renaissance 15, 105
      See also 'El rey de Harlem' ['The King of Harlem'] *under Poeta en Nueva York* [*Poet in New York*]
    religious attitudes 95–96
    Times Square 97
    Wall Street Crash 117
  politics 160–63, 176, 182
  sexuality 1, 181, 181 n.3
    See also 'Oda a Walt Whitman' ['Ode to Walt Whitman'] *under Poeta en Nueva York* [*Poet in New York*]
  works, *see under individual titles*
García Rodríguez, Federico (Lorca's father) 10
Gasch, Sebastià 14
Generation of 1898 26
Generation of 1927 7 n.11, 14
gitanismo [Gitanoism] 22, 26
Gitanos
  Lorca's defence of Gitano culture 25, 26, 27, 34, 34 n.14, 37, 66–8
  See also representation of the Gitanos *under Romancero gitano* [*Gitano Ballad Book*]
  See also Romani people
Góngora, Luis de 7, 14
Guillén, Jorge 14
Hughes, Langston 105 n.11
Huidobro, Vicente 37

'Imagen poética de Don Luis de Góngora' ['The Poetic Image of Don Luis de Góngora'] 14, 32–3, 71–72
'Imaginación, inspiración, evasión' ['Imagination, Inspiration, Evasion'] 14–15, 76, 93
Krausism 133
Larsen, Nelly 105
Libro de poemas [*Book of Poems*] 3
 'Chopo muerto' ['Dead Poplar'] 168
Llanto por Ignacio Sánchez Mejías [*Lament for Ignacio Sánchez Mejías*] 3, 17
Lorca Romero, Vicenta (Lorca's mother) 10
Machado, Antonio 10–12
Mariana Pineda [*Mariana Pineda*] 3, 13, 132 n.2
Martínez Sierra, María 131
Membrives, Lola 17
Modernism 37, 37 n.16
Nelken, Margarita 131, 133 n.4
Noel, Eugenio 26, 37, 67
Novia, La [*The Bride*] (Film) 69
'Oda a Salvador Dalí' ['Ode to Salvador Dalí'] 72–74
Ortega y Gasset, José
 dehumanized art 2, 71
 Teoría de Andalucía [*Theory of Andalusia*] 67, 67 n.22
Ortiz, Paula 69
Pabanó, F. M. 37, 67
 Historia y costumbres de los gitanos [*The History and Customs of the Gitanos*] 24, 25
Poema del cante jondo [*Poem of the Deep Song*] 2, 13, 28–30, 33, 68, 71
 'Adivinanza de la guitarra' ['The Riddle of the Guitar'] 29
 'Chumbera' ['Prickly Pear'] 33
 'Crótalo' ['Castanet'] 29–30
 'Poema de la siguiriya gitana' ['Poem of the Gitano Siguiriya'] 28–29
Poeta en Nueva York [*Poet in New York*] 6–7, 8–9, 15, 77, 79–130, 169, 182
 'La aurora' ['The Dawn'] 88–89, 108
 'Cielo vivo' ['Living Sky'] 123
 critique of modernity 7, 88, 104, 130
 critique of Surrealism 4, 76–77, 88, 104, 128–30, 180
 'Danza de la muerte' ['Dance of Death'] 117–19
 Expressionism 7, 82
 'Fábula y rueda de los tres amigos' ['Fable and Circle of Three Friends'] 123
 'Grito hacia Roma (Desde la torre del Chrysler Building)' ['Cry to Rome (From the Tower of the Chrysler Building)'] 120–21
 'Nacimiento de Cristo' ['The Birth of Christ'] 94–96
 'Navidad en el Hudson' ['Christmas on the Hudson'] 96, 98–100, 103, 169
 'New York. Oficina y denuncia' ['New York: Office and Denunciation'] 100–04
 '1910 (Intermedio)' ['1910 (Intermezzo)'] 121
 'Nocturno del hueco' ['Nocturne of the Void'] 6–7
 'Norma y paraíso de los negros' ['Norm and Paradise of the Blacks'] 104, 105, 106–09
 'Oda a Walt Whitman' ['Ode to Walt Whitman'] 123–26, 181–82
 'Paisaje de la multitud que vomita (Anochecer de Coney Island)' ['Landscape of the Vomiting Crowd (Nightfall at Coney Island)'] 80, 83–85, 86–89, 93, 104
 'Panorama ciego de Nueva York' ['Blind Landscape of New York'] 90–93, 94
 'Poema doble del lago Edén' ['Double Poem of Lake Eden'] 80, 123
 representation of African Americans 104–06, 109, 116
 'El rey de Harlem' ['The King of Harlem'] 104, 105, 109–17, 118, 126
 'Son de negros en Cuba' ['Son of the Blacks in Cuba'] 127

'Tu infancia en Menton' ['Your childhood in Menton'] 123
'Vuelta de paseo' ['Back from a Walk'] 79–83, 87, 169
Primo de Rivera, Miguel 17
Público, El [*The Public or The Audience*] 3, 3 n.6, 181–82
Residencia de Estudiantes [Student Residence] 12, 13, 21, 123, 128, 133, 133 n.4
Rinconcillo, El 10
Ríos, Fernando de los 15
Romancero gitano [*Gitano Ballad Book*] 3, 4, 5, 7, 8, 9, 14, 19, 21–24, 24–25, 30–31, 33–68, 71, 72, 75, 77, 80, 82, 88–89, 104, 128, 135, 161, 165, 176, 180, 182
   Andalusia's cultural heritage 33
   Buñuel on the ballads 14, 128, 180, 183
   camp aesthetic 63–65, 66, 67, 68
   'La casada infiel' ['The Unfaithful Wife'] 31, 55–57
   Dalí on the ballads 21–22, 75–76
   lowbrow/highbrow dichotomy 32–33
   homage to Góngora 7, 32 n.12
   lyricism 5, 23, 30–31, 34, 36, 50–52, 55
   'La monja gitana' ['The Gitano Nun'] 60–63
   'Muerte de Antoñito el Camborio' ['Death of Antoñito Camborio'] 47–49, 63
   'Muerto de amor' ['Dead from Love'] 50
   myth 33, 34, 36, 43, 47–48, 55, 57, 58, 59, 60, 104
   narrative 5, 23, 30–31, 34, 51–52, 57, 71
   'Preciosa y el aire' ['Preciosa and the Wind'] 57–60, 86
   'Prendimiento de Antoñito el Camborio en el camino de Sevilla' ['The Arrest of Antoñito el Camborio on the Road to Seville'] 47
   representation of the Gitanos 54, 55, 43, 46, 47, 54, 55, 68, 104
'Reyerta' ['Feud'] 44–46
'Romance de la Guardia Civil española' ['Ballad of the Spanish Civil Guard'] 38–44
'Romance de la luna, luna' ['Ballad of the Moon, Moon'] 34–36, 38
'Romance de la pena negra' ['Ballad of the Black Sorrow'] 5–6
'Romance sonámbulo' ['Sleepwalking Ballad'] 50–55
'San Gabriel' ['St Gabriel'] 64
'San Miguel (Granada)' ['St Michael (Granada)'] 64, 88–89
   title 23–25
Romani people 3 n.8, 5, 7, 21, 24, 161, 180
Rosales, Luis 18
Rueda, Salvador 24
Salillas, Rafael 26
Salinas, Pedro 14, 67
Sánchez Mejías, Ignacio 14, 17
Santa Ana, Manuel María de 24
Second Republic 17–18, 157, 163
   women's rights 131–5, 151
'Sketch de la nueva pintura' ['Sketch of the New Painting'] 14, 76
Sonetos del amor oscuro [*Sonnets of Dark Love*] 3
Suites [*Suites*] 2, 2 n.5, 3, 13, 71, 181
Surrealism 4, 6, 7, 13, 14–15, 72, 74, 76–77, 82, 88, 104, 128–30, 180
'Teoría y juego del duende' ['Theory and Play of the Duende'] 17, 183
Xirgu, Margarita 17
Yerma [*Yerma*] 3, 8, 17–18, 131, 140–50, 151, 152, 156, 160, 164–68, 169, 173, 175, 182
   childlessness 141–42, 144, 146, 147–48, 164
   honour 141, 142–45, 149
   Juan 141–2, 142–45, 148–50
   limitations of marriage 147, 149
   lyricism 164, 165, 168
   María 141, 145, 146, 165
   Muchacha 1ª [First Girl] 146
   Muchacha 2ª [Second Girl] 146–47
   Old pagan woman 148, 149, 164, 166–67
   symbolism 164–68

tragedy 149, 151, 165
unsuitability of Yerma's marriage 141, 141 n.11
Vieja 1ª [First old woman] 145
Víctor 142, 145

Washerwomen 143, 166, 173
Yerma 8, 141–50, 164–68, 175
   conformity 145–46, 147–48
   obsession with motherhood 146, 147–48

TAMESIS

Founding Editors
†J. E. Varey
†Alan Deyermond

General Editor
Stephen M. Hart

Advisory Board
Andrew M. Beresford
Zoltán Biedermann
Celia Cussen
Efraín Kristal
Jo Labanyi
María E. López
José Antonio Mazzotti
Thea Pitman
Julius Ruiz
Alison Sinclair
Isabel Torres
Noël Valis

www.ingramcontent.com/pod-product-compliance
Lightning Source LLC
Jackson TN
JSHW010147260425
83333JS00012B/81